M000199519

PSYCHOTHERAPY
AS A
MUTUAL PROCESS

OTHER TITLES FROM NEW FALCON PUBLICATIONS

Buddhism & Jungian Psychology
Catholicism & Jungian Psychology
Sufism, Islam & Jungian Psychology
Hinduism & Jungian Psychology
Judaism & Jungian Psychology
Jungian Psychology & the Passions of the Soul
Jungian Analysts: The Visions & Vunerabilities
The Tree of Life: Paths in Jungian Individuation
Reich, Jung, Regardie & Me
The Unhealed Healer
       By J. Marvin Spiegelman, Ph.D.
Undoing Yourself With Energized Meditation
Secrets of Western Tantra
       By Christopher S. Hyatt, Ph.D.
Eight Lectures on Yoga
Gems From the Equinox
The Pathworkings of Aleister Crowley
       By Aleister Crowley
Neuropolitique
Info-Psychology
The Game of Life
       By Timothy Leary, Ph.D.
Zen Without Zen Masters
       By Camden Benares
Breaking the Godspell
       By Neil Freer
The Complete Golden Dawn System of Magic
The Golden Dawn Tapes—Series I, II, and III
       By Israel Regardie
Astrology & Consciousness: The Wheel of Light
       By Rio Olesky
Metaskills: The Spiritual Art of Therapy
       By Amy Mindell, Ph.D.
Beyond Duality: The Art of Transcendence
       By Laurence Galian
Soul Magic: Understanding Your Journey
       By Katherine Torres, Ph.D.
Carl Sagan & Immanuel Velikovsky
       By Charles Ginenthal

And to get your free catalog of all of our titles, write to:

New Falcon Publications (Catalog Dept.)
1739 East Broadway Road, Suite 1-277
Tempe, Arizona 85282 U.S.A

PSYCHOTHERAPY
AS A
MUTUAL PROCESS

J. MARVIN SPIEGELMAN, PH.D.

New Falcon Publications
Tempe, Arizona, U.S.A.

Copyright © 1996 by J. Marvin Spiegelman

All rights reserved. No part of this book, in part or in whole, may be repro-
duced, transmitted, or utilized, in any form or by any means, electronic or
mechanical, including photocopying, recording, or by any information stor-
age and retrieval system, without permission in writing from the publisher,
except for brief quotations in critical articles, books and reviews.

International Standard Book Number: 1-56184-063-7

First Edition 1996

Book design by Sekhmet Books
Cover – *Mutus Liber* in Jung, C.G. *Psychology of Transference*

The paper used in this publication meets the minimum requirements of the
American National Standard for Permanence of Paper for Printed Library
Materials Z39.48-1984

This book is dedicated, with Thanks, to my teachers, Marie-Louise Von
Franz, C.A. Meier, Max Zeller, and, above all, C.G. Jung

Address all inquiries to:
NEW FALCON PUBLICATIONS
1739 East Broadway Road Suite 1-277
Tempe, AZ 85282 U.S.A.
(or)
1605 East Charleston Blvd.
Las Vegas, NV 89104 U.S.A.

TABLE OF CONTENTS

INTRODUCTION
(1995)

Many of the chapters in this book describe my developmental struggle with the phenomena of transference, which, as Jung realized even during his very first encounter with Freud, is "the alpha and omega" of analytic psychotherapy and is the testing fire for all analysts as they learn and practice their calling. And calling, I think, is the right word for this endeavor, as contrasted with craft or profession, since one needs to be "summoned" to do it by the god or gods of healing, just as the priest or shaman is "called". It is not only a joke that one hears the statement that "you have to be crazy to become an analyst" since, like the shaman, it is essential that the would-be depth therapist experience the unconscious in its fullness, which means traveling in those same realms that psychotics are forced to travel. One hopes, though, that the healer will have the added blessing of enjoying an intact and flexible ego which can, like the shaman, bring the treasure back from those same depths, rather than drown there.

I shall say more about this matter in a moment, but I want to add that there are also several chapters in this book which address analysis or therapy more generally, from the point-of-view of content, that is, what the psyche is saying in my consulting room in dreams and fantasies. All of these papers cover a thirty-year period of time and I am glad to say that I am not ashamed of any of them. Indeed, I recognize the white heat of some, beginning with the very first one, and am glad that this heat continues to this day, more contained and alchemically transformed, but still ignited in almost each session with every analysand. Each person brings either new issues and problems or a particular slant to the collective struggle with psyche that everyone faces and, most importantly, a new and unique relationship, with me and with the unconscious, which makes this work ever fresh. It is as if the god of healing is still delighted to make his/her presence felt in the analytic transaction and it is our common task to make this conscious and transforming for both parties.

Jung noted, in his remarkable book, Psychology of the Transference, that the divine spirit, the numen, has made his/her home in the psychotherapist's consulting room. I think that Aphrodite entered into Freud's and Breuer's offices a hundred years ago, accompanying those famous hysterical women who found a powerful love there. Breuer, understandably, was scared off by what we now recognize as the phenomenon of transference, but Freud courageously—at great cost to himself—encountered her as best as he was able. Later analysts have done the same, although it took Jung to realize what was more deeply afoot. Nowadays, rules and regulations—always important as the legitimate respect for the goddess, Themis—threaten to drive Aphrodite out altogether, and it must take that powerful commitment to a therapeutic "calling" for depth therapists to continue this valuable tradition.

That leads me to comment on what I have recently recognized about my own "calling" as a healer. I am not, I think, a natural born healer. I can say this since I have had the opportunity to observe some of these naturally gifted individuals, particularly in my supervisory work. It should come as no surprise that physicians, in particular, seem to be more frequently such natally gifted healers, even though medical materialism and power drives tend to kill or distort this divine direction. But doctors are not alone in this. The healing god, like Aphrodite, comes and goes as he/she wishes and selects as its agent whomsoever it will. Those naturally "chosen" can hardly avoid it. Such folk exude compassion and natural wisdom in their pores and are ever present to healing issues. One need only teach them and go along with them on their journey to make this gift manifest. It is even often shown in early dreams of childhood. Sometimes, though, people have a calling and turn it down. I have seen this in dreams also. The god of healing seems to let some people get away with this rejection of the call and not others, who are pursued and even punished by such avoidance.

I am thinking, now, of the quite young man I saw for only a brief period not long ago. He came to me in connection with his studies in a therapy training program that he was enrolled in—which required him to undergo some analysis—but he was far from believing that this was his own path. He had been deeply effected by the works of my friend, James Hillman, and had recently read his work with the theme, "We have had a hundred years of psychotherapy and the world is getting worse," in which the case is forcefully made that remaining in the confining quarters of individual self-investigation can be counter-productive when "it is the world that is sick."

My young patient was struck by the value of our work with dreams and fantasies in Jungian psychotherapy, so we found common ground with Hillman's interest in imagination. Anyway, when I sent this chap to see Hillman—as perhaps the logical person for him—the latter sent him back to me! So, we had to continue. After some interesting anima-work and an impressive dream in which he saw a statue of the Buddha come to life in a fountain, awakening a religious dimension for him in a new way, he had the following dream:

> My friend, B. and I are in a reality with a history in which the South had won the Civil War. The country had been divided into the Union and the Confederacy, and the two separate nations had been completely separated. No one had been allowed to pass from one to the other since the end of the war. B. and I are in some city which borders both the Union and the Confederacy and, for the first time, people are being allowed to cross over

to the Confederacy, and we go through or over something which is a cross between a bridge and a tunnel. It is night in the Confederate city and the city is extremely beautiful, lit with many colored lights and exceptionally clean. It soon becomes obvious that there are no prohibitions in the Confederacy: gambling, prostitution, drugs and almost anything seems to be legal. B. and I reflect that it is for this reason that the city is so clean. Nothing is suppressed, so everything is dealt with properly. We walk through the streets of the city, admiring the feeling of excitement around, until we come across a book store. We browse the shelves for a while and we are enthralled with the variety of books. There are many books which do not exist in the Union and many of these seem to us mysterious and very intriguing.

As we walk among the shelves of books, our conversation somehow turns to metaphysical healing, that is, the healing of physical wounds or illness through mental means. B. says, "You used to be into that stuff, didn't you?" and I reply that I had, but that I had abandoned it long ago. He then pulls out a knife and stabs a fellow bookstore patron in the back of the neck and says to me, "You're a healer, now heal!" I immediately protest, "No, I don't do that anymore! I gave it up!" But my protestations are to no avail, for Bill has disappeared. I am left with this dying person, and I can find no alternative but to try and heal the person.

The wound is a vertical stab directly in the center of the back of the neck. I put my hand over it and imagine the wound closed. I remove my hand, the wound is closed for a moment, but then pops back open. I try this several more times, until finally the wound stays shut. I say to myself that is the best that I can do and leave the bookstore.

Suddenly, I find myself in a somewhat large room with three large and dangerous-looking men. They tell me that they are going to kill me and that I had better defend myself. I tell them that there must be some mistake, and that I do not want to fight with them. They say that there is no mistake and begin attacking me, telling me again that they are going to kill me and that I had better defend myself.

I dodge their attacks for a while, refusing to enter the battle, but soon they have me surrounded in the center of the room. I cannot escape and I begin to fight. As the four of us struggle, for a moment we are all locked up in combat, but soon we start to turn slowly in a circle. The turning speeds up and I realize that this is no longer a battle, but a dance. Simultaneously, the room and the men are somehow transfigured, and I find myself dancing with two men and a woman in the center of a huge party. It soon becomes obvious that the party is for me and everyone is celebrating that I made it there.

This rather longish and interesting dream has many aspects, but I will only comment on a few of them. The dream begins with a statement of the dreamer's situation. It shows a changed reality. For Americans, the Civil War is a crucial symbol of the division of our country, the battle of North and

South, of continuing opposition in the psyche. In the case of our dreamer, it is a battle between consciousness and the unconscious, a fundamental condition for many. Now, he is one who can "cross-over," that is can reach the unconscious and its contents. He does so, interestingly, via a bridge and a tunnel, from "above" as well as "below," which suggests that integration can take place in both ways, spiritually and instinctively. But what he finds, most unusually, is that the unconscious side, usually experienced as the dark, repressed aspect of the soul, shows openness and freedom: everything is permitted and is therefore clean. I think that a personal level this encourages the dreamer to attend to the unconscious rather than follow his conscious bent of wanting to repair the outer world in some way. Yet I also think that the dream compensates, collectively, for this present time in our country which tends to be more legalistic, repressive and judgmental, while darkness prevails outwardly, everywhere. This is in contrast to the sixties when there was much more freedom and experimentation, particularly for youth, such as this chap.

In the unconscious he finds greater intellectual freedom and much of interest, which is very nice because this is a very bright and rebellious young man who needs to be challenged meaningfully. And here he comes upon the problem with which he came into analysis, namely, should he become a healer or not? The dream presents this as the problem of human physical wounds healed by mental means, the union of mind and body, a central issue in Western consciousness for at least the last three hundred years, about which alchemy was much involved and about which Jung has written extensively.

The dreamer goes from the mental position of looking at books to the physical fact of being forced to address the problem very directly, albeit within the psychic reality of the dream. One can understand B. as his aggressive shadow who forces the action, which the dreamer tries to avoid but cannot. He succeeds, however, in the healing, after which he has to face the three dangerous men who are going to kill him. From a psychological point of view, this would suggest that when the healing issue is confronted, this brings the deeper, archetypal shadow aspect of aggression. Does the unconscious not inform us here that whoever can heal can also kill or be killed? Naturally, the opposite of this is not necessarily true. We need to recall that the great ancient physician, Hippocrates, gave all healers as the first requirement: "Only do no harm"!

Once the dreamer accepts the struggle, he now finds a masculine symbol for wholeness, a quaternity of males. So the battle takes place within the masculine archetype of action, evolving into a circle, a more complete image of totality. The action now transforms into dancing, something which definitely includes the feminine element as well, shown in the fact that one of the four is a woman. Nothing less than transfiguration ensues, which clearly shows that becoming a healer is a religious issue, a spiritual issue. The celebration in his honor, I think, is that he has come home to himself, his own myth and his own "vocation." I do not know if he will indeed ultimately become a psychotherapist, but the dream seems to insist on it and, more importantly, this is in the context of healing the split between conscious and unconscious and between body and mind.

In my case, the healing path as a "vocation" emerged out of my own analytical work and was not the reason that I undertook therapy at the beginning. It may be worth telling that story for other budding therapists or analysts who may be "called" in a peculiar way, but not clearly as healers. When I began graduate school in psychology, in 1948, I planned on becoming a professor and researcher, specializing in social psychology. In one class, entitled "Critical Problems in Psychology", the professor—a charming man but utterly committed to an exclusively behavioral view of psychology—said that he thought that one day we would have a formula for art. Without realizing that I was doing so, I blurted out, "Nonsense!" My professor did not take offense at this sign of insubordination and some discussion ensued. What I remember, though, is what happened afterwards.

I had been sitting next to an "older man" (actually in his early forties while I was all of twenty-two years old!), who commented, after class, that I had "a very interesting handwriting, musical, artistic, imaginative and original." I looked at him as if he were from another planet and asked if he did handwriting analysis. He replied that he had done so before the war, in Europe, where he had also practiced as a lawyer, but was now a Jungian analyst.

"Aren't you Jewish," I asked, to which he nodded affirmatively.

"But wasn't Jung a Nazi?" I continued, in all innocence.

"No, he was not," replied Dr. Max Zeller, for this was his name I then learned, "and I myself spent some time in a concentration camp in Germany."

Now I was really curious and asked if I might speak to him further about Jung and analysis. He graciously replied that he would do so if I wished and invited me to his home. When I asked why a Jungian analyst might be in a graduate psychology class, he replied that a colleague had suggested that he do so since a licensing law for the profession of psychotherapy was likely to be enacted soon and he was trying it out to see if it would be worthwhile for him to pursue this path. He had been accredited as a Jungian analyst in Switzerland, but without undergoing the training that traditional psychology or psychiatry provided. University psychology, it soon turned out, was not his path, and I can certainly see why this was so.

Some days later, I visited Dr. Zeller at his home and was entranced. His house was not in a wealthy area of Los Angeles, but had its own old-world charm with books, paintings, music and a gemüttlichkeit that nourished me.

His family was warm and friendly as well, serving me tea and allowing us privacy for our discussion.

"How shall I tell you about Jungian psychology?" Dr. Zeller began and then answered his own question by saying, "I will tell you a dream." He then related a dream which was like a fairy tale but was also quite personal in its content. He went on to interpret this dream in a way that made great sense to me. Here was food for the soul that I did not even realize that I was missing, pursuing, as I was, the rationalistic academic path. I resolved to come and have analysis with this man when I could afford to do so, just for my own development and without any idea that I might become a psychotherapist or analyst at all. After all, I had largely accepted my university's view that objective science was all that really mattered (see my dream of the sun and the flood in the chapter, "Notes from the Underground"), that clinical psychology was a bit of a scam and that Freud and Jung were largely frauds. It so happens that much in my life that I have scorned I have subsequently grown to value. I scorned Jung and became a Jungian analyst; I scorned Wilhelm Reich and underwent eight years of Reichian body work. I had contempt for chiropractors and have had many years of excellent healing at their hands, including that of my Reichian therapist, Dr. Francis Israel Regardie. So, it behooves me to suggest that one look carefully at what one scorns.

Anyway, two years later, in 1950, when I was now a teaching assistant at the University and earning some decent money, I approached Dr. Zeller and he was glad to take me on as an analysand, at fees that I could manage. That did it. By then, I had studied Rorschach and become an assistant of the world-figure in that area, Dr. Bruno Klopfer, who was also oriented in a Jungian fashion, but I still thought of myself as a social psychologist who was also learning clinical matters.

Within a year, however, all had changed. My analysis went deep rather quickly and I was totally captured by the imaginative and analytic work which revolved around relation to the unconscious. Now I wondered whether I should become a clinician or not but did not decide the issue then, getting my Ph.D. in both clinical and social psychology in 1952. Although I had already been enrolled for a year in a clinical training program, I was still undecided. I had no dreams which announced that I ought to be a healer or analyst at all!

In the meantime, there were Jungian visitors coming from Europe, largely from Zürich, to lecture in Los Angeles, such as Rivkah Kluger (then Schärf), Marie-Louise von Franz, C.A. Meier, Barbarah Hannah, plus Michael Fordham from England, all of whom impressed me mightily with their erudition, skill, charm and humor. I wanted to be among them and imagined studying at the fabulous C.G. Jung Institute in Zürich. How else to do this except by becoming an analyst? In the meantime, I had turned down an excellent academic/clinical job at a prestigious Eastern university, provided by the chairman of my doctoral committee, Dr. Franklin Fearing, wanting to continue my analysis and post-doctoral clinical training. I had also married, just before I was called into the Army at the latter part of the Korean War. I had been in the Merchant Marine for two years during World War II but the government had decided, strangely, that this was not military enough (I had sailed the world and was shot at, for heaven's sake!)—a decision which was only reversed some twenty years later—so off I went to Fitzsimmons Army Hospital in Denver, Colorado (after some weeks of basic training) to be an Army psychologist, newly married and having completed my first analysis.

It was then that I realized that my great commitment was to working with the unconscious, in whatever form it presented itself. That took precedence over being a healer. This was indeed to be my whole life's endeavor. With that insight and acceptance, my dreams now seemed to just take for granted that I would be going to Zürich one day, without any particular emphasis on healing as such. It was clear that the Self wanted me to commit myself to an ongoing relationship with the unconscious, and only then did that same Self "make use" of the analytic path as a good way to continue this work. Only much later, after my training was over in Switzerland, did the "healing God"—presenting itself with a "calling" to me—begin to manifest in my dreams and fantasies. And this was particularly so in regard to the issue of "Mutual Process", what this book is all about. It was as if the main task was the larger spiritual path of relating to the unconscious and only after this was deeply anchored did the healing god appear and take me on somewhat original trails.

I understand all this to mean that my path was clearly in the service of the Self, as a spiritual quest, and the Self ultimately led me also into the healing art, as well as into writing and teaching. All these years since then, I have been glad of the choice and endlessly amazed and impressed at what the Self manages to do in my own life, in the life of those whom I see in analysis, and in the analytical relationship. Both the sequence of chapters on the transference and those on content of the psyche address this theme and indicate what I have learned therein.

It occurs to me that some examples of how the Self shows up as a healer in unexpected ways might be helpful to the reader. I think immediately of two examples. The first comes from the 1960's when I was, in addition to my clinical practice, on the psychology faculty of the University of California at Los Angeles. A fellow member of the department, a researcher with a behavioral perspective, honored me by referring his wife to me for some analytic work. She had a presenting dream in which a behavioral therapist was present and suggesting certain practices of re-learning. I immediately welcomed this presentation by her therapeutic animus and taught this woman the Jungian technique of "active imagination," a way of having a dialogue with the unconscious. She embraced this with alacrity and had her internal relationship with this figure who now handled the therapy, with thanks for my collaboration! After only some ten or so sessions, the therapy was completed and everyone was happy. A Jungian analyst welcomed his opposite number, a behavioral therapist, which the patient approached with a Jungian viewpoint and the work was just right. I take it that the Self, both the patient's and mine, were behind this effort and the honoring of both led to a favorable outcome. Opposites do indeed "touch," as Jung pointed out, and often positively.

Along similar lines, I am thinking of several patients of mine, who were themselves therapists, who worked with me for some time and then went on to work with other therapists, including Freudian-oriented ones. One such person became a Freudian analyst and is now a good friend of mine! Others became Jungian analysts as well, each of whom, I am proud to say, followed the Self as it manifested in their own development. Naturally, not all the people I have trained or worked with have embraced a different perspective, but I wanted to mention these as an indication that the individual "selves" of the parties can be quite different and an unseen Self transcending both may well take us as far as we can go together and then help us to move on. I have had the pleasure of also doing analysis and/or supervision with Freudian, Kleinian and Reichian analysts, so that this interchange is not only a one-sided "love-affair" for me, as it is alas, for many of our Jungian colleagues, whose fascination with Object Relations is complete but whose collegial love-object does not return the interest.

The main thing, however, is that relating to a guiding "third" in the analytic relationship, whether a healing presence or the larger Self, is the modern understanding of the ancient idea of following a "calling." This conception that the Self is present as a "third" in the analytic relationship is hardly original with me. Let me here quote the famous statement of Jung (in 1929), which provides the crucial background for this realization:

> What does this demand mean (that the analyst be analyzed first)? Nothing less than the doctor is as much "in the analysis" as the patient. He is equally a part of the psychic process of treatment and therefore equally exposed to the transforming influences. Indeed, to the extent that the doctor shows himself impervious to this influence, he forfeits influence over the patient; and if he is influenced only unconsciously, there is a gap in his field of consciousness which makes it impossible for him to see the patient in true perspective. In either case the result of the treatment is compromised.
>
> The doctor is therefore faced with the same task which he wants his patient to face... This therapeutic demand can be clothed in a thousand different formulae, according to the doctor's beliefs. One doctor believes in overcoming infantilism, therefore he must overcome his own infantilism. Another believes in abreacting all affects—therefore he must first abreact

all his own affects. A third believes in complete consciousness, therefore he must first reach consciousness himself. The doctor must consistently strive to meet his own therapeutic demand if he wishes to ensure the right sort of influence over his patients. All these guiding principles of therapy make so many ethical demands, which can be summed up in the single truth: be the man through whom you wish to influence others. Mere talk has always been counted hollow, and there is no trick, however artful, by which this simple truth can be evaded in the long run...the fact of being convinced and not the thing we are convinced of—that is what has always, and at all times, worked.(Jung, 1929, Coll. Wks. Vol. 16, "Problems of Modern Psychotherapy", ¶166-7)

This potent statement of Jung provided, early on, an accurate observation of what the analytic relationship consists in and was further spelled out in depth in his great book on the transference (Coll Wks. Vol. 16, "Psychology of the Transference"), written in 1946, which made use of the images from the medieval alchemical text, the Rosarium Philosophorum. It has taken many years and many analysts' efforts, from all schools, to work out the "implications" of these facts. The early psychoanalytic attitude of "maintaining objectivity" and trying to stay apart from these effects gave way to the realization by Melanie Klein and the subsequent Object Relations analysts, such as Bion, Winnicott, etc., that the analytic process did indeed draw the analyst fully into the psyche of the patient. They dealt with this fact by using the concept of projective identification, of the patient "putting into" the analyst those aspects of himself/herself which were troublesome or pathological, etc. This process is either conscious or unconscious and is surely present at times. But, as I spell out (together with the astrophysicist V. Mansfield, in the 1995 paper, "On the Physics and Psychology of the Transference as an Interactive Field"), this causal perspective must also give way, at deeper levels, to an acausal, synchronistic, "mutual process" perspective in which the archetypal content is constellated by the relationship itself. But I shall leave the reader to see how this is arrived at and developed over the course of the years. Suffice it to say that the archetypal perspective, which Jung discovered, shows us that the Self is both the guiding force in the work and is that which is worked on, requiring, ultimately, "mutual process."

I think that the therapeutic community is now more ready to embrace this idea of mutuality than it was thirty years ago, when I wrote my first paper, or even ten years ago. The Logos position of needing to separate from the analysand and teach him/her to relate to the unconscious via active imagination and other solitary tasks (in the classical Jungian perspective), or to maintain separateness and objectivity and reveal nothing of the analyst's inner workings (in the classical Freudian perspective) has been either augmented (in the Jungian view) or displaced by the Eros position of focus on the relationship itself.

My understanding of this change is enhanced by the realization that the continuing manifestation of the feminine aspect of the Self in collective consciousness (announced in Jung's "Answer to Job" in 1952), is showing itself in the therapeutic field by greater focus on the relationship and on the body. The Goddess is friendly to these aspects and to mutual process, in my experience. And so the climate, now, is better than it was some time ago (see the chapter on The Image of the Jungian Analyst and the Problem of Authority) to consider these things. I recall showing a copy of the first two papers in this book, many years ago, to a respected, senior Jungian analyst who then proceeded to go through them and mark the items "true" or "false"! I realized that he did not have a clue about what I was dealing with, despite his erudition and deep Jungian commitment. I hope that I will not, in turn, be so blind to the next generation's discoveries or experiences.

So, here is the record of the investigation, the ideas and examples. Some of these papers have been published in various journals, and some in abstruse publications, or not at all. The record of publication and translation can be found in the Appendix. It is indeed a bit wry that some of these papers have appeared in Japanese without having been printed in English! A couple have also been translated into Italian. Like my Zürich teacher, C.A. Meier, my work has been more popular with Japanese and Italians, why I can not say. Yet my dreams, years ago, did announce this fact. Long, long ago, I dreamt that I was talking with C.G. Jung intently when he was called away to have serious discussions with the Pope. In the meantime, I was to do analysis with an Italian artist/poet who needed healing for a wounded heart. And my last dream upon finishing training in Zürich in 1959 (see the chapter on Report to Alma Mater), announced my being open to the "Land of the Rising Sun", following which, in reality, I enjoyed the opportunity of working with several analysands from Japan when I returned to Los Angeles. So, the Self seems to know the future as well as the past, sometimes giving us glimpses of it in dreams and visions.

It has been my task and good fortune to continue in the spirit of Jung and to advance our understanding of the mutual effect of analyst and analysand and to see how the archetypes manifest in that relationship and how, particularly, the larger Self has chosen our own little therapeutic rooms to appear as a numen. In conclusion, I find that I can do nothing better than quote the final two paragraphs of Jung's discussion of the second picture of the Rosarium, where he cogently places this work in psychological and historical context (Vol. 16, ¶ 448-9):

> Individuation has two principal aspects: in the first place it is an internal and subjective process of integration, and in the second it is an equally indispensable process of objective relationship. Neither can exist without the other, although sometimes the one and sometimes the other predomi-

nates. This double aspect has two corresponding dangers. The first is the danger of the patient's using the opportunities for spiritual development arising out of the analysis of the unconscious as a pretext for evading the deeper human responsibilities, and for affecting a certain "spirituality" which cannot stand up to moral criticism; the second is the danger that atavistic tendencies may gain ascendancy and drag the relationship down to a primitive level. Between this Scylla and that Charybdis there is a narrow passage, and both medieval Christian mysticism and alchemy have contributed much to its discovery.

Looked at in this light, the bond established by the transference—however hard to bear and unintelligible it may seem—is vitally important not only for the individual but also for society, and indeed for the moral and spiritual progress of mankind. So, when the psychotherapist has to struggle with difficult transference problems, he can at least take comfort in these reflections. He is not just working for this particular patient, who may be quite insignificant, but for himself as well and his own soul, and in so doing he is perhaps laying an infinitesimal grain in the scales of humanity's soul. Small and invisible as this contribution may be, it is yet an opus magnum for it is accomplished in a sphere but lately visited by the numen, where the whole weight of humankind's problems has settled. The ultimate questions of psychotherapy are not a private matter—they represent a supreme responsibility.

CHAPTER ONE

SOME IMPLICATIONS OF THE TRANSFERENCE (1965)

In his paper on transference, (1), C. A. Meier has focused on a dark and puzzling area, emerging with ideas which seem to me to be decisive in their clarity and fully borne out in my own experience. In this paper, I wish to highlight these formulations and present some implications which, I think, are rather far-reaching and shed some light on current questions of psychotherapeutic training and practice.

Meier visualizes the analytic relationship as two partners, A and B, who, in the course of the work and by the very nature of it, are influenced by the third factor, C (the unconscious), which comes into play. Thus far, this is not particularly new, nor is there anything here with which analysts of any persuasion would cavil. What Meier does bring in which is new, is the observation that in the subject-object relation, A, the analyst, in investigating his patient, B, ever more intimately and deeply, soon finds that the "cut"—that is, the distinction between subject and object, between himself and his patient—becomes blurred. As he moves more and more into the object, the analyst eventually finds that he cannot distinguish between what belongs to him, as his own complexes, and what belongs to the patient. This condition is fertile for the activation of the collective unconscious. Therefore, the attribution of C (the unconscious), is that, in truth, it belongs to both partners. Meier has hit the nail on the head, I think, in ascribing the activation of the collective unconscious to the very effort of the analyst to understand and help his patient.

When one comes to consider the mutual projections involved, we have to admit that there is always the "hook" in the person projected upon, as well as in the projector. Meier concludes that it is on this basis that the analyst needs to be analyzed before he conducts analyses, in order to know himself and the "hooks" as much as possible. Equally importantly, the analytic process compels the analyst to continually work on himself, as well as the patient.

Meier shows that when this condition of activation of the unconscious prevails, there is a symmetrical relationship between the two partners. He recognizes that not all therapeutic relationships have this quality of symmetry. Many are of the traditional, asymmetric type in which, say, the analyst maintains a firm separation between himself and his patient. He also emerges from such a process relatively unchanged. In my experience, the symmetrical type of interaction occurs rather frequently—almost always in those analyses which are of long duration and not infrequently even in encounters of only a few interviews.

The implications of this observation and formulation are vast. First off, it brings into great question all those methods and attitudes of the analyst which prevent him from becoming subjectively involved with his patients. Whether he uses a "blank-screen" approach of chair-behind-the-couch, or whether he sits face-to-face, he can not really go deeply into the psyche of his partner without discovering his own unresolved complexes and confusions as to what is patient and what is himself. Should he stubbornly resist this realization about himself and the situation, he will either never constellate the unconscious in its deeper forms or will require that the patient carry the whole burden of the contents activated.

It is this latter point which has aided me in understanding why the material which Jung has described does not find more common recognition among psychotherapists generally. My thought is that they have not run across it because they have not opened themselves up to the implications of their own involvement. Naturally, this extreme position is probably rather rare, since therapists generally are quite aware of what is called "counter-transference". Freudians, by and large, greet this problem as lamentable and, at least traditionally, see this as a consequence of the analyst having been insufficiently analyzed. Fenichel, for example (2), suggests that the principal task in the transference is "not joining in the game." He agrees that it is impossible to be exclusively a "mirror" for the patient, but dismisses the problem in a brief discussion about smoking!

It is true that most Freudians have departed from this extreme position, but, as far as I can make out, even now counter-transference reactions are something to be "used", something to indicate to the therapist what the patient is doing to him, and definitely not to be revealed to him as they occur. In other words, the analyst needs to have a rather sterile—or, at least, aseptic—psyche which works as a surgeon's knife in unraveling the complexes, defenses, etc. of the patient. It is this attitude, I maintain, that either precludes the appearance of the collective unconscious or forces the patient, like the surgeon's sick object, to carry the whole burden, while the analyst both protects his patient and himself from anything not quite right in his own condition.

Jungians, by and large, are not so fearful about revealing themselves and their reactions. Indeed, they are inclined to do so in order to "humanize" the process to some extent. They also know that the archetypes are behind strong reactions and that the analyst is as much a victim of these factors as is the patient. Practically, however, in my experience, Jungian analysts will reveal something out of their past, give emotional reactions, and be much "in" the process, as far as the patient is able, but the "openness" is limited. They do not, for example, reveal their own fantasies, or desires, nor do they acknowledge their shadows very willingly, except where a dream seems to insist on it, or the patient confronts. Most importantly, we do not tend to analyze the transference situation as it actually exists. We may, like Freudians or Sullivanians, point out how the patient sees us as parent, savior, or some other figure, but how many of us acknowledge to the patient the child in ourselves that needs the patient's fathering or mothering, for example? I have never heard this analytically, though I suspect it to be true, from my own experience.

Gerhard Adler (3) has asserted that the analyst must have an "impersonal Eros", selfless, containing, to succor the patient. I react in a strongly negative way to this assertion and suggest that, if Adler does this, he is identified with the positive mother archetype. That is lovely, no doubt, for the patients who need mothering, but does it permit a woman patient, for example, who needs to come to her own maternal function, to experience that in the analytic relation? I doubt it, for she is too busy being mothered. I think that Adler's viewpoint suggest the obverse of what we have criticized among the Freudians, namely their Father-God identification. The latter view, as we have seen, requires the patient to carry the unconscious; the one that Adler suggests is merely the obverse, where the analyst carries it all. In either case, analyst or patient or both become possessed by the collective unconscious and suffer the effects of inflation.

My experience teaches me that many, if not all, patients, come to a genuine "I and Thou" relation, in which there is real equality, and that at this point all enjoinders as to how the analyst ought to be are irrelevant. He simply is what he is, in his heights and depths, wisdom and blindness, shadow and light, just like the patient. It is at this point, I believe, that a clearly Jungian analysis, in the sense of the individuation process, begins. It is at this point also, I think, that the material that Jung describes, in his paper on the transference (4), shows itself. The solutions found, of course, are then perforce individual. I think that for this process to occur, the analyst needs to give up his claim to authority and even his desire to defend himself from exposure. Otherwise the real mutuality will not take place.

Perhaps many Jungian analysts would agree with me thus far, but some will say that "Only a few of my patients need or come to this; most of mine require traditional doctoring or teaching" or something like that. I have found, to the contrary, that most of my patients require this mutuality ultimately, if not at the very outset. In short, I find that individuation is involved in practically all those patients that I see for more than a few interviews and, not infrequently, with those I see only briefly. I am not clear about this difference in my experience and that of the aforementioned colleagues.

I would like, however, to stress the idea of equality. If this is so, then there is no ground for the analyst holding rights to the "maternal eros" idea. I find, for example, that such an unconscious identification led me to experience exhaustion at the end of the work day. I submit, in addition, that the commonly heard complaint of "exhaustion" among analysts may rest on such an identification. Being positive mother all day leads to being martyr mother and letting other people know about how one suffers. Better, in my view, acknowledge one's fatigue, boredom, or anger to the patient when it occurs, and analyze it, jointly. Only then can we see if it may, in truth, belong to the analyst, patient, or both and be overcome. Also, I find, one can really learn from patients and not just the stuff from which routine acknowledgments are made in papers and books. To learn, one must be ready to submit to the other and expose one's ignorance. Thus, analyst is also pupil, as well as teacher, analysand as well as analyst.

The answer, in short, is to recognize the presence of C, as Meier calls it, and acknowledge that the unconscious is effecting both partners simultaneously. The analyst, therefore, is willy-nilly involved as a human being and must relate to the objective psyche, just as the patient. In other words, once committed and open to what is happening, he is as much "in" the analysis as the patient.

But what does it mean to be as much "in" the analysis as the patient? Is the relationship, by means of its symmetry, really one of equality. Does the analyst need the patient as much as the latter is need of the former? These questions, although crucial, are hard to answer simply. Let us return to Meier's formulations of the symmetrical process. He speaks of the "oscillation" which is set up between the two partners. He states (5):

"When things are going well, and A and B are in phase, there is a building up of oscillation; when things are going badly, a destructive interference. The last named effect narrows down the personality and is found, unfortunately, among not a few analysts, a fact which says much for the 'totalistic' character of the situation."

I know of a particularly apt symbolic expression of this oscillatory character. A patient dreamed that a beautiful bird wove a thread about herself and me when things were going well, but when I was "out of it" (retreated, too objective, etc.), the bird continued to weave the thread about herself, but it had the effect of choking her, enmeshing her and, if unchecked, killing her. Such a symbol is also convincing of the truth that Meier refers to when he avows his experience that Eros is a "mighty daimon". This dream reveals that at that particular juncture, the patient was in greater need of the analyst than the latter was of the former, or he would not have retreated (though one can make a case that the analyst was not as aware of his need for connection as the patient was). But the analyst's need to help, to rescue the patient from this terrible state, brought him right back into the web. Thus different needs were being served through the same symbolic relation. The eros need of both is thus fulfilled. And, I think that this is often the case: the same relation or symbol is satisfying to the two partners and fulfilling a need, but often in a different way, or, in the obverse, different needs are fulfilled in one way. Through the confrontation with the other, both analyst and patient are compelled to see themselves and each other as they really are. These needs and conditions can not be subsumed under any "ought" or collective standards. This, of course, is what we expect from our patients and, naturally, we have to take our own medicine.

Meier points out that, in the initial situation, the analysand is moved out of a labile or stagnant condition and the analyst moved out of a stable one, as a consequence of the emotional charge of the archetypal images constellated. Transformations of personality therefore occur and both are changed.

From whence arises the analyst's stability? Obviously, from his own continued work with unconscious. I submit that the fundamental need of the analyst, as met in the analytic situation, is to deal with the unconscious, whether in himself or others, and this is the common thread of analysts' individuation processes. It follows that the analyst is always "in analysis", and with many people (all of his patients), so that he becomes an "old hand" in these encounters, knows more, and can remain more stable, even under pressure. His analytical needs, also, are met by several different sources so that he is not dependent upon any one patient as much as the particular patient is dependent upon him. But this is only generally true and at any given time, or with any given constellation of complexes, the analyst's need for the particular patient may be as great or greater than the patient's.

This latter situation seems to be a great bugaboo among analysts. I have found, however, that acknowledging this fact when it occurs (and admitting it is not the case, when that is so), is a tremendous humanizing factor in the situation. Rather than burdening the patient, such an acknowledgment of need on the part of the analyst gives the patient a feeling of genuine importance and value to the analyst which is not to be underestimated. Naturally, the patient then has the problem of what to do about it, just as the analyst has. As a matter of fact, the very independence and stability of the analyst, and his lack of need of the particular patient, may be a source of the "destructive interferences" of which Meier speaks. I think that is the personal, individual need of the two partners for each other that serves as the balancing opposite for the impersonal and collective material which arises from the unconscious. Thus, the equality consists in the mutual fulfillment of needs, primarily that of the individuation process, as it effects both partners.

Faced repeatedly with the foregoing observations and reflections, I somewhere decided to abandon myself to this process of openness and follow the flow of talk, imagery, and impulse going on in myself as well as the patient. I found it necessary to acknowledge my personal involvement and to speak out of what came to me. Thus far, this is standard experience for Jungian analysts. I found, however, that I had to go farther in even coming out with my reactions when they seemed to be immoral, unaesthetic, inopportune, untherapeutic (from any rational standpoint), indeed, at times all wrong. I expected this, after all, from my patient. How often my reactions matched what was going on in the patient was startlingly high and this encouraged me to proceed in this manner. When there was a matching experience, one could interpret (and thus raise into consciousness) what the actual transference situation was at the moment. Even when I was alone in my reaction, I found that there was no great loss, but that I, too, was shown to be human, limited, have complexes, and not be responding to the patient or the collective unconscious, but to my own complexes.

I recall, for example, revealing a fantasy of mine to a patient which contained some infantile sexual material and found, to my chagrin, that her own fantasies were of a more adult kind. When she, characteristically, would then berate herself for being unconnected and inadequate, I was able to point out that it was my own infantility and that, in this instance, she was far more grown up than I was. This was enormously beneficial for a person who tended always to see others as better, more advanced, etc., than herself and proved to be freeing for a greater openness to herself.

The kind of flow that I am describing becomes, at times, like the Free Association of Freud, but more directed in that the response of the other person is taken into account. Perhaps it is a mutual free association which includes dialogue. (At this point, a little voice tells me that I may be misunderstood, that some may think that I am advocating a new technique, or suggesting that the analyst come out with all that is going on inside him to the patient—a kind of reversal of what Freud advocated. I hope that this is not the case. I am skeptical of all techniques, certainly do not propose the reversal that the little voice suggests, but am rather trying to describe an attitude of openness in which the analyst can be much freer with his patient than has heretofore been suggested.)

I came to examine what interrupted this flow and found that this had to be analyzed in the usual way. I also found that I was increasingly making interpretations out of the experience of what was happening at the moment. In this, I find a parallel with the experience of C.T. Frey (6), who discovered that the effective dream interpretation was dependent upon an irrational factor, the meaningful moment. The meaningful moment, I think, is very often the transference situation. I find that the best interpretations come out of what is actually transpiring in the relationship, where both are in the grip of the same complex, which seems to travel back and forth. The implication of the foregoing is that the relationship itself is central and that the desired objectivity, individuality, and understanding come out of it, out of the actual experience, rather than out of some presumed knowledge or objectivity (intellectual or feeling) in the analyst. I am not certain if this is what Fordham is alluding to in his writings (7), but I believe that it is out of a similar experience of mutuality of the transference and its importance that he writes.

The experience of the aforementioned openness in the relationship has led me to give full assent to the contents of the psyche as described Freud, Adler and Jung. The nearest model to what actually goes on in the analytic work as so conducted is given by Jung's alchemical opus. The process is where the gods come down to earth, making it hell and heaven as they wish. Hells of infantile sexuality, domination, violence, hatred, greed, inertia, chaos—all deadly sins—and the heavens of love, mutual understanding, respect, value, dignity, intensity, consciousness. Yes, heaven and hell; the opposites in all their glory. And the dilemma is, indeed, for two benighted human beings to somehow maintain the flicker of consciousness in the midst of all this assault; to protect themselves from the world while being open to the gods. Yet to protect themselves from the gods and from each other as well. And why? Just because. Utter truth becomes more and more apparent because the Self mercilessly reveals the natures of both and is itself revealed— and we defend ourselves with labels, titles, and accusations of each other by calling it projection. No one wants the witch, but she also stands behind "el amor brujo" and transforms only when both silent and shared sufferings are acknowledged. All injunctions that this is a spiritual task, for the development of consciousness, to heal, etc. become pallid and wormy in the mouth. No one knows what it is for, though we hope and pray that it has a positive outcome...

So it seems during the work. End results do generally produce the positive effects of increased consciousness, healing, and the enhanced capacity for love that is desired, but there seems to be no guarantee of this.

Despite its trials and dangers, this kind of work seems to be of brutal necessity to not a few patients, to say nothing of analysts. Whether this is the inner demand for individuation on the part of many people, as Jung seems to think, I am not sure. I find, however, that the emphasis on this being a joint work, in the fullest sense, is especially and increasingly apparent. Perhaps this is to compensate for the sorry state of relationship and kinship in our time. I am inclined to think so.

If this is the true character of the analytic work and its ultimate model is the alchemical opus as Jung demonstrates and as Meier elaborates, there are some further questions and implications regarding who should undertake this work and what the training should be. I wish to use the remaining part of this paper to discuss this issue.

The most common models of the analytic relationship are those of doctor-patient and teacher-pupil, with analysts tending to identify with one more than the other of these models. There has been a growing dissatisfaction with the doctor-patient model among psychotherapists (e.g., the Existentialists), with the psychoanalyst Szasz delivering the most cogent criticisms. Szasz's main idea (8) is that the concept of "mental illness" refers to a mythical, non-existent condition, that it is based on a false analogy with medicine, and that the real work of the analyst is to help people cope with "problems in living." His criticisms are well-taken but will not be gone into here (I will subsequently present some other criticisms of the "doctor" viewpoint), other than to observe that Szasz rejects the one model to embrace the other. Helping someone to cope with "problems in living" results in a teacher-pupil model.

All of us know that the doctor-patient archetypal relation, as well as the guru-disciple relation, is constellated analytically all the time. We know, too, that a competent therapist needs to connect with both of these patterns or he is terribly limited. But many other archetypal relations are constellated as well. To mention only a few crucial ones, there are parent-child, sibling, lovers, all kinds of incestual relations, savior, hero. In the forefront of these constellations is the problem of Eros. This is just what Freud and Jung found. In our day, when relationships are often perfunctory, exploitative, devoid of spiritual content, it does not surprise me that analysts should be required to focus on this as a most necessary factor of human growth and significance. One could, with equal importance, reverse Jung's emphasis and state that God can be manifest where there are two as well as one, "among you" as well as "within you."

Now, if the analyst's mettle is tested in the eros problem, how can we describe the model? The shadow side of it seems to be whore or gigolo, since we charge a fee for our analytic relationships. But it may also be priest or priestess, serving the Self in an Eros capacity, as well as Logos. We are not the Goddess, however (as Gerhard Adler seems to advocate), although disidentifying with the God seems to result in becoming the Goddess. No we, like the patient, are the benefactors or victims, depending on our attitude, to what goes on.

I am deeply impressed with the experience that the archetypes, particularly the Self, apparently wish to incarnate themselves in the human relation, as well as in the individual, and that we are both fortunate and harassed by these profound events. In these days of mass action, it is also a source of great significance that two individuals participate in such a quietly momentous event, giving it all their best—and worst.

It is this experience which brings up my chief objection to the doctor-patient model. We, as Jungians, know that some God-image is always present and being served, whether we know it or not. If one is a doctor, one serves Apollo, as in modern medicine or, for other Jungians, Aesculapius (9). The "modern physician", including the physician-psychotherapist, is technique-oriented, impersonal, often mechanical, cut-off from or not aware of his profound connection with the spiritual factor. The rare doctor who has the spiritual attitude implied by serving Aesculapius is far more profound, but his objectivity and impersonality, compassionate or not, seems to preclude his being in the process as an equal. This, I think, would be the chief criticism of the "incubation" model shown by Meier in his earlier book (10). The incubation events occur, of course, but the model is not general enough to include the relationship of symmetry which Meier demonstrates in his later article.

Another criticism of the doctor-viewpoint has been given by James Hillman of Zürich, who shows (11) that the physician's effort to save life at all costs and to reduce pain misses the service of the psyche or soul. Thus analysts may give drugs, L.S.D., and all such extra-analytical care, which may be all right, even necessary for cure, but it is not analysis in the sense of the study and service of the soul. The additional criticisms of doctors as often too authoritarian, too concrete, too unionized, seem well-founded to me— and all of these shadow qualities can be traced back to the doctor-patient model.

The teacher-pupil model seems equally inept to me. However wise a guru, however brilliant an objective scientist, he is never quite human. The teacher and observer, in the traditional way, is always outside his object of observation and doing something to it, just like the doctor. The main difference is that the scientist-teacher wants to know or teach, rather than to cure. Psychologists, as the current carriers of this model (although many physician-analysts are also identified with it), get criticized—and justly, I believe—for being too remote, impersonal, objective, and theoretical. I know full well, for example, how young psychologists feel when first confronted with a patient as someone to be helped, rather than as someone to be studied. It is even taboo to touch this human being (no problem for the physician). It seems to take psychologists a long time to simply react to the situation and the person with some naturalness and not out of a theory. I experienced this myself with considerable discomfort. A further inadequacy of this model is shown by the observation that the very aim of the scientist is not fulfilled in the analytic relation when he stays remote. It is clear that those who have significantly advanced our knowledge of the psyche have been physicians deeply immersed in the work with patients (Freud, Adler, Jung, Rorschach, to mention only the pioneers).

In short, to become analysts, it would seem that doctors have to overcome being doctors and psychologists overcome being psychologists. Both need to embrace what the other has to offer. Combined, the two models have much to recommend them. Perhaps we have to have to find an equivalent in modern times for the old shaman. But even this, I think, is inadequate. For both models, in their best sense, serve a God, but where is the Goddess? To become her is a gross error, especially for a man, but even for a woman. I have the impression that we Jungians are almost as guilty as the Freudians for espousing a patriarchal male psychology. The spirit is always the focus, rather than the body or soul. Our women patients and analysts often also embrace this view, unfortunately, so that the animus has a bad name, unless he is doing some intellectual or artistic work (12). That Eros is a center of life, and that the animus might serve it, indeed a feminine Goddess, is a gross heresy. But my experience teaches me that this a fundamental need of both men and women and that there is no coniunctio until both principles are of equal status.

If the foregoing is a correct assessment, there are several implications. First, that analysis is a mutual unveiling ultimately and no use making bones about it. Second, that our requirement that analysts should previously have been doctors or psychologists is anachronistic, patriarchal, or merely a persona-type requirement and not in line with the reality of what occurs or what is needed. We all know that some of the best analysts have no degrees at all, as well as degrees in the humanities, which, after all, might be the best preparation for a humanistic endeavor. Third, that our training programs be geared to helping the prospective analyst cope with this reality which ultimately faces him.

This last implication deserves a full amplification, but here I am in a position only to make a few remarks. Clearly, the best and continuing preparation for the analyst is his own analysis—as long as necessary and with as many analysts as he can conveniently and usefully work. We can trust the continuing work with his patients to either drive him back for more analysis and/or arrive at the point where he is, indeed, constantly being analyzed by his patients, as well as analyzing them—a condition which both suits his needs and contributes to his development.

Secondly, we need to emphasize the transference more in our teaching and supervision. Jungians are, by and large, not in the situation described by Fordham (13) from his experiences in 1933, when the transference was "taken for granted", but we are far from focusing on the problem sufficiently during the training. One important practical viewpoint, in my opinion, is to take the dreams that the patient has of the therapist as true, and for the therapist to find where it is true, acknowledge it to the patient and only then deal with the projections. I am in full agreement here with Meier's statement of this attitude and have found that the practical effect is enormous.

In conclusion, I wish to re-affirm my belief, as Jung once said to Freud, that the transference is the "alpha and omega" of the analytic process and that, as Meier has observed (14), "...Any intellectual advance in psychology today depends very much on whether it is possible to revise these old-established concepts in the light of the experience that has accrued through their practical application."

NOTES AND REFERENCES

1. C.A. Meier, "Projection, transference and the subject-object relation in psychology," *Journal of Analytical Psychology*, Vol. 4, 1959, pp. 21-34.

2. Otto Fenichel, Problems of Psychoanalytic Technique, *The Psychoanalytic Quarterly, Inc.*, Albany, New York, 1941.

3. Gerhard Adler, "On the question of meaning in psychotherapy," *Spring*, 1963, pp. 5-30.

4. C.G. Jung, *Psychology of the Transference, Collected Works, Volume 16*, Bollingen Series XX, Pantheon Books, New York, 1954.

5. loc. cit.

6. C.T. Frey, "Problems of dream interpretation," *Journal of Analytical Psychology*, 1962, 7, 119-140.

7. Michael Fordham, *New Developments in Analytical Psychology*, Routledge & Kegan Paul, London, 1957.

8. T. S. Szasz, *The Myth of Mental Illness*, Hoeber-Harper, New York, 1961.

9. I am grateful to Robert Stein, M.D., of Los Angeles for his discussion of these points.

10. C.A. Meier, *Antike Inkubation und moderne Psychotherapie*, Studien aus dem C.G. Jung-Institut, Rascher, Zürich, 1949.

11. James Hillman, *Suicide and the Soul*, Hodder & Stoughton, London, and Harper and Row, New York, 1964.

12. I am grateful to Jane Wheelwright of San Francisco for discussion of this point.

13. Fordham, op, cit,.

14. Meier, op. cit., 1959.

CHAPTER TWO

NOTES FROM THE UNDERGROUND
A View of Love and Religion from a
Psychotherapist's Cave
(1969)

I think of my consulting room as a cave—a place where people retreat from the light of the sun and come to gaze at the dark world of their psyches, that place of dreams, fantasies, secrets, worries, desires, fears. After eighteen years as a psychotherapist, ten as a Jungian analyst in private practice, I think of myself as a groundhog in that cave and, therefore, these notes come from Underground. I am surfacing now, after years in the darkness below, to see whether it is safe to come out. I am afraid that the nuggets of dreams and visions which I have been privileged to observe will not be received, or will be seen as fool's gold rather than the real thing. The groundhog is said to be sensitive to shadow—should it cover him as he emerges, he goes back into the ground.

Before I speak about the gold, a word about the place of the psychotherapist in a discussion of love and religion. What can he say about these huge issues which has not already been said? Before Freud, the issues of love were left to poets; and before Jung, religion was the province of theologians. After these two giants of psychology had reported their observations of the soul from the viewpoint of their own caves, the situation changed. The revolution of depth psychology in the twentieth century had shaken and removed the old institutional authorities, substituting itself briefly as an all-knowing, scientific priesthood. But now we are at a time when most modern men find no one particularly authoritative in either love or religion.

For the most part, the Freudians and Jungians, revolutionary in their day, have become part of the Establishment; the young gravitate to them less and less. I have yet to hear positive words from my older colleagues about contemporary youth's ways of love and worship. For them it is "dissociated group-sexuality" and "doped-consciousness religion." Nor are the young less negative about their elder's "hypocritical morality" and "loveless lives."

So, as there are no experts, I shall speak of the psyche as shown to me over the past years in the dreams, fantasies and problems of my patients—and myself. Together with the demise of the expert there is a death of that shaky belief in a thing called pure objectivity. We are all creatures of psyche, as well as of our time; we all speak out of our own condition; we all speak ultimately about ourselves. Therefore, it is incumbent upon us to acknowledge that sub-jectivity and to speak from it and about it when we address ourselves to such important matters as love and religion.

Patients complain of too little love, giving and getting. So, by love I mean the need for emotional closeness, for sexual gratification, for relation-ship—fundamentally, the need for union at various levels: spirit, body, soul. Patients suffer from problems of religion: the need for meaning, for answers concerning who one is, why one is here, what it is all about, where is the numinous and awesome, is there a God, and what is He like?

Because of their reflective and soul-searching needs, people who are forced to "tune in" on their psyches and become aware not only of the spirit of the time, but also experience and intuit that which others in the culture tend to discover only after. Freud's interest in sexuality, for example, despite the academic outcry at the time, reflected only that which was going on in the unconscious of Western civilization. He anticipated long in advance and helped create a new attitude toward love and sexuality. The same holds true for Jung in the religious field. We are still a long way from grasping all these giants discovered. Although with the help of our introspection and soul-searching, I believe we may approach this immense task, and glimpse aspects of the future.

Let me give an example from one of my dreams. Eighteen years ago, when I was studying psychology in graduate school and was already in analy-sis, I dreamed:

> I was walking on campus on a bright, clear day. Many others were strolling, too. Suddenly, there arose from the sea a tidal wave which swept toward the campus. Other people were distraught, and ran in anguish. I was fascinated by the sea, particularly by the white caps and foam of the waves. Finally, the sea began to inundate the campus, and I climbed the scaffolding of a building that was just being constructed. I was uncertain if this scaf-folding would protect me from the tidal wave. The feeling was, however, that once the water had flooded the campus and receded, this would a new and better place than before.

The dream speaks of my situation: it hints at the impending end of my days as a student, as well as an end, as a consequence of analysis, of those clear-skied, rationalistic, academic attitudes with which I had been trained. But the dream also portrays a larger than personal event. The unconscious in its collective form as the ocean invades the institutional area of light, of rational consciousness. I am fascinated by the unconscious, particularly in its foaming, eros aspect. Aphrodite was foam-born, you recall. The wave sweeps the campus and I finally climb a new structure that might survive the invasion. The lysis or end of the dream is uncertain, but there is hope for a new consciousness to emerge, one which will survive the seeping away of the detritus of the old rationality, perhaps. The wave may fertilize like the inundations of the Nile; it may be occasion for a rebirth of a feminine, eros aspect.

All this was certainly true of my personal psyche at the time and mirrors accurately what took place in my development for some years afterwards. But the dream also speaks of a collective level, of a campus, of an institution, of a flood, all greatly beyond my personal concerns.

As I see it, the dream anticipated the flood that subsequently hit many college campuses. To me it is not too fantastic to think that the tidal wave of passion and love which I glimpsed at that time, in the relative safety of analysis, slumbered also in the souls of my contemporaries. Since that time, the flood of revolution has increasingly swept the campuses. I am inclined to believe that the dream had objective significance and that its lysis is going on right now. It is an open question whether there will be a new attitude on the campuses, a place where the feminine principle will also reign. Is not the emphasis of the students upon love, and beauty, upon emotion, and nature? That flooding took me far from the University, and eventually brought me to my own cave.

What is it that I have found in my careful attention to the psyche? (That, by the way, is another and valuable definition of religion: the "careful attention" to the numinous, to that tremendum which fascinates us and frightens us, wherever it occurs. My own piety may be, indeed, a religion of the psyche). I have found that the old images of God have died or fast dying—hence the "God is dead" ideology. This means that the authority, creativity, power for good and evil which was previously experienced or projected upon a "God out there" is no longer viable, and that God has taken up residence in the human soul. Thus we are fascinated with the psyche. But this God who dwells in the psyche is not so readily apparent. He makes Himself known first in the images and forms of the past, e.g., Greek, Jewish, Christian. Moreover, these psychic parts war in ways which are astonishing. Freud saw this already as the battle between the superego—a judging and punishing Jehovah—and the id, a daimonic child who seeks pleasure amid the breakage of all rules. Jung saw this—more accurately, I think—as the mythological play of archetypal images, man living out a myth unawares.

Jung saw that the God-image in some men pushed them towards realizing the "God-within." This he called Individuation—that process of struggle between nature and nurture, the given and the possible, a road which winds a long way, resulting in uniqueness. The symbols which emerge on such a path, the exciting, miraculous, and painful steps of so profound and often lonely a journey, are graphically described in the example of Jung through his autobiography, Memories, Dreams, Reflections.

Jung thought the process of Individuation was aristocratic, limited to the few. In the years since I have been watching this in myself and others, however, I have found that Individuation is much more common than Jung believed. Indeed, I have found that many—most, even—of those people in analysis for more than a year have been fundamentally gripped or plagued by this process. The evidence comes from their dream symbols, their interminable struggles that, on the surface, should be readily reconcilable.

The slang for Individuation might well be "doing your own thing," which, of course, many people now embrace. And there is a strong sanction to take this path. But to do one's own thing as a conscious process, to follow the course of one's uniqueness and creativity, to branch out and away from established patterns, be they of family, country, profession or religion, really to Do One's Own Thing, is very difficult and painful. Nevertheless, I think that the conscious taking up of one's psychic development is increasing and partly accounts for the breakdown of outer authority and old standards.

What, then, of the previously accepted images of God "among us"? Rejection does not sweep them away. The abandoned Gods of the fathers continue to exist in oneself as autonomous devils or take up residence in the many "isms" which abide in the world. Communism, Scientism, Psychologism, Drugism are just a few of the dead Gods of Judaism, Christianity, Greek Paganism that have survived in other forms. The compensatory and evolutionary nature of the psyche, however, suggests that new, collective images of God would appear. Also, man's social nature requires a new image of the Divine.

Will this new image be another variation of the Christian myth? I think it will; for the image of God in a particular culture rises naturally out of the antecedents. The next development in Western man may well take its source from the religion which has been dominant for two thousand years, Christianity. Even if the Christian religion "dies," its seeds could take an underground path of growth so that the new myth will continue certain Christian features. Let me illustrate this direction from a dream of a non-Christian man who, all the same, had to struggle internally with Christian symbolism:

> I am standing on a hill overlooking a valley. Just beyond the valley is another hill, as high as the one I am on. The region is semi-arid and dry, but has the atmosphere of a beautiful desert region in either New Mexico or Israel. Many people are gathered on both hills, walking about expectantly. There is tenseness and electricity in the air. Far down the valley, and upwards towards some high mountains, there is a small group of people. They walk together, seemingly following one man. As they come closer, one can see a certain radiance around the heads of all these people. I am startled to see that these must be halos. It is a light, a glow about them. I feel glad, as if I understand something by experiencing, by seeing, that which had been puzzling to me.

As they come closer, I see that the man in the lead is Christ, but he is nothing like the pictures I have seen. He is tall and dark and quite muscular. He even resembles the movie-actor Charlton Heston. He walks firmly, even angrily. Nothing is said, but as they come close to us and directly before us in the valley below, all of us, on both hills, know that Christ is returning and that he is returning angrily. His anger is because he has been misrepresented and he is now returning to the world to change all that.

The Christ of this dream is far, indeed, from those sentimental paintings popular during the last centuries. I think of Philip Roth's novel, Portnoy's Complaint, in which the Jewish hero recalls seeing these pale pictures in a Catholic home; he wonders how Christians can conceive as God what Portnoy considers "The Pansy of Palestine." The Christ of the dream is as angry as the one who drove out the money-changers; he is also muscular, strong, and handsome—even if still slightly tainted by sentimentality, now in Hollywood colors. But this Christ has body! That seems the great change of the new aeon: the God of Love can have a Body. Perhaps this new God of Love will even make love as well as preach it.

In contrast, I would like to show another aspect of the changing Christian myth. This time the dreamer is a young woman in her early twenties. She has come for therapy because after having given birth to a child out of wedlock, she suffered from anxiety and bodily vibrations which made her feel as if she were going to die. What emerged in the analysis was not that she had unconscious guilt about having a bastard child; rather, that she had been deprived by her modern, very competent physician from experiencing the actual birth of her baby. She had been knocked out and had the baby taken from her both in the birth process and afterwards. She needed to have that natural experience, not to be treated like some freak, object, or "fallen woman." The young woman dreamed as follows (the boy-friend of the dream, incidentally, is not the father of the child but a current relationship):

> My boy-friend and I are in bed together, making love, but having some trouble. At that moment, Jesus comes into the room, stark naked, and announces that this is "The Age of Immaculate Conception."

The dreamer was raised agnostically in an enlightened, formerly Christian household. The dreamer enjoyed sex and had no apparent "hang-up" with it. She also was in a reasonably good relationship with her boy-friend. The meaning that emerged from our work was that Jesus was speaking about the need to have a God within. She was being pressed to give birth, within herself, to a God-man. Not only she, the dreamer, was so pressed, but what is emerging Jesus says, is a whole "Age of Immaculate Conception." Men and the new God-image can be born in a state of grace, not through "sin." This has a very deep and far-reaching implication: nothing less than the redemption of men; or as the Bible anticipates, when all men will "be as Gods."

Lest you think this is a sweet story that causes the dreamer no pain, let me assure you that the coming-to-be of the Christ image is far from pleasant, edifying, or marvelous. Mostly it is hell. For it means crucifixion, an inner torness between opposites of desire versus duty, of morality versus love, or even of one duty against another, one love against another. Such people do perform an imitatio Christi, but they do so not out of a wish nor because they are Christians, for such a God-image occurs among Jews, Christians, Agnostics, and even Buddhists! It is a syncretic thing that is happening.

Let me give you an example from the dream of a woman who was born Jewish and given a Catholic education, subsequently to become, like moderns of her day, agnostic. This woman dreamt that she saw Christ upon the cross, but that he was dead, or nearly dead. She then began to make oral love to him, fellatio. The Christ stirred and gradually came to life. He then descended from the cross and, despite the dreamer's desire that he remain with her, went off "about his father's business," although he was much appreciative of her love. Her dream ended at that point, but the subsequent experience of her life, of being torn apart in loving a man, in trying to be true to her own love at the cost of her security, her family, her reputation, showed how she experienced the "coming to life" of the God of love within her. She drank deeply of this spirit and was often abandoned by it. She had many agonies until a feminine Self could be born which could encompass this great spirit of love.

You will note the rather uncanonical presentation of Jesus being loved orally. Such things do happen in dream and fantasy. This imagery is not so far afield even within the tradition of the Church. In the sacrament of the Mass, the God is incorporated: he is eaten, body and blood. This deep cannibalism of the soul is one of the most profound expressions of the idea that one assimilates, takes in, integrates a particular psychological or experiential content. However, the oral love of the dream is a taking in, a loving which is not cannibalistic. It takes up that which Victorians thought of as pathological and even Freud considered "infantile," and makes such love holy, special and profound, not pathological.

The dream of this woman is not unique. A comparable series of dreams from one man shows a similar development. Furthermore, these dreams indicate that the archetypal background for the God of love does not restrict itself to Christian symbolism and dogma alone. The man dreamt that a dark and powerful, demonic figure was going to teach women to love by first compelling fellatio and then requiring that the women lick up the remains of the semen. This was followed by a vivid illustration with various women. The dreamer awakened with sexual desire, fear, and disgust. He was confronted with a dark Eros, a "mighty daimon," as Plato tells us. Some time later, this same man dreamt of a peculiar priest-wizard who had a number of women around him, all of whom were being instructed in the ways of love-making as a religious rite. Again, the main ritual for such expression lay in oral love. Still later, the man dreamt that a 'Redeemer had been born of a sweet, but passionate young woman, unknown, yet one that the dreamer had been intimate with. The dream father, however, was both "unknown" yet related to this same demonic God hovering in the background.

I believe the unconscious picks such "polymorphous perverse" sexual symbolism in the portrayal of its new God images, because the psyche is trying to restore and re-divinize those aspects of bodily love which have been rejected as taboo. This was anticipated by D.H. Lawrence. In *The Man Who Died* Lawrence beautifully describes the experience of the man, Jesus, going from the crucifixion to a priestess in Egypt, who teaches him love in the flesh. In a similar vein is *The Holy Sinner* by Thomas Mann and some of the works of Henry Miller. However, in our time, where has sex has become almost blasé, it is no longer the opening up or even the valuing of sexuality which can shock us, rather the new shocking thing for our western consciousness is the re-divinization of sexuality. That God can have a penis as well as an all-seeing eye! That God can make love as well as preach about it!

I think these are hints of the new God-image. He is a demon and from the Underworld, but he is not the devil, nor even a devil. The devil of Christian tradition is an unavoidable negative brother to the all-positive Jesus-image of God. The emerging image is different. He is demonic as passion and love and sexuality can be demonic, with their aspects of jealousy, rage, possessiveness, desire. This demon is no devil; he simply includes those aspects of love previously rejected by the conscious acceptance of love as purely Agape. This demon is from the Underworld in that he is a spirit which dwells in the flesh, emerges from the flesh as in the spiraling upwards of the serpent-like energies of the autonomic nervous system in Kundalini Yoga. But he is also romantic and gentle.

Some years ago, I dreamed:

> I had been on a long journey and had come to a place in the Underworld. I entered a room which was much like a cave. This cave was dark, but I could see on the wall a very beautiful tapestry which seemed to have its own sources of light from within itself. The tapestry looked something like those pictures of Columbus discovering the New World, but this was a Knight-Soldier-Discoverer, accompanied by an American Indian, stepping ashore under a bright sun. But what they were finding ashore was a figure which looked like the alchemical Mercurius, a hermaphroditic being with golden light about him. I was impressed by this beautiful tapestry but then became aware that in this room was a living figure, large and awesome. I cam closer and found a dark, powerful man, chained to the floor by means

of a circular handcuff. An unknown source made me aware that this figure was a God-man and related to the Mercurius of the tapestry. I had in my own pocket the key that would unlock the chains and free him. The choice was mine. I hesitated for a moment as to whether to free such an unknown and powerful being, and then did so. At the next moment, this being and I were going at great speed, like arrows, the dream suggested, towards the City. At the same moment, I was aware that the God-man was himself like an arrow.

The God-man of the dream seemed to me none other than Eros, the mighty demon of love who had been rejected by Christianity and gone underground. This God of Love was somehow related to Mercurius, about which Jung has written so much, and which involves the chief labor in the alchemical work in the individuation process. Further, there is a hint of another sort of discovery, similar in kind to that of Columbus of the New World, but this time the Indian is accompanying Columbus! I concluded that the realization of this tapestry, the work of art, devotion and love, is to bring back to the city, to society, to life, the demon Eros, the love-God.

The subsequent course of my life has, indeed, involved such struggles, realizations, dismemberments and crucifixions as difficult and trying as those of my patients. My understanding of what has resulted over the years of coping with these demon Eros, this archetypal representative of aspects of the self which have been overlooked in our culture, is that this God wants to become Man, just as Jung hypothesized. It is as if the living of these conflicts both humanizes the God-image and divinizes man. We have had God the Father, God the Son, and now God the Holy Spirit has descended into Everyman and is becoming God the Brother. God becomes more human and men become more God-like when they take up this dismembering struggle to allow God to live in their own souls rather than to project him elsewhere.

Along with the new image of God, there seems to be emerging an image of a Goddess. Because the old image of God is dead, the psyche seems now to be bringing up repressed and ignored aspects of the soul. Among these discarded parts of the psyche, much will be feminine, as would be expected from depth psychological theory. We have evidence also from our culture in the recent enhancement of what have been thought of as feminine values: feeling, intuition, body, the personal, the irrational, beauty—in contrast to their masculine opposites of thought, fact, spirit, the impersonal, the rational, utility. To shed some light upon what historical transformations these changes are alluding to, let me begin by telling a dream.

This dream is from a woman who is herself a practicing psychotherapist, has had many years of analysis with various analysts, is Jungian in her orientation. I mention the Jungian orientation for several reasons. First, Jung plays an important role in the dream. Second, among modern psychologists, Jung has been most aware of the feminine principle in the psyche and has gone further systematically to include and accept this aspect.

> The dreamer is informed by Jung that he can see her if she wishes. She has been having an analytic hour with an old woman analyst, a trusted friend as well, and now prepares the room for Jung. She is competent and at home in it, but has difficulty lighting the fire. She finally does so as Jung comes in. She laughs, but feels exasperated. Jung mimics her and she feels that he is picking up something deep within her. She says that she feels dissatisfied, that there is something deep within her she wants to get at. She is aware of being connected with ancient women, Babylonians. The deep ironical laughter has something to do with the Whore of Babylon.
>
> Jung and the dreamer sit close together, and Jung asks if the dreamer has thought about what is behind the archetypes. The dreamer starts to respond from knowledge in a previous dream and Jung is delighted and comes close. He then speaks of a grandson, but not his biological one. After that, Jung complains of pain, seems to grow old and rigid, his hands blacken and fall away. It is a shock and horrible to the dreamer. Jung is matter of fact and dispassionate about it. He has lived long enough, but can't tell how long it will be before he will die.

This is a long and complicated dream, but I will relate some of what we both concluded as to the dream's meaning. She has a deeply feminine, ancient thing within her which "Jung" can pick up, but which can not yet be expressed. It has to do with Babylon and the Whore. I shall come back to this symbol later. "Jung" then asks her about what is beyond his own theory and the dreamer has some ideas. He speaks about future generations knowing his ideas, males, his grandson. Finally, he grows hardened, rigid, and ready for death. Jungian psychology in general could be reflected in this dream as having become unfortunately rigid, and just because of this inability to get access to the deep and ancient feminine principle which wants to express itself. It seems to take several generations, according to "Jung" in this dream, for such an assimilation. I think that this is true. Very few of the colleagues of my generation, Jung's "grandsons," so to speak, have been compelled to take up this challenge of the ancient feminine. The dreamer herself, however, has already done considerable work in this area and, I believe, it will be women who will be carrying the expression, the coming into being, of the ancient, neglected feminine aspect.

What is this aspect? The qualities of the Goddess which are being re-awakened can be subsumed under the name, Witch. The Witch, this dark and magical principle, ancestress of the matriarchal religions, this threat to the austere disciple of Protestant Christianity, to the monotheism of Judaism and to the rationality of science, brings with it the occult, such as astrology and magic and the darkly sensual, such as is recalled when we think of the Whore of Babylon.

This Witch figures appears in dreams in many guises. When negative, she can be like Mrs. Portnoy in the book by Roth I mentioned earlier—unloving, unconscious, negatively self-involved, hostile, bitchy. She can also, in her deeper aspects, drive a person crazy. I have seen many people, including myself, in witch-states of enormous pain and frustration. These are the negative emotions of love: jealousy, hatred, envy, rage. There is the negative feeling of frustrated life: feeling impotent, unable to act, torn apart. There is the pathology of fear and distrust—suspicion all the way to paranoia, twisting of reality, feeling, often rightly, that one is a victim. There is also the darkening of consciousness which blots out memory of anything good.

Such is the experience of one who is caught in a witch-complex, in the negative feminine of the emerging dark Goddess. One terrible aspect of the witch-complex is the inability to express in words. Remember what happened to the Babylonians? Their tower of Babel, their multiform modes of expression, along with the attempt to reach Heaven itself, was struck down by the patriarchal God. And Babylon, including the Goddess, was left speechless. She is beginning to return, but is having trouble expressing herself.

The agnostic woman I mentioned earlier, who took on the oral love of Christ, dreamt that she saw the witch suffering terrible agony in hell. But she was unable to utter a sound, and one could sense her agony only from her eyes and face. This inability to say what is happening occurs commonly. Sometimes the words are not available; sometimes the words would hurt too much if they came out. Sometimes one must not speak or cannot. This is a hell of dismemberment.

Just as the male Eros-God has in his Christian form an aspect of pain and horror, symbolized by the suspension between the opposites in the Crucifixion, the female Witch-Goddess has the symbol of being roasted in the fire when she is alone with the agony of her state, and the symbol of dismemberment. The breaking up of one's psyche into pieces is horrible. I recall a dream of my own of this kind. I saw the mother of an old friend of mine, dark and dreary, with flat, suffering eyes. She seemed to be accusing me of something; I was guilty. I awakened feeling depressed, lifeless, worried and full of obsessive rumination—just as the woman used to be, and vaguely guilty. That was a witch state. And her flat suffering eyes were mine: I had lost all vision, all perspective of my situation. This loss of reality is a feeling of dismemberment.

I have mentioned only the negative of this Goddess. What of the positive? This might be seen as an image of a new feminine Self—a beautiful and passionate Gypsy, for example: a woman of spirit who can also love and be independent. I recall a dream of a woman who had worked hard in analysis for several years:

> She had been on a long sea voyage with many people, all those whom she loved, cared for, was involved with, including her analyst. At one point, she knew that she would have to leave all these people in order to find herself. She chose to accept this fate, despite the pain, and leaped over the side of the ship, sinking down into the depths of the sea. After having difficulty breathing, she finally saw a beautiful golden flower, growing from the depths of the ocean, and that gave her peace, serenity, and primarily, a deep acceptance of herself as unique, an individual different from all others.

This dream shows the aspect of the witch which compels the woman to go against eros, love, and relationship, and to be alone. She has to be alone to find her spirit and also to come to her deepest feminine self, the biological plant level of the flower. The dreamer did not know of the symbolism of the oriental golden flower, about which Jung has written a commentary, but she experienced in her soul that profound union of male and female, yang and yin, which brought her the serenity of self-acceptance. Later on she dreamt that she was being hounded on all sides by the people she loved and who loved her; she could handle it only by feeling, just at her back, this same golden flower. Thus does the feminine self, this mandala of tender wholeness show itself.

There are many dreams from women which show that they must travel the road of their individuation via love. And their love will be painful, unconventional. Emotion, passion, irrational intuition must all be included. The witch is bringing back a darkly feminine love of deep personal involvement, of the endurance of pain and the dismemberment of being unable to take action. It is the love of Aphrodite in all its forms, sensual, dark, full of intensity.

This also means taking one one's opposite in many ways. Here, I am reminded of a woman who could always love, tenderly and passionately, but who had difficulty expressing herself verbally. After a painful period of struggle such as I have described, there emerged in her, almost perfectly, whole poems of love. This woman had never had training in writing of any kind, but the level of struggle produced an expression of deeply beautiful and philosophical poems, expressing primarily the paradoxes of love. We see, thus, that the witch, with her phallic nose and aerial broom, is also united with a maleness, a being which expresses itself in spirit.

The lack of communication in words also suggests the feminine need for non-verbal expression, for touch and taste and smell, as well as talk. She is there, is she not, in the current sensory awareness laboratories?

The archetype of the witch is also bringing forth a new form of con-sciousness—a new Logos, as well as a new Eros. This new form of con-sciousness is quite different from that having prevailed for many hundreds of years. It is personal rather than impersonal, concrete rather than abstract, individual rather than collective, magical rather than scientific, irrational rather than rational. Even though feminine and different from the prevailing consciousness, it is yet consciousness. It is already found in fields such as the healing arts, which combine science and art, require intuition and the per-sonal touch. Psychotherapy itself is just such a field.

This old-new consciousness is associated with the occult, with astrology, Tarot, and all kinds of divination—with what has been called the Black Arts. They are coming back, despite being driven out by science. And now, hope-fully, there is enough of the scientific consciousness and reason among all of us to be able to look at, to reintegrate that which has been rejected and repressed. From where I sit in my cave, the popularity of astrology, of all the occult books, of Eastern ways of religion, of meditation, and the like, as an awakening of the feminine, of the mother as opposed to the father, of the sister as opposed to the brother, of the mother-daughter myth as opposed to the father-son myth of Oedipus. All these are ways of saying that a new kind of consciousness is being born. But this new feminine God-image is not yet fully clear, partly because, being feminine, she never will be "clear" the way our rational, scientific, blue-skied consciousness would like. But partly, too, because her outlines are not fully apparent but are developing along with us. In short, I think that God the Sister is emerging along with God the Brother, and that we all, men and women, are partners in helping to realize this event. That is what is meant to me by the hermaphroditic character of the Mercurius in my dream and in alchemy. I think, too, that this is what the process of indi-viduation is about: for each of us to realize in our souls and in our loves an emerging and self-realizing He-She God. For is not the totality a union of equals, of male and female, of yang and yin, of father and mother and also, in the coming time, of brother and sister, as the alchemical imagery puts it?

I have portrayed this event in a book of mythical-psychological tales which tells about ten people of different religions who meet in Paradise. After they have pursued their individuation processes, they find communality in the experience of the God-Goddess becoming manifest within them. My own psyche resonates particularly with that aspect of Jewish mysticism called Kab-balah. The Tree of the Sephiroth, with its imagery of male and female unions of various kinds, is a tenfold image of God. This goes beyond the Trinity in its apparent polytheism, but it still holds the oneness, the monotheism, for these ten aspects of are but the faces of the One God. Also, the Kabbalah image of the wedding of God with his own feminine Shekhina, which lies in the soul of man and must be realized on earth in the community of humankind, suits me psychologically very well.

Much more could and needs to be said about this emerging consciousness of feminine Logos and masculine Eros. I am aware that I have not differentiated the two from each other sufficiently and that I have only sketched their portraits in outline. But time requires that I leave it at that now. I mean both the time permitted for the presentation tonight and also this time in history, when we are touched with only glimpses, with hints, with intuitions of the future and discern only outlines.

CHAPTER THREE

TRANSFERENCE, INDIVIDUATION, MUTUAL PROCESS (1972)

Some years ago, I wrote a paper, called "Some Implications of the Transference" (15), in which I explored the consequences of what seemed to me the fact that as analytical work progresses, there is an activation of the unconscious, affecting both analyst and patient. This results in a mutual embroilment in the work, the archetypes manifesting in both participants and in the situation itself, leading to a condition of symmetry. This symmetrical condition was originally formulated by Jung (8), elaborated by Meier (11), and represented a significant advance over the previous psychoanalytic view of transference as largely perceptual distortion and inappropriate response, asymmetrically directed from patient to analyst.

In my paper, I maintained that the symmetrical relation required a greater degree of openness on the part of the analyst than was usually acknowledged, and that the work eventually became a truly mutual one, in which both participants were changed. By openness I meant not merely disclosing facts about oneself or mutual free association, but that each partner disclose his feelings and fantasies in relation to the other primarily. I believed that the mutuality was happening anyway; both parties were now required to focus upon it, make it conscious and shared. The analyst who resists this fact of mutuality, I held, makes the patient carry the whole burden of the activated unconscious and forces him into the role of "sick patient" or "unknowing pupil." I found that the symmetrical relation occurred quite frequently in my own practice and was of central importance in the individuation process. In my paper, I explored the implications of this fact which, I believed, required analysts to go beyond the traditional doctor-patient and teacher-pupil healing and learning models.

Although published in a not-easily-available Festschrift, the paper was greeted with a lot of response, both positive and negative. It is even translated into Italian (16). As I collated the criticisms of my paper, I found that they mostly had to do with the fear of loss of control by the analyst: sexually, aggressively, emotionally, or ideationally. The analyst should maintain his composure, his objectivity, and he must certainly never "act out." I discovered that not a few analysts had, indeed, "lost control" during their experiences.

There had been emotional or sexual involvement with a patient that had been disastrous or, at least, very painful. They gone "gone with the process" and had been deeply wounded, inwardly or outwardly, by ethical violation, by betrayal, or by the breaking of the temenos, the analytical vessel. Indeed, I had the impression that this injuring of the healer was a fairly common occurrence, even a necessary part of the experience of the archetype of the "wounded physician".

The particular nature of the wound was not written about—indeed, was hardly even talked about among colleagues, since there was some fear of further hurt, but it was a commonly hinted at experience, nonetheless. Patients, too, were wounded by such experiences, of course, but, surprisingly, were often less hurt than the therapist! Some colleagues thought that I was encouraging a freedom and openness which would lead to a painful and destructive outcome for both patients and therapists.

I was encouraging openness, it is true, but in the context of a joint work, a shared struggle with the opposites, a mutual process with patients who were capable of it. I was hardly speaking of imposing something or inviting destructiveness. I was speaking out of my own experience at the time, as well, and not only from a theory. I, too, had been deeply wounded by the consequences of my own necessity for openness and "going with" the truth of the process, but I was also much helped in my own development, thereby. Indeed, my individuation both demanded this direction and was deeply nourished by it. I think that some of my colleagues, faced with the kind of conflict, pain, and uncertainty that all serious and dedicated analysts must face, had to either avoid this confrontation, in my opinion, or were broken by it. Some seemed to do a "regressive restoration of the persona," as Jung describes it, in his second of the Two Essays on Analytical Psychology (5).

In the ensuing years, I think that I have learned something more about this mutual process that I would like to report. First, however, I wish to acknowledge where I found my critics to be right and I was wrong. At that time, full of the excitement of the work and my own involvement, I believed that most of my patients were in an individuation process. I noted this in my paper and admitted puzzlement about this, as contrasted with my colleagues. I was mistaken. Most, if not all, of my patients were trying to deal with their problems and pain psychologically, but that is not necessarily individuation. A smaller number of them looked upon their lives as ones of spiritual development, and it was this group that led me to believe that individuation, as Jung had described it, was involved. But I, in my need of partners in mutual individuation and in the joy of discovery, exaggerated. Individuation—in the sense of a conscious and active dealing with one's psyche in a committed way, pursuing the goals of wholeness and self-realization with a continuing relation with the unconscious—this was rarer than I thought. So, my critics were right about that. I can go even further. The number of people who are either capable of pursuing a long-term mutual individuation process, or desire to do so, are even smaller!

But, lest you think that I have retreated from the egalitarian and democratic stance of my earlier paper, and have fallen once more into the aristocratic attitude of "individuation for the few" or "mutual individuation for even fewer", I hasten to add that I think that the numbers of people who need both Jung's individuation and the mutual individuation of which I am speaking, are numerous and increasing. Not everybody is at that point, but I am encouraged that there is a definite evolution of a process of mutual growth which, I think, is important at this time in the history of the development of consciousness. I also wish to add that there are other modes of spiritual growth, of course, which are equally valuable. I am laying no claim for the ingrained superiority of processes which enhance psychological consciousness. The methods of meditation, such as in Buddhism or other religious structures, as well as in the variety of psychotherapeutic and magical approaches, are also productive of growth. Indeed, I am interested in comparing these modes with individuation. For example, a colleague and I are working on a comparison of Buddhist Enlightenment and Jungian Individuation, by a study of the Zen Ox-Herding Pictures. But one wants to be clearer about what all these modes can and cannot accomplish, what is fostered by them and what not, in order that all of them can develop. It is in this spirit that I am working.

Before discussing mutual process or mutual individuation in greater detail, I want to speak about what I have experienced as the limits of Jungian psychology and individuation itself. This will both make it clear that I am no mere propagandist for individuation, and will also further prepare the ground for our understanding of mutual process.

Individuation is a natural process, observed at work in the human psyche by Jung, who also developed some methods of facilitating it. He particularly stressed the consciousness-raising aspect by the work with dreams and fantasies and, ultimately, in the use of Active Imagination. This activity is focused upon the individual alone with himself and his unconscious, although, of course, there is the life necessity of confronting and relating with other people in one's process of growth and development. This devoted dialogue with the unconscious is soul-making and creative in its deepest sense, as all of us who have worked along these lines can acknowledge. It leads to enhanced consciousness, to creative work, to deep insights, to fundamental inner change. I can fully attest to its value, having been actively engaged with this inner work for more than twenty years! For me, this has developed into a literary form which I call "psycho-mythology," and is also central for my life.

But active imagination, I have also found, does not solve or even put a dent into those problems which lead to concretization, on the one hand, and to the outer world, on the other hand. Let me explain further. Through working with the unconscious, one "makes soul," as Hillman has described it (4);

one transforms the realm of passions and desires into ideas and images. This is spiritualization and sublimation, just as Jung maintained. This, however, leads only to the unio mentalis, as the alchemists described it and as Jung discusses in his Mysterium Coniunctionis (7). This state of "mental union" is achieved when projections are withdrawn from matter, from the body, and from the world. It is a stage of union of mind with soul. This unio mentalis precedes the unus mundus, the "one world" where psyche and matter are united, where inner world and outer world are again experienced as the same. Jung describes the latter condition as occurring in synchronistic events— which most of us know and have experienced at times, especially during our work with active imagination and other deep involvements with the unconscious.

Not many of us, I dare say, have found this union as a daily experience of life, where concreteness and symbol, image and reality, are normally experienced as One. That is the stage, we remember, when the union of mind and soul, the unio mentalis, becomes joined with the transformed "body", which is also the "world". That is the unus mundus, where the split between spirit and matter is overcome. And it is just at that point of development, I am maintaining, that the methods of work with the soul, of the person alone with himself, come to their blurry limit! And, I further aver, it is here that the horrible problems of my colleagues, with their fear of loss of control, occur. Are not they—and we—continually led toward concrete satisfaction, toward literal fulfillment? Does not the flesh, finally, defy all efforts after its total spiritualization? We all know this. We also know that it is, at last, the union of the opposites that we seek, and not spiritualization alone.

Analysts also know that they must be alert in these areas with patients. They believe that they must be the carriers of consciousness. The loss of control that analysts fear is that if they do not carry consciousness, it is gone, for the patients surely can not do this for both. Is that not so? Is that not the deeper anxiety? And this fear, of course, keeps analysts in the parent-teacher-guru-conscious role and keeps the patient as child-pupil-patient-unconscious role always. Well, some patients can get to the place of being carriers of consciousness, sometimes, where the analyst cannot!

(Two women friends, themselves therapists, have commented here that analysts do not like to give up the role of guru, and do not like to be acted upon, either. In other words, it is a question of power and control, of the person and the unconscious, and not just benevolence).

But I digress slightly. My point is that individuation, as usually described, comes to a certain limit in the problem of the realization of the Self concretely. Active imagination is soul-making and brings a union of ego and soul, but does not automatically result in union with the body. It is possible, however, I am maintaining, to individualize the specific ways of concretization of psychic union, and this mode is notably absent in Jungian literature.

I wish to put forward the notion that it is in these two areas, the concrete relation to the body and its energies, and to relationships and their complexity in group life, that Jungian psychology has, thus far, been insufficient. I also wish to state that what I am speaking about as "mutual process" is one attempt to advance both our knowledge and development in this area.

So then, having examined the limits of individuation as thus far described, let me go into greater depth and detail about mutual process or mutual individuation. I shall first present a general definition and then explore it.

Mutual process is characterized by being a psychological relationship in which the partners recognize and work with the unconscious as it manifests itself within them and among them. It requires an increasing degree of mutual openness, of intersubjectivity, and a recognition of their equality before the gods, the archetypes. It normally enhances both relationship and consciousness by promoting both differentiation and union. It results in a creative work, often one of joint concrete products, such as in art or science, or in aspects of relationship itself, such as mutual healing, mutual deepening. It is recognized as a spiritual task, a relationship requiring work. Each process, like individuation itself, is unique, and requires that both partners recognize that there is a potential for uniqueness at the outset which remains to be realized, made manifest. There is, therefore, always an uncertainty in the relationship, both between and within the partners, just as there is in individuation, and this provides part of the motive power for change. Mutual process recognizes all the trials and joys of individuation, including the characteristic struggle for union of the opposites of spirit and flesh, mind and matter, and continues this struggle as a shared experience, with mutual individuation, alone and together, as the outcome.

That is the general description. To amplify these points, I wish to begin with how I described this mutual process in my earlier paper, which focused particularly upon analysis itself and the transference. I spoke of the necessity that both parties become aware that the archetypes in general, or a particular complex at the moment, was affecting both of them, that they were in the grip of an image-event-process which goes back and forth. They are both observers and participants in this exchange, and it is this aspect which is central for mutuality and also is difficult to describe. But this participant-observer requirement was exactly that which enhanced consciousness, logos, and served eros, the relationship.

In my earlier paper, I described this as the gods coming to earth and incarnating in the relationship, making it heaven and hell as they wished. I think that I spoke truly, but somewhat dramatically. Not every incarnation of the archetypes is so dramatic or poetic or life-and-death in character; that depends pretty much upon where the particular participants are personally and also on how they affect each other. Yet there is a true drama in the interaction, just as the dream itself is a drama, a portrayal of the psyche. Now the drama is mutual, and it is shown in the difficult work of sorting out—by the use of dreams and fantasies—who is who and what the archetypes are doing.

One image I used in my earlier paper to describe this process was that of a bird weaving a thread about both parties. When both are in synchrony, there is a positive oscillation, a "build-up", as Meier had called it in his paper. When one retreated, or got too objective 00/0or "outside", the bird goes on weaving, but now merely chokes the other! The image comes from an actual experience of a patient of mine. From it, I can see very well that dis-synchrony can result, as Meier also observed, in the narrowing down of the personality of either patient or analyst or both. This is not so uncommon an occurrence, unfortunately, among some analysts.

Thus the process requires, by its very nature, the joint work of both parties. This mutual embroilment necessitates an openness to what is going on inside oneself, a sharing of fantasies, a speaking of impulses and ideas, a joint struggle in keeping the transformation process going, of uniting the opposites. And this is done by both following the flow, surrendering, and directing one's awareness and control, as well.

I have found that my concept of openness, and of surrender and control, were not entirely clear to others. By openness, I mean not the self-disclosure of facts about one's life or problems, necessarily—though these are not excluded—but the bringing forth of those fantasies and dreams, particularly, but also impulses and ideas, which have to do with the other person, analyst or patient. It is an openness of the subjective aspect of one's self which entwines the other person in some way. It is work with these images and impulses, jointly and openly, which is at stake.

As to surrender and control, there has been even more suspicion. Surrendering to the flow of imagery and impulse is not "acting out," since I assume that in this imagery there is also fear as well as closeness, retreat and withdrawal as well as advance, conscience as well as desire. Attention to surrender and control in one's self, as well as in the other, and going with the flow, will tend to preclude violation or hurt. It is this same Self, flowing back and forth, this same third factor, which is being served. The aim of this service of the Self, "among" as well as "within", as Jung was also careful in asserting, is one of uniting the opposites.

Now, that is the whole point. What is involved in mutual process, I am maintaining, in extension of Jung's work, is the union of opposites, both within one's self and in the relationship. I characterized this, even in my earlier paper, as the attempt at becoming conscious of and realizing the God "within" and the God "among". The God "within" is clearly the work of traditional individuation; the God "among" is enhanced with mutual process. The imagery for this is quite apparent in alchemy, which describes the work of the alchemist and his soror mystica, his mystical sister. Remember the pictures in Jung's books on this? Where the two adepts are fishing, and each hooks his opposite number beneath the water? And they are both being fished from above at the same time? Well, that is how it is. The man is both relating to his anima within, and to the person across from him, with whom he is having a psychological relationship. The same is true for his partners. All the complications of projection and connection take place, as is described by Jung in his Transference paper (8). But now both participants acknowledge their involvement in this process and work on it together. Nor is it just man and woman, or animus-anima underneath, of course. This same process can happen among men, and in all other types of relationship, including even parent-child, doctor-patient among them. It requires that the analyst realize that when he is doctor, for example, there is also the "sick patient" inside himself, and that the patient has the "healer" within himself, too.

Adolf Guggenbuhl has discussed this aspect very well in his book, Power in the Helping Professions (2). He has come to some conclusions similar to my own, at least as far as recognizing the danger of the analyst becoming caught in identifying with the doctor archetype. He uses the excellent concept, "split archetype," for the phenomenon of one person identifying himself as the doctor, for example, the other as the patient. The truth, of course, is that the opposite is in each and in both! I fully agree and can appreciate the vivid and convincing way that Guggenbuhl describes the destructive aspects of such a situation. I would add that the doctor would do well not only to recognize the "patient" within, but to also speak about it and from it, when it emerges in his work with the outer patient. I also think that what I have been describing as mutual process is one remedy for the destructiveness that Guggenbuhl is profoundly aware of in analytic work.

Guggenbuhl goes on to conclude that analysis itself is dangerous in that the analyst gets too wily, too tough, and eventually becomes impenetrable, cannot be touched. I think that this is often the case. The wounded analyst, hardened and tough with his scabbed-over wounds, becomes disillusioned, a wily old goat, a Saturn and senex, and with a regressive restoration of his persona, no longer vulnerable. I think that this is likely to happen if the analyst does not acknowledge the mutuality contained in our work. Guggenbuhl hits upon friendship as the antidote to this lamentable state. Friendship, of man and man, of man and woman, is the way that the analyst can still develop, be confronted and changed. This suggestion of Guggenbuhl is surely a valuable one, though I must remark that, as far as I have seen, many therapists tend to get rather isolated in their work and their friendships are not especially creative.

I would agree with Guggenbuhl's recommendation nonetheless, but I would like to add that there is a particular kind of friendship that can take place, despite his doubts in the matter. That is the psychological relationship which can emerge in the analysis itself. Psychological relationship is not limited to analysis, but is any relationship in which both parties recognize the unconscious background going on within them and between them, and that they both share this realization and work on it. That is mutual process.

Psychological relationship has been described as possible in marriage by Jung early on (9), and more recently attested to by Verda Heisler (3). It has not yet been described as developing in the analytical relationship itself, as occurring also in friendship and, indeed, in any kind of relationship. I am claiming that this is possible. I even have the seeds of such as relationship with my children, neither of whom is yet in their teens. Clearly, an active psychological relationship can occur in marriage or in the rare friendship, but it is not limited. My main point here is that the analytical vessel, when it is truly alchemical and recognized as such, provides the initial laboratory, the first experience, which then leads the analysand to be capable of this in other relationships. Indeed, I think that the fascination, in the twentieth century, for analytical work is because that particular kind of fostered psychological activity has been the seed of many creative developments in both logos and eros. Among these, I hold, is the fostering of psychological relationship.

Now it seems necessary to give examples, but this is hard for me to do. Not only is this difficult because I am mostly intuitive in type and examples, as facts, get lost for me, but also because the evanescent character of mutual process, as it changes from moment to moment, from relationship to relationship, is as difficult to pin-point, to nail down, as is the process of individuation itself! We know that Jung rightly resisted speaking about "stages" of individuation, and those of us who have struggled so hard for so many years know perfectly well that one does not move from persona understanding to shadow confrontation to anima-animus development to mana personality to Self, as is suggested in the Two Essays (5). We know that the whole thing is not even like the alchemists described their stages from the massa confusa and nigredo, through albedo, rubedo, to the finished Stone. And yet, what both Jung and the alchemists say, as we also know, is true.

The paradox here is that there is a certain truth to these general statements, but these generalities often break down in the individual case. Jung has shown us that. And this uncertainty and relativity holds even in chemistry and physics, as the Einsteins and Heisenbergs of modern science have demonstrated. Remember how it was in high school and college during the laboratory demonstrations in chemistry and physics, that the experiments would often fail? Even the general principle of gravity only works perfectly under very special conditions, in a vacuum. So then, in the case of the psychological field, where the observer is inextricably bound up with the observed, this uncertainty is even greater. Indeed, my formulation of "mutual process" is a variation on this same contemporary realization!

Yet one needs these generalizations, these collective formulations, at least as a guide line. I wish that I could provide them. But the truth is that I have not seen enough long-term mutual processes to be able to describe them generally as yet. I have, indeed, been blessed with a number of relationships of this kind, some now lasting five to ten or more years, but each seems utterly different to me and to connect with both special aspects of myself and my totality. In one relationship, for example, much of me as a writer is involved; in another, there is a joint work with art. In a third, there is the interplay between Buddhism and psychology. In still another, there is a movement toward magic, ritual, and the understanding of mediumistic phenomena. All of these mutual processes have emerged out of long analytical relationships to become psychological friendships. This seems to be my own pattern.

My wife has not been in analysis with me, and our mutual psychological process has a different character, of course. We not only share our children and life together, but we have the particular way in which our joint process works. It seems less turbulent than that described by Heisler (3), but that, I think, is because the interrelationship of our psyches and the nature of our characters is different. I am much impressed, I would like to add, that a comparison of the horoscopes can be very helpful in understanding how people in any mutual relationship affect each other.

In speaking of marriage, I think that the symbol of marriage itself can be one paradigm of the mutual process. The syzygy, a symbol of the union of opposites in the Self, appears frequently in such processes, just as it does in individuation. In addition, however, there is the emergent "third" in mutual process. Just as children usually result in a marriage, there are "children" in a mutual process. In several instances, for me, this has resulted in a joint artistic or intellectual work, an etching or an essay, for example. But there is also a creative work in the establishment of the relationship itself, or in group work. It is in this area that I am now exploring and experimenting. I am leading a group jointly with an art therapist friend, for example, and am planning a group on psychological problems of mediums with another friend. And I have already mentioned the work on Buddhist Enlightenment and Jungian individuation with a third person.

This leads over into a consideration of mutual process as not only occurring with two people, but with three or more. That is an area in which I am greatly interested, but I find it even more puzzling and difficult to work with than I have found with a single person. One way this has developed for me is in my analytic work with couples. Usually, this takes the form of seeing a marital couple, or parent and child, or lovers, or friends, for brief periods, in a kind of counseling. What I do is to describe and analyze the kind of interaction going on between the partners, to show how the complex or archetype is affecting both of them, interfering with their communication, their being able to see each other as real people and not as images. This consciousness-bringing work seems to facilitate not only the solution of particular problems and blockages, but to help the partners work together more psychologically as well. So far, however, the extent of mutual embroilment, including me, the analyst, seems limited. This is not because I am so wise and capable as to not be drawn in, but because the people do not stay around long enough for it to become a three-way or four-way mutual process.

I am quite interested in the possibility, even, of an analysis going on with two or three people simultaneously. Not only does this save money for the people, but new effects can emerge. There is the constellation of the archetype in the concrete relationship, for example, and its working through directly with someone a person is deeply involved with. This is analysis, I repeat, and not only traditional marriage counseling, since the unconscious is taken into account, and attention is paid to it as it appears in dreams, fantasies and in the relationship itself. I am speaking now of group work as analysis, and not group therapy or encounter groups. The latter normally work quite differently, I think. I believe that ultimately there will be a kind of work which can encompass the values of depth analytic effort in individual analysis along with group processes in a variety of ways.

In my work with groups in other ways, I can thus far report only little. Ongoing meditation groups, of which I have been a member, are instructive for other kinds of connection than mentioned heretofore, but it is too soon to say. What these meditational or magical or mediumistic groups have in common with mutual process groups that I have been describing is that they are intersubjective. One is alone in deep quiet with several others, or one shares the fantasy that emerges, or the mediumistic connections. The intersubjectivity is also found in mutual process, in working with the unconscious, in contrast to other types of group work, psychological or otherwise. Even the sophisticated encounter or gestalt groups, that work with fantasy or dreams, focus upon, as they are fond of saying, the "here and now." This is exampled in the kind of statement, "What you said me feel angry," or "I am experiencing pain in my heart right now." This approach is an excellent antidote to the usual distancing and depersonalizing, even dehumanizing techniques of much psychological work or ordinary conversation, but it leaves out the depth factor. Indeed, it leaves out the relationship itself. The leading lights of such groups, as in gestalt, emphasize that one is responsible for oneself, neither of us should hang on the other. The fact of the interaction, the nature of what is happening between the partners, both subjectively and objectively, is not mutually explored. And it is just here that depth psychology has its main interest. I am encouraged that this can be included in group work also.

I am aware that I have stated several times that it is difficult to provide examples of mutual process, even though I have been consciously pursuing such an activity for at least seven years. I gave given several reasons for this difficulty, and now I wish to mention two more. These are uniqueness and uncertainty. Just as each individuation process is unique, by definition, the same is true for each mutual process. This particularity precludes predictability of direction or outcome, and thus results in uncertainty.

These characteristics of uniqueness, uncertainty, and inter subjectivity bring me to my difficulty in conveying the idea of mutual process to others. Often the idea seems incomprehensible. Or, if it is comprehensible, the other person says that is nothing new. I am unable to make clear to myself whether this is, indeed, something new or not. The statements of others is not much help here since the pattern of most new things is first incomprehension, then rejection, then comes the acceptance with the statement that everybody knew it already. Thus, too, perhaps, with mutual process. Luckily for me, I am not inordinately possessive of holding the discoverer's pennant in that area and would prefer others to know what I am talking about and to share in our mutual enlightenment. In short, I believe in mutual process in the area of discovery of same!

[A social scientist colleague, familiar with related work by Rogers, Bion, the Tavistock group, Gestalt, as well as with my viewpoint, says here: "The part that is new, as far as I can see, is the (1) contract to (2) work (3) together (4) consciously on the (5) interaction of (6) unconscious transference and counter-transference, which, of course, is always present in varying degrees in any important interpersonal relationship."]

I have found that the understanding of the idea and its attractiveness varies with sex and age. Many older people either do not understand or are antagonistic, whereas the young people, under 25, both understand it more readily and like it. That is consistent, I think, with their revolt against the impersonal, dehumanizing aspects of our culture, and their desire for deeper and more meaningful subjective life, both alone and in community.

I recently began analytic work with a young woman of twenty who had undergone a number of months of therapy with a Freudian analyst. He had helped her, indeed, but her complaint was just in the area that I have been speaking about, so I would like to quote her very expressive words about it (my added words in parentheses for clarity):

"My pain is the pain of not being in connection with myself and not connecting with others. So, I went to a therapist, and he constantly told me to look into myself to find the reason for a question, and maybe when I knew that reason he would answer the question. That constant turning (me) back (to myself) denies that there are two people involved, that the therapist's emotional, physical being is also present. That must be acknowledged, for I can take in a look, a mood, the subtlest of things as being a response to what I am saying, to what I am. That (lack of response) is wrong. That is destructive of my being. I have the right to ask for clarity in what is happening. If I am projecting, tell me; if not, tell me.

"I am disconnected, and all he gave me was that I was disconnected. He would not connect with me, risk for me, be with me. That was too hard, so he played with knowledge. All I could give him was my sickness, which kept me sick out of my need of him."

That last line, "all I could give him was my sickness, which kept me sick out of my need of him," is, in my opinion, terribly poignant and important. This young woman had no knowledge of my paper or Guggenbuhl's book. She spoke from her own pain and experience and that, perhaps, is the most convincing of all.

So, the young understand the need for mutual process and connection better than older people do. But I also have found that women understand and appreciate it more than men do. That, I think, is because they are generally more tuned into the value and problems of relationship than men are. Relatively few men have spent as much time and effort on the anima development which would lead them to a care about relationship as such. Many men, of course, have developed the anima into creative areas such as art, science, and self-expression, but how many can really carry and struggle mutually with a relationship? Even analysts stay pretty much in the traditional anima roles of helping and healing, rather than in mutual work. I trust, however, that there will also be a change in that soon. The growing emancipation of women, enabling them to rightfully embrace and enjoy the fruits of independence and having their own spirit will, I think, compensatorily require that men develop their feminine capacities more, and among these will be the valuing of and interest in relationship. Just as the integration of the animus results in a spirited, independent woman, the increased integration of the anima required of men will result in animated, loving men! As I said in my earlier paper, the cultivation of eros and the service of the Goddess will become increasingly important as the New Age, with its technologically produced possibility of both freedom and leisure will both permit and require this, if we are to survive in this overpopulated world. As men become more involved with relationship, I foresee that male-male relationships will take on new creativity as well. But that, like the "new woman" emerging with liberation, is another topic in itself. I want only to hint at that development for the sake of completeness of presentation.

I want to return, now, to the limits of mutual process. Here, again, I wish to make clear a concept rather than propagandize it. Mutual process, despite its depth and intensity, can never replace individual process since each of us is, finally, alone. We are born into the world and die as separate beings, in a mortal body. And all our unions are only communicative or exchanges, at some level. We are, in the end, alone with the aspects of ourselves which are utterly unique. Indeed, we desire to remain not only unique, but also enjoy being solitary. Even the Goddess of Relationship, Hera, has a deeply solitary nature. Zeus's wife, mistress of monogamous marriage, required utter solitariness for herself, at times, or she became terribly bitchy! So, then, we shall always be partly alone with ourselves. One might even say thank God for this fact, since we can not really know the value of union if we do not know the value of aloneness. This is a pair of opposites that require each other, the God "among" as contrasted with the God "within". So, then, mutual process finds its limits in the person alone, in individuation for itself, in the God "within."

There is also a limit, I think, to mutual process among people. With how many pairs is it possible to have a meaningful, creative mutual process? Even though I am a born Gemini and am inclined to the "many", and even though my Taurus ascendant and Scorpio Moon give me both considerable energy and a need for depth and intensity, I am limited in the number to whom I can truly connect and relate with at any given time. There is also the danger that the "many" will not embrace the "one" and just fragment it. Pairs are limited, finally, and must give way to groups of greater numbers. I tried, indeed, not long ago, to realize my image of a Round Table of individuating people, Knights and Ladies sharing the common quest of the Grail of the new image of "God, "within and among." It did not succeed. Too much individual difference, too much that the people were all friends of mine and not of each other, were the reasons for failure. In any case, pair-processes must also find their limit and make room for threesomes, foursomes and more. The greater number of people, the less possible it is to keep in touch with the individuals, or to know what is happening among pairs.

We must deal, then, with the archetypes of multiples, with the larger God-images of people in groups. I know that this is possible. It is apparent to all that it happens, for we could not have organized religion or other rituals, for example. It is not apparent, however, if the underlying archetypes can be worked with, made conscious, in such large groupings. Perhaps group meditations are likely to be a good way into such work with more than four people. In that situation, at least, it is easier for us to hold on to our aloneness amongst the many.

So, then, mutual process leads over into group process and then into institutional or organizational process, about which I can say very little as yet. I have been analyzing some creative sociologists, however, and hope that they will ultimately do original work in this area. Indeed, perhaps that area will be a mutual process of these sociologists and myself!

Another limit to mutual process comes in the area of choice. By this, I mean not only that many people seem to incapable of taking on such a task, but that even those who are quite capable of this may not choose to do so. Or, they may limit the number of such involvements drastically, to only one person, perhaps. I have several examples for this. The first of these has to do with a close friend ands colleague of many years whose views I respect and whose friendship I value, and with whom I have had many deep and important psychological encounters, but who does not choose "mutual process" at all. The reason for this is that he believes that people, or groups, come together because they are serving a common image, or common God, consciously, whereas I believe that a common image is usually being served unconsciously and is revealed when there is mutual difficulty. He also does not recognize the "third," between the two, as occurring, but takes place within each person. These differences have been worked on by us over the years, almost, I am tempted to say, as a mutual process, but it has not been resolved.

Furthermore, there have been several patients in my practice, a nun for one and a competent specialist in group work for another, who have understood mutual process but have declined it for good reason. Neither of them wanted a relationship with me which involved mutuality. They already had enough of that elsewhere. They came to me for specific expertise and help, and that was that. I could really appreciate their straightforwardness, even though it hurt my image of mutual process. It made me aware that one could also choose, one could say to no mutual process as a conscious act, even though the archetypes are involved anyway. A conscious saying "no" can bring back a creative asymmetrical relationship, in which there is a deeper appreciation of what is involved, a clearer apprehension of just what is looked for and received in the relationship.

I now wish to describe an extension of mutual process that I can foresee, even though this is hardly more than conjecture as yet. This has to do with the deeper or more accurate assessment of what is going on in the mutual relationships that I have been describing. You can see quite clearly, I imagine, that thus far the essence of mutual process has been described as the contacting of archetypal factors via the use of imagery and ideas. The other person and myself are open with regard to what is going on inside ourselves and express it primarily by means of images and words. This is necessarily so, since we are engaged in a work of transformation, of soul-making, and consciousness-raising, just as was done within the traditional analytic process. But there is another sense in which the exchanges, the underlying archetypal connections between people are not only in image or work or idea, but are also concrete. By concrete, I mean not the concreteness of physical contact or sexual union or aggressive damage, as is generally feared, but the concreteness of a true energy exchange. I am speaking now about the psychophysiological energies described traditionally in Kundalini Yoga (as an example of the "within"), or by healers who transmit their healing energies. The book by Shafica Karagulla, for example, (10), gives many instances of sensitive people who are able to see this energy exchange in force fields.

What I am saying is that ultimately what we describe as "transference," and which I have tried to deepen by asserting the necessity of intersubjectivity, is truly an exchange of psycho-physiological energies. My own beginning experimentation with these energies of the various chakras of Kundalini (1), or the centers as described by the Edgar Cayce group (17), is rather promising to me, and I do think that this is what happens between and among people, even though they may not be aware of it. If, indeed, we can become aware of this interchange of energies, altogether new ways of psychological-physiological work are possible. This in no way, however, reduces our work with images and words, it merely adds new dimension and new levels. This extension of mutual process into energy links up with the work of Wilhelm Reich (13,14), for example in his understanding of muscular armoring as a mirror of character structure, as well as his general bioenergetic theory which posits these energies both in the body and in the atmosphere. That his work, like that of Jung and Freud, was sneered at, is no test of its worth. It is quite likely that we will be able to test these outlandish notions more adequately in the years to come. There is already positive evidence from Russian para-psychology (12).

Finally, I wish to indicate that there are no automatic limits to the growth of the asymmetrical type of relationship either, analytic or otherwise. One can easily conceive of new land creative ways of enhancing the doctor-patient and teacher-pupil models most valuably. For example, the physical work with character armoring in Reichian therapy seems to be largely asymmetrical. Likewise is this true of behavioral modification. One must ask, however, that the asymmetrical procedures no longer be inhuman, that the practitioners be aware that both parties are being affected and interchange is happening anyway, even if it is not attended to or worked with, else all the destructive effects described by Guggenbuhl and known to us all as the shadow of analysis will merely continue in the newer forms.

Having discussed the limits and nature of mutual process, I want now to take up the problem of "equality," as I mentioned in my earlier paper. That was a sticky matter, then, for it was hard to see how the two partners in analysis could really be equal, since one of them was paying money in the relationship, and one of them was presumably equipped with more knowledge and experience about psychological matters, else why pay? Was there equality really and, if so, what was its nature? In my earlier paper, after considerable reflection, I concluded that equality was on the basis of need. I put it as follows:

"It is the personal, individual need of the two partners for each other that serves as the balancing opposite for the impersonal and collective material which rises from the unconscious. Thus the equality consists in the mutual fulfillment of needs, primarily that of the individuation process, as it affects both partners."

Now that was a brilliant solution, I think. I can be immodest about it since I also think that the brilliant solution was not adequate. I have never been able to reconcile the paying of money, for example, as the patient becomes equal, yet I am even more chagrined when I do not get paid! Yes, one can say that the analyst is a servant of the patient, hence asymmetrically lower to the latter, and that the patient knows less than the analyst, hence asymmetrically lower in that regard, and that these high-lows balance. But that is not sufficiently convincing to me.

And yet mutual process seems to require some level of equality or the mutuality is meaningless. To speak of mutuality when one is superior to the other is senseless, unless one speaks of the archetypes themselves doing that. For example, the doctor-patient polarity, or the superiority-inferiority polarity at any level can be mutually experienced (just as with parent-child), and worked through by both partners. This happens, as we have said, when the parties realize that both parent and child, doctor and patient, superior and inferior reside in each of them, and that the interplay between them, within and across, can be attended to. But even that is not enough of a solution to our equality problem, I believe. The partners must arrive at full equality, whatever it is.

Is the equality that of mutual need for individuation, if for nothing else? I do not know. But my thoughts are that the equality is like that spoken of in our American Declaration of Independence: "All men are created equal and are endowed by their Creator with certain inalienable rights..." How, indeed, are they created equal, since they certainly are not equal in stations of life, in ability, in achievement or in anything else? Well, the idea is that they are equal under God!

Now that is the point, I think. Equal under God translates psychologically as equal before the archetypes, the chief of which is that of the Self. The Self is ubiquitous, residing in each and every person and plant, animal and object, even. But most clearly, says Scripture, the divine spark resides in people. Each of us has an aspect of the divine, the Self, and all parts of the Self are equal. Therefore, the analogy from the first principle of our country and from Scripture hold in the psychological realm. We are equal before the archetypes and have to struggle in relation with them. And nobody, as they say, is "more equal" than anybody else. It is only that some are more experienced in the struggle, more conscious about it. And that is why analysts get paid: because they are experienced—and, just as important, they need to live too; that is how they earn their living.

There is another aspect of the equality issue which is important. The archetypal relationship, as it begins, is unequal. There is "patient" and there is "doctor." The analytic relationship should, in my opinion, move toward equality if its aim at fostering individuation should occur. They should ultimately move out of the asymmetry into symmetry and equality. As the patient grows in independence, understanding and in the ability to cope with the unconscious, this other sense of equality, that of mutuality, can occur to a greater degree. So an aim of analysis can be that of helping the analysand toward a true independence of spirit and, at the same time, of enhancing the capacity for relating equally.

(The aforementioned social scientist, reading the foregoing, comments here: "Although relating 'equally' may not be more effective in producing growth-individuation than other methods, it may be a result of growth and choice on the part of the patient and analyst.")

The whole problem is one of working toward that true mutuality of sharing the work with the unconscious. When the patient knows this, when he is in connection with his own spirit, his own pursuit of individuation and his God, then we can be glad. For then, we have another person who might share our hope of a larger mutual process, of Knights and Ladies of the Round Table, seeking the Grail of common individuation and wholeness, of realizing the God "within" and "among", together and alone.

That brings my comments about mutual process to an end at this time. I realize that there is much that I have not taken up, such as the problems inherent in mutual process itself. Among the latter, for example, are the crucial questions of the interference between one relationship and another, the problems of primacy, of betrayal, of openness and closedness with regard to other mutual processes, or the danger of "going over to the other", losing oneself, rather than forming a true third. All of these questions are very important.

In addition to these, there is much that should be said about the factor of time. It would seem that individuation, once taken up consciously, can not be set aside without serious consequence of psychological arteriosclerosis, whereas mutual processes seem less demanding in that area. It may well be rhythmical, in that a particular mutual process may require a good deal of work at times and then rest easily for an indeterminate period. But all of these questions must be reserved for a future time, when one can explore them fully.

REFERENCES

1. Avalon, Sir Arthur. *The Serpent Power*. Third Edition. Ganesh & Co., Madras, 1931.

2. Guggenbuhl-Craig, Adolf. *Power in the Helping Professions*. Spring Publications. New York and Zurich, 1971.

3. Heisler, Verda. "Individuation Through Marriage" in *Psychological Perspectives*, Vol. 1, No. 2, 1970.

4. Hillman, James. *Suicide and the Soul*. Hodder & Stoughton, London, 1964.

5. Jung, C.G. *Two Essays on Analytical Psychology*. Vol. 6 of Collected Works.

6. Jung, C.G. 'Transcendent Function'. In Vol. 8 of *Collected Works*.

7. Jung, C.G. 'Mysterium Coniunctionis'. Vol. 14 of *Collected Works*.

8. Jung, C.G. *Psychology of the Transference*. In Vol. 16 of *Collected Works*.

9. Jung, C.G. 'Marriage as a Psychological Relationship' in Vol. 17 of *Collected Works*.

10. Karagulla, Shafica. *Breakthrough to Creativity*. Devorss, Santa Monica, California, 1967.

11. Meier, C.A. "Projection, Transference and the Subject-Object Relation". *Journal of Analytical Psychology*, Vol. 14, 1959.

12. Ostrander & Schroeder. *Psychic Discoveries Behind the Iron Curtain*. Prentice-Hall, New York. 1970.

13. Reich, Wilhelm. *Character Analysis*. Orgone Institute Press. New York, 1949 (original, 1933).

14. Reich, Wilhelm. *Function of the Orgasm*. Orgone Institute Press, New York, 1948.

15. Spiegelman, J. Marvin. "Some Implications of the Transference" in *Speculum Psychologiae*, edited by T. Frey. Rascher, Zurich, 1965.

16. Spiegelman, J. Marvin. "Alcune implicazioni del Transfert" in *Rivista di psicologia analitica*. Vol. 1, No. 1, Marzo, 1970.

17. Sugrue, Thomas. *The Story of Edgar Cayce*. (There is a River). Holt, 1942.

CHAPTER FOUR

THE IMAGE OF THE JUNGIAN ANALYST AND THE PROBLEM OF AUTHORITY (1980)

In the spring of 1966, my colleague Robert Stein and I were rejected as Training Analysts by the Certifying Board of our local Jungian Society. We were told to wait six months, with the implication that we should undergo further analysis with one of the older analysts. This was a shock for which we were unprepared; both of us were constitutionally qualified, members of the Executive Committee, and I was already engaged in judging Candidates as Director of Studies and I was previously a member of the Certifying Board itself! And we were unprepared because those judging us were friends, colleagues, teachers and analysts—the people with whom we were closest.

We spent years trying to comprehend this act and its consequences. The intervening years [fourteen at the time of this presentation] have dulled the pain but failed to answer our questions of the time. Stein's was: What image have they of how a Jungian Analyst or Training Analyst ought to be? Mine was: How can Jungians be so irrational, unjust and violating of personal relationship? I believe analysis of this event and the images underlying it can contribute to the understanding of training, the sum of our notions of what we expect analysts to be like.

What kind of image have they of how an Analyst ought to be? This question of Stein's continued to haunt me long after he abandoned it as unproductive. When I read Barbara Hannah's biographical memoir of Jung, I got a hint. She described Jung's centrally important encounter with Richard Wilhelm and the now-famous story of the "Rainmaker" the Sinologist told him, which moved him deeply (1):

Richard Wilhelm was in a remote Chinese village which was suffering from a most unusually prolonged drought. Everything had been done to put an end to it, and every kind of prayer and charm had been used, but all to no avail. So the elders of the village told Wilhelm that the only thing to do was to send for a rainmaker from a distance. This interested him enormously and was careful to be present when the rainmaker arrived. He came in a covered cart, a small, wizened old man. He got out of the cart, sniffed the air in distaste, then asked for a cottage on the outskirts of the village. He made the condition that no one should disturb him and that his food should be put down outside the door. Nothing was heard of him for three days, then every-one woke up to a downpour of rain. It even snowed, which was unknown at that time of the year.

Wilhelm was greatly impressed and sought out the rainmaker who had now come out of his seclusion. Wilhelm asked him in wonder: "So you can make rain?" The old man scoffed at the very idea and said of course he could not. "But there was the most persistent drought until you came," Wilhelm retorted, "and then—within three days—it rains?" "Oh," replied the old man, "that was something quite different. You see, I come from a region where everything is in order, it rains when it should and is fine when that is needed, and the people also are in order and in themselves. But that was not the case with the people here, they were all out of Tao and out of themselves. I was at once infected when I arrived, so I had to be quite alone until I was once more in Tao and then naturally it rained."

Miss Hannah relates that not only was Jung profoundly affected by this tale but he encouraged her to tell it whenever she gave a lecture on Jungian psychology.

Here is to be found a central image of Jung's psychology, one that informs us an ideal. One of our colleagues, de Castillejo, wrote a paper extolling this approach to life, entitled, "The Rainmaker Ideal" (2). This image reminded me of a story told about Jung's attitude when I was a student at the Institute in Zürich in the late 1950's. Jung was said to have remarked that after the age of thirty, men are really alone, each pursuing his course like ships which pass in the night, blinking a greeting light but no more. This was said approvingly albeit a trifle sadly. Even then, however, I recall that Stein and James Hillman and I did not like this image of grand aloneness and challenged it, pointing out that it merely led to a parting of the ways, à la Freud, Adler, Jung, Rank, Reich and the rest. We felt that brotherhood and comradeship could be an important part of the "journey" as well. I recall adding, as a veteran of the Merchant Marine some years earlier, that ships had crews of least thirty and demanded mutual effort and tolerance both to sail the ship and provide privacy in close quarters.

Here was the image that underlay such a vision: man alone and recon-ciling himself with the powers of the universe, alone, retreating and healing himself in the face of social dilemmas. And here was Jung, suspicious of groups and institutions, advocate of internalizing the conflict of nations as a way to grow in individual consciousness. How often did Jung not say that ten or a hundred savants together were one huge fool, and that the hope of mankind lay in the individual, not the group (3)? Here was the image: The Rainmaker Ideal. Was I not also a follower of that ideal? Had I not practiced active imagination all those years since first beginning analysis at the age of twenty-four? Did I not share Jung's suspicion of groups? I was worse with them than Jung was—consider the trouble I often got into. Further, I shared his belief that the individual was the locus of consciousness. What then was the difference? What was my image?

I realized that I was always emphasizing dialogue and mutual work, and recalled that the paper I wrote for the 1965 Festschrift for C.A. Meier, "Some Implications of the Transference" (4), emphasized this character of analytical work and the necessity for mutual openness. I remembered the suspicion with which this paper was greeted by these elders at the time, and realized that my image of the analyst was based more on the alchemical model, the Alchemist and his Soror Mystica. This, for me, was not just the alchemist and his inner anima, but an actual sharing of a work of transformation of the prima materia, beginning with the unconsciousness brought in by the patient but soon affecting the analyst as well, and requiring the two, in work and prayer, in struggle and devotion, to attend to the gods as they manifest in their work, within them and between them.

I realized that this alchemical image also underlay the Jungian ideal of how an analyst ought to be, and that this emphasis frightens and offends even Jungians who accord recognition to the alchemical model. In Britain a student said he would never tell a patient a dream, particularly sexual, he had about her but would work on himself to change his attitude. I would have felt a moral obligation to tell the patient, feeling this was a joint matter and the telling would reduce the impression of impersonal authority and show that I was personally involved in the process as well. Jung often indicates that he agrees with mutuality in analysis, at least in any deep, fundamentally transforming work. He says in his paper, "Problems of Modern Psychotherapy," published as early as 1929 (5):

> What does this demand [that analysts undergo analysis] mean? Nothing less than that the doctor is as much "in the analysis" as the patient. He is equally part of the psychic process of treatment and therefore equally exposed to the transforming influences. Indeed, to the extent that the doctor shows himself impervious to this influence, he forfeits influence over the patient; and if he is influenced only unconsciously, there is a gap in his field of consciousness which makes it impossible for him to see the patient in true perspective. In either case, the treatment is compromised.

Jung goes on to state that the doctor is faced with the same task he expects the patient to face—strong words in support of the mutuality idea.

So there are two canonical images of how the analyst sees himself: the Rainmaker, alone and self-transforming, and the Alchemist with his co-worker, sharing and dialoguing. For some, even the latter has a Rainmaker quality—he knows that the archetypes affect both parties, but transforms himself in order to produce changes. He does not attend to the "third" in the work, namely the relationship itself and the unconscious "between" them. As for me, I was a Rainmaker when alone and Alchemist with patients.

Why did my colleagues shrink from my view of mutual process? I think they rejected what I understood to be some natural implications of Jung's view of the transference. For me, at the moment the analyst begins having fantasies about the patient, or is experiencing an obstruction or strong affects, he or she is entwined in a mutual process with the unconscious and is no longer in possession of "objectivity." Rather, the two partners are wrapped in the anima/animus or other archetypal conditions of unconscious relationship. My conclusion was that I had a moral responsibility (in the name of honesty) to tell my fantasies, as well as to hear the patient's. It was this, I think, that frightened or offended colleagues. From such sharing, however, both patient and therapist gain insight as to what is transpiring in the relationship (as opposed to "my" or "your" unconscious) and we are now mutually connected to the "third" or the relationship itself. I have called this third the "god among" (as opposed to the "god within"). Objectivity and authority is hence transferred to the unconscious itself, as revealed in the fantasies and dreams of the participants, as partners, who can now attend to themselves and the other as well as to this third, thus performing the work of alchemical transformation Jung was writing about.

Let me give an example of such an exchange, which occurred as I was working on this paper. A patient was having sexual fantasies about me but was unwilling/unable to tell what these were. I found myself alternately excited and repelled without knowing what was affecting me. Her withdrawal produced either a withdrawal on my part or impersonal, aggressive sexual fantasies. I also had a dream in which I had intercourse with her. I told the dream and the fantasies, along with the interpretation that I was both trying to penetrate her resistance and unite with her and was also afraid of this. She then dreamt that the therapist was holding a gun on her from the genital region and then she invited him to lie down on the floor with her and make love. He responded he could not. End of dream. I acknowledged the accuracy of the imagery and she added that her own intensity frightened her as well as the fear of rejection. Then she told her fantasy of being alone before a fireplace, nude and dancing. The therapist appears and she gradually becomes the fire itself. As fire, she draws toward the therapist. My reaction to her fantasy was one of withdrawal, fear of being burned, which I told her. Then I saw that we were involved in the alchemical fire-water union, the attempt of the unconscious to unite the fire of passion and desire with the water of feeling. The play of these opposites was going on both within each of us and in the relationship itself. The fire-water image and the union in steam (fantasy, spirit), proved a saving "third" from the unconscious to which we could both relate.

After I had written the foregoing, the patient appeared once more and told me that she been a fool to believe that stuff, she now had her personal power back, and that she had felt me judging her for her physical desire. I was astonished and hurt, not to mention feeling a fraud for using the event in my paper. I told her my feelings and also mentioned that I had even used the incident as an example in a paper I was writing. She was clearly moved and told me that after the last session she felt taken over by a sneering, suspicious, cynical spirit, which said I didn't really care about her and that she was a worthless, undeveloped form of life. As we worked, it became apparent that the fire-water union had indeed occurred, but that another dimension, that of earth and air, got opened up and showed its split. She felt identified with the body, earth side of concrete fulfillment and the spirit (air, judge) camel in as a negative, denying power. Our discussion seemed to clear the air, particularly her felt reassurance that I really did care about the relationship.

She then dreamt of a lovely princess who lived in a magnificent castle but was lonely. A handsome prince, whom she admired and loved deeply, was guarding this castle, riding back and forth on his horse, his powerful sword unsheathed and ready to fight anyone who approached. At last, the princess asked the prince to lay down his sword, come inside and be with her. She didn't want to be alone any more and did not need protection. End of dream.

Following this, the patient dreamed that the therapist was standing in front of her, smiling and holding out his arms to her. This dream was similar to one she had early in the analysis, a year before, in which the therapist stood at the head of a long flight of stairs, arms outstretched and welcoming. She had to ascend this long flight, with no banisters, to reach him. In the current dream, she sensed the power of the therapist, but also his humanity and vulnerability, and felt a tremendous amount of loving and caring. Later that same night, she dreamt that the therapist came to her house, met her family and played the piano. The next night she dreamt that she came to therapist's house also.

These dreams are transparent, I think. In the castle dream, she finally makes connection to her animus and is ready for her own inner union—a Rainmaker work! With this shift away from the defensive use of the animus, she is ready also for "mutual process" with me, at a deeper level, as the following dreams show. I am also struck by the presence of the Judge archetype, which intrudes into the work and tries to destroy the union which did take place. This Judge, about which I will have more to say in the next section, is very much present in regular analytic work, particularly in transference problems, as well as in the training/assessing process. But here it was essential that I was willing to "unveil" my own fantasies and dreams in relation to her, as she was doing until blocked. I do not see how the union could have been otherwise effected.

Once more, after the paper was already in the hands of the editor, the patient dreamed that she came to the therapist's office, but found both it and him changed. He was dressed in a green Elizabethan costume, a little chubby and foolish-looking. An authoritative voice said that the therapist could not help her. End of dream.

The patient was devastated by this dream, as was I, once more feeling the fraud. But no. As we worked, it became clear that the "fool" was now I, as she had felt herself to be previously, and this was correct insofar as I foolishly dependent on her psyche for validation of my views about mutual process. Her authoritative voice, it emerged, was really insisting that she not give herself totally to the relationship, as she was in danger of doing, but to stay, too, with her inner Self, the "god within." She was being tossed back and forth between these opposites and was compelled to honor both her own Rainmaker and the alchemical process between us.

That insight helped me to realize how foolishly dependent I had become upon patients' dreams as revelatory of objective authority, so my patient and I were really in the same boat. We are taught in Jungian training that dreams about the therapist are largely projection. I, with my mutual-process idea, had often gone overboard in the other direction and accepted the patient's dreams of me as "true," thus losing my own inner authority.

It is this unveiling of fantasies, I think, that my colleagues had great doubts about. The material revealed may include content which is sexual, aggressive or infantile and they may fear that such openness can lead to "acting out" or a loss of control on the part of the therapist. This is a legitimate fear, but one must realize that such fears are also instinctive and perform a regulatory function, as in the foregoing example. If I have a fantasy of slapping a patient, I also have a fear of hurting or being hurt myself, which restrains bodily action. This, too, is part of the "unveiling." Moreover, when we understand that therapy is a psychological relationship aiming at the enhancement of consciousness and the capacity for loving, such natural limits as provided in the mutually agreed upon aim prevent—or at least make less likely—damaging events. In any case, I think it is better to be open about such processes (making mutually conscious), than to let them fester in the dark to cause mischief from being handed over to the witch and devil archetypes.

A colleague has suggested that therapists shrink from mutual process and openness because of their unwillingness to show their weakness, vulnerability or need. Once you do this, he says, you lose your authority and the other will hurt you! I am afraid that this is true; I have been so treated more than once. Yet the therapist can speak about his hurt or rejection, perhaps evoking the compassion of the patient and thus enhancing the latter's inner authority as well.

This holding on to authority is a not infrequent experience among therapists. I have encountered many, including Jungians, who were judgmental, inflated with the archetype of Old Wise Man or Woman, impenetrable and invulnerable. Indeed, I am grateful for the work of Guggenbühl, who has shown so brilliantly in his Power in the Helping Professions, that therapists can readily succumb to the rigidity and impenetrability our profession seems to produce. Guggenbühl's portrait of this malady, I feel, is an apt picture of the shadow of the Rainmaker. I think my colleagues' fears were largely a dread of openness, as I discuss in my papers on transference.

I am well aware that other images, such as being "closed," are also of great value. The fantasy of growth, in the silence and darkness of earth and womb, is an obvious example, as is the Hermetic stance of "indirection." If I emphasize openness, it is because this has been grossly neglected in our field.

We turn, now, to the second question that arose in response to our rejection, namely: "How can Jungians be so irrational, unjust and betraying of personal relationship?" How could they, indeed? One might just as well ask why they should not be, since we are "all too human" as Nietzsche said, and we all share the "ugliest man" who does these things. At that time, my belief was that people on the conscious road of individuation would not do such a thing.

It was not so much that I was more innocent then than I am now, but that I had no adequate conceptual tools to differentiate between my personal shock and the larger impersonal issue of judgment. Nothing in my training or experience equipped me to penetrate the meaning of this event. In retrospect, I can see that neither the Rainmaker model (not conscious at the time), nor Alchemist could help me understand better. I knew that I was in the grip of an unjust judge and this was central to my experience. My own inner image of the archetype of the Judge was perfectionist, harsh and demanding, and it was to that figure that I turned in trying to deal with my pain and disbelief. This Judge was very hard on me at the time for violating its standards in my personal life, and I bore an intense conflict of my own. I could readily see a Freudian interpretation of what happened to me. I had unconsciously produced or provoked these betrayals and judgments from without in order to punish myself for my infractions. That would also account for my failure to stand up for myself more forcefully and protest the action's injustice. The causalist Freudian interpretation must be true. After a time, I could see the merits of a finalist, Adlerian interpretation. Despite the fact that I was rejected as a training analyst, I continued to have therapists come to me for analysis (at least half of my practice has been with therapists ever since). Was this, then, an "arrangement" in Adler's sense, so that I had to sacrifice the power-drive of being the "training analyst" only to become one in a non-recognized, power-shorn way, thus contributing to a genuine "social interest"? That made good sense too, and it has helped me to appreciate the Adlerian viewpoint.

I could also see the value of a Jungian finalist interpretation—that I needed to break away from the group, at the age of forty, and pursue my individuation. This made sense on the basis of dreams and my later fictional writ-

ing. This individual imaginative work would very likely not have been produced had my inner figures remained only in the service of the Jungian collective, hence the validity of the Jungian finalist interpretation.

But these three interpretations were not enough. They retained an inner-
oriented viewpoint (i.e., still Rainmaker) and did not give sufficient weight
to the dialogic, relational, and group needs involved. This is where Stein and
I attempted some consciousness-raising and healing on our own. We knew
that both of us were heavily affected by the inner Judge and we tried, in our
relationship, to deal with this. But despite the apparent successes of my
mutual process idea with my patients, particularly the younger therapists and
those with an existentialist background, I still suffered the wound and hurt
of the "Unjust Judge." The several interpretations—causalist, finalist, and
relational—all seemed helpful and true, but I could not isolate the image
and myth I was struggling with. I sensed it, but it seemed too grand to be connected with the small-scale issues and relatively minor agonies I was coping
with. I refer to the Job story and to Jung's work with that important myth of
our western consciousness (7).

In that work, as we know, Jung took on what he felt to be a central myth
of western culture: God's injustice, his need of man in dialogue with him to
advance his own consciousness, the continuing incarnation—the humanization of God and consequent divinization of man. These weighty matters, and
Jung's passionate explication of this development in the western image of
the divine, have been as central in his psychology as his preoccupation with
alchemy as the precursor and symbol-carrier for modern consciousness.

It was this story that I felt to be at work in my experience with my Jungian colleagues, in my own work with myself and in my practice. For me,
the Board was an embodiment of the Sanhedrin of Jesus' day, arrogating to
themselves a retrogressive judgment out of fear of the prevailing collective
and in subservience to their own power needs. And I was partially identified
with Jesus, a man who had an inner relationship to God, denied the authority of the "elders", was himself combining divinity and humanity! I certainly
felt crucified and abandoned.

My approach to healing lay in the idea of mutual process, of working-
through this complex so that as a group we all would emerge relating to the
God-Among. I thought this combination of the personal and the impersonal
would do the work of humanization of the archetype. That is not how the
original story went, of course, nor did my colleagues cooperate, so I was stuck
in myth and could find no satisfying alternative solution. Gradual dis-identi-
fication from the God-man archetype was difficult, I found, since the conscious carrying of such an image was precisely what Jung had concluded was
contemporary man's condition, in his *Answer to Job*. We in western civilization
are living through this myth in some fashion, and I think that those of us in
Jungian psychology have a particularly close affinity to it. The problems of

judging, of being "human" and dis-identifying from archetypal possession are very much in the forefront of the training process, in therapy, and in life.

Some features of the myth pertain to the analytic and training situation. These are: (1) Personal-Impersonal; (2) Subjective-Objective; (3) Power—Assertion-Submission.

Personal-Impersonal: The image of the divine figure in the Job story is passionate, personal, single-minded, and apparently unreflective. He identifies with his power while disregarding its effects. He is personal in his intensity and passion, but impersonal, not affected by, the reality of his human partner. He plots in the background and justifies himself with his own power and lofty aims. Throughout he makes judgments.

This authoritarian image dwells in many of us. When not humanized, it can muddle the therapeutic situation and cause great pain, but the need for healing and some sort of union can bring about a satisfying humanization of the archetype. In the training situation, however, particularly if some judgment of the rightness, adequacy or "readiness" of the candidate is at issue, the worst aspect of this archetype can obtrude. Should either party insist on his own righteousness (often the case), it is hard to see that any resolution is possible. Should they accept the idea of mutual process, they can attend to the personal reactions, viewpoints, dreams, and fantasies of all parties, and the "third" can manifest from the unconscious to show the possibility of union of the personal and impersonal.

Objective-Subjective: The emotionality in this archetypal pattern of Job/Jahveh and its consequences of unjust judgment have led many to substitute for it an objective viewpoint. The difficulties are enormous, especially if we deceive ourselves that we are truly "objective" and have overcome the personal affects and biases which distort the judgment. This is particularly apparent in the training/assessing situation and causes the kind of distancing and violation Jungians complain of in Freudians and patients complain of in both. The difficulties are particularly great since the Judge usually considers itself quite correct and in touch with ultimate truth. At the same time, the distancing from emotionality and subjectivity brings on an illusion of objectivity from having "overcome" the affects. Yet each view sees the inadequacy of the other, and the judged scratches his sores like Job. The prologue in heaven with light and dark sides of the authority having sway results in the split archetype we see in the human situation.

The way to overcome this split archetype is to sacrifice one's claim to exclusive objectivity, just as I think it wise to sacrifice impersonality. One can permit the conflict of objective-subjective in one's self and know that greater objectivity can arise when the views of all parties are connected, once more, with the third of the unconscious itself.

Power—Assertion-Submission: In Jung's description of the psychological process going on in the divine, recognizing its own injustice and lack of consciousness of "what it means to be human," there comes a sacrifice of its power and a surrender to the frail human condition. This "incarnation" brings about an advance of consciousness which can contain the divine and human, in psychological terms a union in consciousness of the archetypal and the personal. Presumably this process is a continuing one for us, psychologically, but in the training/judging situation it is only too easy for the archetype to split, and the student/trainee must submit to the power and authority of the trainer/judge. I suggest, once more, that this split can be overcome by recognizing it. I suggest that to overcome the negativity and destructiveness of the split archetype of divine/human, judge/judged, assessor/trainee, etc., we follow the process we do for ourselves alone and for our patients when we, as Jungians, submit to the unconscious itself and to the process of its unfolding! But here the unconscious is also "among" and not only individually within each person. I realize that there are other approaches to this dilemma (which can be characterized, I think, as the problem of authoritarianism) and it is these various solutions I wish to examine next.

Antidotes to Authoritarianism in the Therapist: The problem of authoritarianism in our field goes back to its modern beginnings. Jung's conflict with Freud in this regard is well documented in both Jung's autobiography (8), and in his Two Essays on Analytical Psychology (9). Jung, of course, felt that the conflict was a type-problem, but in his memoirs he shows only too clearly that Freud's view that it was a "revolt against the father" was also true. The breaks by Adler, Rank and Reich, can also be seen as stories of a newer spirit unable to stay contained in the older vessel, or to be accepted by the older spirit. Jung has described this process well, and both von Franz (10) and Hillman (11) have explored the archetypal background of such conflict.

It was Guggenbühl, however, who first described this issue in the context of the therapist and the struggle with power (12). His answer to the danger of the therapist becoming invulnerable, rigid, and increasingly impenetrable was the cultivation of eros in the form of friendships outside the therapeutic relation. Friends and close colleagues are the antidote to one's isolation and empire-building, says Guggenbühl. That seems most heartwarming advice, but I have doubts about it as a single solution. Friendship is certainly a desideratum but the archetypal image of father-son, separation and individuation seems more powerful than comradeship, despite the presence of societies to foster the latter. My own position has been to enhance eros in the analytic relation itself by the emphasis on openness and mutual process. This type of eros seems to have worked for me, as friendship has worked for Guggenbühl, but what is the experience of our colleagues in the struggle with authoritarianism?

Hillman, in his "Psychology: Monotheistic or Polytheistic" (13), attacks the authoritarianism of monotheistic consciousness, equating it with a kind of theologizing, in contrast with psychologizing, and holds that a polycentric view is more in line with the facts of the psyche, thus truer to the soul. He realizes that his either/or position is itself an indication of the type of consciousness that he is rejecting, yet he refuses a more inclusive position. Kathleen Raine's response to his view, in terms of William Blake's system, is that the enemy is the arrogation of power of one function or "god." My response to his position derives from Kundalini Yoga: the "Place of Command" is not and need not be the highest authority.

In the Kundalini system (14), each chakra has a divine syzygy of god and goddess, representing a type of consciousness and energy. Since the energy rises and descends in a circulation bringing enlightenment, no chakra is superior to the others and no divine manifestation carries hegemony. Even Ajna, the "third eye", is called the "Place of Command," but is subservient to Sahasrara, the highest lotus at the crown of the head. This chakra connects the yogin with the most sublime experience of the divine and his ultimate enlightenment. But even "ascent" itself is not the desideratum, since circulation of the energy is the aim, and all the images of the gods are seen as aspects of the one divine pair in union. This multiple image of authority offers a model for the de-literalizing of our authority symbol.

One might ask how an image of multiple centers squares with the vision discussed in Jung's Answer to Job, the humanization-of-God—divinization-of-man? I have attempted such a reconciliation in my fictional work, *The Tree: Tales in Psycho-Mythology* (15). In that book, ten people, each representing a different belief system—Catholic, Pagan, Atheist, Taoist, Hindu, Gnostic, Jewish-Kabbalistic, Alchemical, Zen, Muslim—recount their own stories of individuation in connection with their myths. They meet in Paradise and it seems apparent that even such diversity has a commonality in the experience of the "humanization of the divine—divinization of the human" paradigm Jung explored in his Job work.

It seems to me that the problem is not one of authority alone, since each function, type of consciousness, religion or "God-image" has its own sphere of power. Rather we are faced with the arrogation of authority and the unwillingness to relativize claims. Neil Micklem of London has suggested (16) the idea of "de-training" as an antidote to rigidity and narrow-mindedness in the therapist. He has pointed out that just such a detraining occurred in his own transition from physician to analyst at the Jung Institute in Zürich. He also notes that there are many Jungian analysts who have undergone other kinds of analysis, both before and after their Jungian work. The Kleinian experience of many in London is well-known. I, too, have undergone extensive Reichian work (eight years as a matter of fact) and can testify that "detraining" can have enormous effect on the personality. Each therapeutic system has something specific to offer, hardly attainable whole in another modality. So, too, each system has its shadow: the achievement of any system's main aim also entails its opposite, failure. There always seems to be further work to be done.

In our Jungian field, the shadow of the individuation process (isolation, rigidity, invulnerability) is perhaps best approached in an eros manner. This eros is found in relationship, perhaps even in group work. Jung, of course, was very much against group therapy and on strong grounds. We all know how group can use the power of the archetypes to destroy individuality and reduce the membership to the lowest common denominator of consciousness. But is this necessary? Can there not be groups composed of individuals each seeking his or her own individuation, yet sharing a common quest as well?

Some might reply that there are Jungian groups all over the world which believe precisely that they are doing this. This was not true in my own experience with a particular group many years ago, and my occasional forays to Jungian enclaves both in the United States and abroad, lead me to doubt that even now many of these groups differ markedly from the usual professional societies or clubs, with the typical power struggles and politicking. F. Riklin once said, in Zürich, about the Jung Club there, "It is not a club, it is a battlefield!" But there is every possibility that something along the lines of common quest is happening or can do so.

What further can we do, beyond the suggestions of Guggenbühl, Micklem, Hillman and myself? I think we can return to the image of Jung's Job, which instaurated our now declining era. Perhaps the next step for us Jobs (the "many" as heir to the "one" sufferer) is not only to see the flaws and the shadow of the authorities and gods, and internalize our own, but to no longer "cover our mouth" (as Job does at the end), but speak out. It seems to me that we very easily slip into unconscious identification with that authority and we do need each other to point it out in some way. In the very act of pointing this out, the partner can slip into such identification himself, causing no end of trouble.

For me, the emphasis on eros, on connection with the soul of the other, is the best antidote to identification. I grow increasingly aware of how subtly we slide from stating were we are personally, or connecting to the other, to the assertion of what "the truth" is. Mutual process is one way to deal with this in a relationship of two, but is often not adequate in the group connection. In the relationship of three or more, the complexities increase. I am fond of the story told by Hannah in her memoirs about Jung in his days at Burghölzli (17). Jung gathered together three people, each of whom thought he was Jesus Christ. Each thought the other two were crazy. Our next step, I think, is for the many "Christ-bearers" (those who experience an inner connection with the Self) to acknowledge the other selves and to listen to their truth speaking as well. I see this as the individual carrying the dilemma of being both with the personal and the transpersonal, with his inner authority, yet open to others, working alone and in groups, living his own conviction but knowing the relativity of his experience.

What has this to do with our theme of training? Everything, I think. An analyst clan only train and influence according to his being, rather than according to his words, persona or authority. We train by what we are. It behooves us, then, to follow Jung's advice to be both aware of what we are and not hang a curtain of "transference" or "projection" to protect us and our patients from our condition. I realize that I am an advocate of a personal stance in analysis and this in itself may prove inimical to some. But these ignore the question posed in this paper at the risk (as Jung says) of "compromising treatment."

I think that Jungians are particularly heirs of the Job problem. We are willy-nilly in the boat of judging and being judged. As heirs to Jung, we are heirs to Job. Thus the conscious and unconscious horror that is happening to candidates—and to judges—should not be banished, once more, to heavenly prologues and hellish sequels, to unspoken plots and opinions followed by pronouncements and one-sided decisions. Rather, we need to examine these issues, I think, and not "compromise" training either.

When we come to training, we know that deep distrust can be constellated with the problem of judging. Because of this, the personal analyst is often not called on to be a judge, but judgment is not avoided on that account. In light of these problems, I would like to suggest that once candidates have been accepted into training, the judging process no longer resemble the patriarchal, asymmetric model. I think it better understand that there is a mutual commitment to the process of helping the candidate to determine when he or she is ready to go from stage to stage. Particularly when there is doubt, I suggest that the mutual process model be applied to this process. This means that the participants openly give their views and feelings, that no authority is claimed beyond such statements and that more than one meeting be given over to such discussions. In this process, the relevant dreams of candidates and judges need to shared. The image, then, is that the Judge becomes the "third," the God-Among to which all relate.

NOTES

1. Barbarah Hannah, *Jung: His Life and Work, a biographical memoir* (New York: Putnam's, 1976), p. 128.

2. Irene Claremont de Castillejo, *The Rainmaker Ideal* (London: Guild of Pastoral Psychology, Lecture No. 107., February 1960).

3. Most powerfully affirmed in *The Undiscovered Self* (CW X).

4. In *Speculum Psychologiae* (Zürich; Rascher, 1965). The sequel to this paper is "Transference, Individuation, and Mutual Process," a talk delivered to the San Diego Jung Group, 1972.

5. CW XVI, p. 72.

6. Adolf Guggenbühl-Craig, *Power in the Helping Professions* (Spring Publications, 1971).

7. *Answer to Job*, in CW XI.

8. C.G. Jung, *Memories, Dreams, Reflections* (New York: Random House, 1961).

9. CW VII.

10. M.-L. von Franz, *The Problem of the Puer Aeternus* (Spring Publications, 1970).

11. James Hillman, *Senex and Puer: An aspect of the historical and psychological present in Puer Papers* (Spring Publications, 1979).

12. See note 6 above.

13. James Hillman, "Psychology: Monotheistic or Polytheistic" in *Spring* 1971, pp.193-232.

14. See Arthur Avalon, *The Serpent Power*.

15. *The Tree: Tales in Psycho-Mythology* (Los Angeles: Phoenix House, 1975). [Now *The Tree of Life: Paths in Jungian Individuation,* New Falcon Publications, 1993].

16. Personal communication.

17. B. Hannah, see note 1.

CHAPTER FIVE

THE IMPACT OF SUFFERING
AND SELF-DISCLOSURE ON THE LIFE OF
THE ANALYST
(1988)

In the bathroom of my office hangs a poster portraying a life-size statue of a nude woman, before which stands a man wearing only a hat, coat and shoes, his back toward the observer. He bares himself to the statue, and the poster carries the inscription, "Expose Yourself to Art." I have certainly been troubled by the issue of self-disclosure. Over the years, I have had any number of dreams of being in a public situation with either the wrong clothes or no clothes, and I have spent lots of time trying to sort out this issue of my persona in some decent way, without a huge amount of success.

One resolution of this issue, to expose to and for art, has resulted in several books of fiction I have written, and my style, even in scholarly articles, has been personal and often self-revelatory. In the following comments, I shall both reveal and conceal, for that theme, I maintain, along with suffering, is a chief feature of the life of the analyst, particularly in our work.

Patients come to us and reveal their secrets, their lives, their concerns, and we listen carefully, thoughtfully, and appreciatively, trying to be non-judgmental, if we can. Even if we can not, we have exposed our own shadows and secrets to our analysts enough so that we are less inclined, by and large, to condemn patients, if not each other.

This self-revelation of patients, we realize, is ultimately Self-realization with a capital S, since we understand that this exploration, thus begun and continued, becomes an arena in which the Self is gradually made manifest. Jung has taught us that it is not only the Self of the patient which is being revealed, but it is also the analyst's Self which is constellated and we are not only "in" the work with patients but are required to reveal ourselves as well. For myself, I have found that what needs to be revealed are not facts and secrets about my life—which does not usually produce much of value therapeutically—but what I am thinking and feeling in relation to the patient, since the unconscious is mobilized in both parties. Therefore, the Selves are ultimately exposed, to one degree or another.

Not long ago, I added another little card, next to the poster I mentioned earlier, given to me by my wife for a birthday. On this card is shown a rather meek, elderly gentleman wearing a proper suit and carrying an umbrella. He glances rather startled at a woman whose back is toward us. She is a fulsome creature, wearing a very luxurious fur coat, and she bares herself to this shy soul.

This card balances the picture. The two, together, express my views about the process of analysis being, ultimately, a mutual one, in which both parties are exposed to each other and, more importantly, to the unconscious itself. This fact, peculiar to our profession, has far-reaching effects upon us. I shall be noting these effects in the further course of this paper. Now, however, I wish to examine the second theme of the paper, that of suffering.

We can approach this theme, perhaps, by asking: What is it that makes the life of an analyst different from that of a chiropractor, astronaut, interior decorator or chef? The first thing that comes to mind is that we are connected with, fixed on, devoted to, suffering. We are totally and intimately confronted by the suffering of those who come us, since they do not usually bring—at least at the outset—their joy, achievements and delights. This strange involvement with suffering already makes our lives different from the last three occupations, but not different from the chiropractor and, for that matter, from the physician, nurse, social worker or clergyman. These other healers, however, have quite a different outlook on human suffering. They are armed with techniques to alleviate pain or ameliorate the environmental strictures which causes or aggravate the pain. Physicians and nurses are skilled in the precise administration of drugs and procedures which cure or soften. Social workers and priests are allied with institutions which make life-in-pain more bearable. Clergy, furthermore, have instruments and sacraments of belief and practice which give them direct access to helpful forces. Should these interventions prove unsuccessful, they do not consider themselves to blame, nor do their constituents.

Only "shrinks" can not shrink from nor evade the direct, powerless encounter with suffering. We are armed with our concepts, to be sure, and the strength resulting from endless years of training-analysis, but ultimately, as Jung taught us, we are equipped only with our Selves. We encounter this suffering as both symptom and event, as condition and person, and our central question is always, "What are we—and they—going to do about it?" The answer for us is always individual, although the repeated encounter with this dilemma profoundly affects us. In order to understand the life of the analyst, we need to comprehend this endless confrontation with suffering, a feature which contributes mightily to our own "deformation professionelle."

How are we to approach this issue of suffering and what does it do to our lives? We all know that confession is good for the soul. We encourage our patients to fully and deeply express all that makes them suffer, to associate to it, to round it out and, together with us, to examine the causes and purposes of such pain. This work usually alleviates the suffering or ultimately provides meaning to make it bearable. It can also transform it. We are in the position of a caring and intelligent friend, but we are also knowledgeable and skilled in communicating non-judgementally and with some objectivity. Furthermore, as Jungians, we are committed to the view that the ultimate healer and authority lies within the person. We address our efforts to link this sufferer with his inner world, and we try to read the messages of the Self of the patient, in dream and fantasy, which leads toward healing and understanding.

But what does this repeated exposure to suffering do to us? We, too, are infected, as Jung pointed out, and our own suffering inevitably comes into the picture, both induced and activated, both similar to that of the patient and different. Finally, it is or becomes our own.

Could this fact account for the high suicide rate among psychiatrists? Perhaps it underlies the common wisdom that those who work in the area of mental health do not generally possess much of it themselves. We try to fend off such suffering, of course, both consciously and unconsciously, but the resultant rigidity and closed-offedness, as described by Guggenbühl, in his *Power in the Helping Professions*, is not attractive either. In short, the issue hinges on what we call the transference, seen by many of us as not just the projections of the patient on the therapist, but as the unconscious co-mingling of the psyches, in which the archetypes are constellated and the analyst is affected as well as the patient. All this we know from Jung, who also told us that there must be some reason for us to have chosen such a dour and bleak vocation, that our psyches must need it. Indeed, we are all very much aware of the proffered image of the "wounded healer" and that we even heal from our own wounds opened up in the work.

I have never been happy with this image of the "wounded healer." I am aware that I am, indeed, continually wounded by patients and their psyches, that I help in the healing by finding my wholeness in the face of the fragmentation and distress which patients bring and which divides me, even splits me. The image is too dark and heavy, however, and leaves out the healing effects of joy and laughter.

We will remain with the issue of suffering, however, and examine how this effects our lives in a number of areas. I will address eight of these, and then return to our general themes of suffering and self-disclosure and the myths which underlie them. The areas which I have chosen are anxiety, depression, aggression, sex, money, alienation, community and religion. A large handful, naturally, and perhaps too much to include, but I shall be offering reflections rather than essays on these issues. I can venture to offer these reflections on two grounds: First, I have always had a number of patients who have been therapists, so I speak not only idiosyncratically. Second, my own suffering as result of forces external to the work has been relatively mild, compared to many other people. So I think that I can speak of the suffering of the therapist which is a consequence of the work itself and the personality of the therapist who, by either fate or choice, is immersed in such a vocation. Indeed, since my subjective impression is that I have suffered a lot in this work, I wonder how some of my colleagues, less blessed than myself in the areas of relationship and security, survive the assaults on the soul which our work brings.

Anxiety

The first step in our eight-fold path of examination of the suffering of therapist is that of anxiety. My own experience of anxiety, outside of the therapeutic hour, has been that of it being attached to other topics of my chosen list, namely aggression, sex, money, alienation, community and religion. I have only rarely experienced—outside of analysis—what we called in my Rorschach days, "free-floating anxiety," or the nameless dread of which Kierkegaard speaks. Yet I have had patients, of course, who have suffered from this condition, and such a dread has indeed frequently manifested in the work. Jung believed that anxiety was associated with the numinous: dread and awe are the necessary concomitants of facing the gods. I recall Madame Jolande Jacobi, in a course at the Institute in Zürich in the late 1950's, solemnly intoning that such anxiety arises as a consequence of not being in touch with one's shadow. If your shadow is with you, providing the earthy grounding of its instinctiveness, for example, your anxiety will change to a specific fear, a realistic apprehension of present danger. A true statement, this, and one that we unconsciously assent to when we encourage patients to "go with the anxiety," to see where it leads and to what it refers. Name the god, as it were, accept the fear, and we are half-way there.

Yet what about our own anxiety, awakened during the analytic hour? Are we alert, we rightly ask ourselves? Are we connected, doing the "right thing"? Is this patient going to be all right, will he/she quit or commit suicide? Now, as I contemplate this anxiety of my patient and experience my powerlessness to alleviate it, to interpret it, even cope with it, my own anxiety arises by induction. As I experience this, I think, shall I reveal that I, too, am anxious, powerless, helpless? Will this self-disclosure make things worse, make him/her feel even more helpless and also feel that I can not assist or even cope with the nameless fear? Or, if I do reveal my own anxiety, will this be beneficial, alleviate the condition by a sharing, by an indication that I can stand it, endure it? And, if I do disclose, will it be the feeling of anxiety itself, or will I also reveal that I am afraid that I can not help, that I will be abandoned by the person who, perhaps, is feeling the very fear of abandonment which is now assaulting me?

In my own analytical stance of "mutual process," in the belief that the archetype is now constellated between us, I will likely reveal any or all of the above and wait for the reaction. And the result? Sometimes very helpful, sometimes not. Sometimes this self-disclosure on my part leads to a deepening, a capacity to move onward and more meaningfully, with a therapeutic effect. Sometimes, however, I am greeted by—and I think now of a particular patient—a look at me from previously downcast eyes, with non-understanding, a further dread and a sense that I, too, can not help him just as no other therapist could.

So, with this patient I am powerless and even the confession of our mutual powerlessness makes things worse. I then suggest that we both ask or pray together for the source of this dread to reveal itself here in the room. And now, this rationalist who has been successful in his life but in his sixties is nearly broken and defeated, is so fearful of praying together and, probably, finds this erstwhile rational therapist to be a superstitious and dangerous fool, wants to bolt. Yet he also has a little hope and wants to please me. I feel the same thing, I say, in a further orgy of self-disclosure, and the hour ends. Soon, not in that session but in several more, he terminates the therapy, and I feel like the fool. Now, many months later, as I write, I feel the need to telephone him and find out if what I said above was true for him. So, I call and he is delighted to hear from me. Yes, he is still surviving, just the same as before, only just barely. He is with a previous therapist, one who gave him drugs. Yes, I was right that the demon was just too much and that he was even more terrified of being together in prayer. He feels that he should have stuck it out. But that is not why he left. He ended because there was just too much gloom and doom in our relationship, nothing upbeat. No, it isn't better now; the demon of which he was afraid is still there, it neither leaves him nor kills him. We share a few words of mutual appreciation and hang up. So, here I am with my paper, once more, my own anxiety alleviated by a connection with him and by the healing power of self-revelation. The demon-god, dark and unforgiving, relents for one moment and my ex-patient is grateful for the care and contact and I am grateful that I need not feel guilty for the failure, nor feel abandoned. So, whose therapy is it? For whom do we do this work?

I turn, now, to my colleagues, toward whom I direct these words, and acknowledge that it is the self-disclosure which seems to be at issue here, whether successful or not, whether it assists the patient or not. I conclude from this that what is mobilized in such events is, indeed, the god itself, which we dread. It is the darkness of the dread, and the dark side of the Self which is being revealed. The self-disclosure about which we are ambivalent as professionals is actually disclosure of the Self (capital S). This is what is at stake in our work. We reveal and conceal, just as the Self is revealed and concealed. Our struggle is to find the right attitude with which to address this revelation. The Self-manifestation of the images of the divine, which usually remain in the background for others, haunt us. The aspects of totality which want to be seen and incarnated also defy all our efforts at approach, whether we placate, command, cooperate or submit. Ultimately, I think, with each patient, if we go deep enough, we discover aspects of this god of Self, and anxiety is just such a condition for its encounter.

I wonder, then, if my other anxieties, apart from the therapeutic vessel where it is induced, are also manifestations of the god? Is the god which I fear out there in the world the same one? When I am anxious over money, over abandonment, over performance, do I experience the self-revelation of the god? The same demon that plagued the patient with whom I failed? Am I, too, merely hanging on, surviving the onslaught, neither relieved nor dying? At times it seems that way. But I also find, unlike my patient, my capacity to kneel to the higher power, to regard it as Other and greater, to do all I can with my ego, but also to surrender this ego, is what brings relief, meaning, continuity. Do I teach this to my patients? I suspect that I do.

What is the difference between anxiety considered in the therapeutic process and that encountered in the workaday world? Everyone suffers anxiety about money, performance, security, and we all dread the unknown. But how we handle it alone and with friends and loved ones is a different matter than how we do this patients. With the latter, we are participatory, we are induced, we are willing victims. We are part of that stoked alchemical process which even heats the feared and rejected content. Some colleagues, mostly Freudians, want to increase anxiety, turn up the heat, providing motivation for greater and more sincere work. I do not share that view. The god comes of its own accord. Just work away and the unconscious, if so inclined, will appear. The hard part, as it was with my anxiety-ridden patient who had positive dreams and deep dread, is to integrate it, to endure it, to survive it.

And that is how our lives as analysts are different from others: we are partners in the plague. We submit to the darkness, to the "emotional plague," as Wilhelm Reich called it, willingly, with consciousness, even gladly, because this, we think, will heal or transform or bring more light. What is more, we do this because it is our calling, our vocation, our life. This does make us strange in the eyes of the world, and makes it difficult for us to communicate what we do, how we are. This makes us, too, like scientists and prostitutes, not ordinary. And, as with the vocations just mentioned, we are admired and despised, sought after and feared.

Depression

This psychological condition is, in my experience, the most typical and frequent form of psychopathology found among our fellow therapists. Most of us experience down-goings and despairs in the course of the work, and more than other professionals do. Witness: the high suicide-rate among psychiatrists. Witness: the later works of Freud, Adler, Reich and, in a more profound and worked-out way—as, for instance in *Answer to Job*—Jung. Pessimism and the problem of evil is the lot of the advanced worker in the vineyards of the soul.

So, to, has this been my own most typical psychopathology, particularly since the age of forty. How many mornings have I awakened in darkness, gloomy and distressed! Everything seems laden with uncertainty and pain. Why is this so? I remember telling Michael Fordham that his work was certainly brilliant, but it usually left me feeling depressed. He responded, heartily, that he thought it was a good thing, since I was too high up in the air and needed to be brought back to earth. My fiction-writing, for example, was unfoundedly optimistic. Well, he had read only my first psycho-mythology book, *The Tree*, which is surely upbeat, but he had not read my book called *The Failures*, a story of an unhealed healer, an unpublished writer, an empty teacher, and an unfrocked priest, all of whom go for healing to a powerless magician!

Yet Fordham had a point. Many therapists, Jungians particularly, tend to be intuitives or intellectuals and we are, indeed, "high up" or "in the head," not enough connected with the body and the earth. But, then, what about the most important body-therapist and theorist, Wilhelm Reich? He ended up with a very pessimistic attitude, as shown in his book, *Reich Speaks of Freud*, if not downright mad. And what of Freud and his feelings of "discontent" and "disillusion"? Non-Jungians are bleak, too.

One reason for this depressive and disillusioning condition is to be found in what our colleague, Robert Bosnak of Amsterdam and Boston, has discovered in our images of inferiority. Starting with Freud's first "Irma" dream—the archetypal beginning of the work of analysts—Bosnak shows us that it is the analyst's image of inferiority, defeat and incompetence which dogs us endlessly in our work. His paper was the first I ever read which spoke to the condition I have usually had, no so much in therapy itself (although I do occasionally experience it there also), but whenever reading Freudian-style work. Feelings of inferiority, failure, and incompetence come with the reductive attitude, I believe. It is, all the same, true. We are archetypally conditioned to experience this lamentable condition. But the writings of Jung, I find, with its synthetic attitude toward darkness, provides the necessary complement to the reduction. Not only is the analyst's anima, as in Irma, badly treated, too much for us, and sick, she is also, as in Jung's anima of his doctoral dissertation, a medium for the depths, fascinating and revealing.

However we conceive of this depression which dogs most of us, how do we deal with it? Following the Jungian procedure, we go down with it, we let it speak, we follow the movement of the soul into the depths. But many of our patients can not or will not do this. It is not their way, especially in the earlier years of the work. So, then, what do we do, or suggest to them? Well, we burn it out, in the American method, through activity: jogging, swimming, exercise. Here the image of coping with the "nigredo" is to burn away the dankness and heaviness of Saturn, which sometimes works, sometimes not. How different from the attitude toward depression taken by the Asian! One Japanese psychiatrist who worked with me told me that the treatment of choice for depression in his country was rest, to be quiet, to retreat and to allow nature to restore energy and wholeness. How different from us! I am reminded of the poster offered by an American monk to contrast the western and eastern viewpoints. It suggested: "Don't just *do* something, the Buddha said, *stand there!*"

In my own experience, all of these methods—rest, activity, active imagination and consciously moving away from the dark moods—do help the condition. All are right at times and ineffective or inappropriate at others. How do we know which and when, and how do we know when to ask our medical colleagues for help with drugs for those patients with whom none of these is effective? Well, we don't know, although there are books about depression and increasing knowledge about its physiological concomitants and antecedents.

What we do know is that we therapists experience more of it than do other professionals. Is this through the induction I have spoken of? Or the initial condition of our psyches which attracts us to the work in the first place? Or the necessary compensation to our heights and intuitive soarings? As it is with all the treatment modes, so are all the explanations true. Furthermore, we seem to experience more failure than do physicians or lawyers, more frustration in achieving goals of wholeness and creativity. We are willy-nilly tied to extreme ambiguity and uncertainty in our work. Very little is certain and even that is always relative to that particular individual who enters into our offices and our psyches. The blessings and curses of individuality, like that for art, depend on the soul and its achievement. But how do we gauge the latter? Are we like van Gogh, geniuses who produce great work and are not recognized, or like Boucher, precious and talented, successful but shallow? How many of us look to highly recognized or more successful colleagues, particularly those from other schools, and see them as shallow, or catering to the public triviality?

That competitive and envious shadow is to be solved, I discovered, by sacrificing it, abjuring it, consciously, in the outer world. Give up the competition and embrace the simple life. I suspect that many of us come to such a solution privately. We go to work, come home to family and friends, read our books, write papers, tend our gardens, listen to music and enjoy pictures, look forward to those weeks of vacation in the mountains and seashore, and are content. "Work and Love," said Freud, and resolve competition that way. Yes. In this, we are like many other people, yet we come to this, I think, out of the heat and drama of our work, the deadness and vitality of the analytic process, in which the alchemy is secret and contained, for we can not even talk much to others about what we do.

No wonder we are inferior and superior, and no wonder so many us opt for the simple life outside, to compensate the complexity and uncertainty of the inside—that is, the inside of our offices and the inside of our souls. We are specialists in the darkness of the soul, and in that we can join no other vocation that I can think of, not even that of most clergy. We are more like monks or hermits in that regard, but we are neither totally alone nor in groups, as they are. We are with an "other" and each "other" who appears. What a profession! What a blessing and what a curse! No wonder we seem strange, and no wonder the simple life is so attractive to many of us.

The answer then—or, at least my answer—to the depression evoked in our work, is the simple life. Brought down from ambition, greed and competition, to joys of the simple life. Brought down, too, to the divine darkness which enters into our work and wants to be included in our lives, lived as an undercurrent to our simplicity.

Aggression

We move, now, as a depth psychologist might be expected to, from depression to aggression. Have we not been told that the former is a repression of the latter? And that the expression of anger and its concomitants is the cure of the same? Well, yes and no. We do know, from Reich, that anxiety and sexuality are mutually exclusive, physiologically and psychologically, but I am not at all sure that depression and aggression are in the same polar connection. I have spent lots of time on a Reichian couch, yelling and hitting, which has been relieving, but that, in itself, did not "cure" depression as much as the "simple life" has. Nor do I generally have much trouble being in touch with my own aggression and being able to verbalize it or visualize its images in fantasy. These capacities to imagine and verbalize, however, have been only partly effective against what I conceive as my greater problem, that of muscular tension.

Muscular tension, in turn, in my opinion, is very much a consequence of our work. Sitting there, day after day, attending to the psyche of the other, is certainly *contra naturam* and requires lots of physical exercise and non-concentration on others as an antidote, but even that unnaturalness is not the cause of this stress. Rather, I think, that which produces stress is the endless alertness required of us, the perpetual attention to what is happening in self and other, so that mere relaxation and unconsciousness is a luxury indulged in all too rarely. Furthermore, the poison of the process seeps into us; the unacknowledged rage and aggression of our patients is what claws at us from below and from behind, bombards us hourly, daily, weekly, yearly. After some years, I found, our bodies, so assaulted and alerted, become tense, rigid, inflexible. Tennis and running won't do it, although they help. Even Reichian therapy and conscious connection with the body is not enough either, although very helpful to me.

I really do not know any remedy for the stress and muscular tension, although we each have many methods for coping. But what are we to do about the restraint of our natural aggression? Not that we need to hit patients or yell at them, but we might need to say to passive-aggressive folks, for example, "Wake up and acknowledge your negativity and hostility, damn it!" And even if we did, it would not help much, even though it could conceivably be consciousness-bringing for a particular patient. No, the poisons which seep into us go deeper and our constraint against running away, or against natural reactions—fight or flight—even if we allow ourselves verbal expression in the hour, are such that we can never overcome the "analytical stance." That analytic stance, unnatural in the extreme, is full-attention, alertness, care for the other, and restraint of our natural reactions and movements, all in the name of compassion and consciousness.

Nor would we have it any other way. That *contra naturam* is what we do and what we teach. Our releases come from insight and union of soul. They also come when we can effectively be natural and whole with our aggression with the patient. But still, what do we do about the body and this unnaturalness? Luckily for most of us, analysts are not by nature inclined to be particularly aggressive physically or even strongly athletic. Most of us are contented with our week-end tennis, swimming and walking. We add to that by going into nature when we can, and being healed of these poisons of the soul by the Great Mother Herself, as we hike in Her precincts, smell the trees and revel in the silences.

But the tensions persist anyway and Jungians, in contrast to Reichians, are said to be insufficiently "in the body," or even seen as "dead." At some conventions, alas, I have seen what they mean. But I have also been at a Reichian convention or two and I am not impressed with what I have elsewhere called a "P.E." (physical education class) approach to life.

The reasons for this persistence of tension, as I have said, are not only the restraint and alertness of the therapist, but also the endless taking-in of the poisons, via the unconscious in particular. Transference does indeed "absorb" us, and we are absorbed into this endless *nigredo* and mercurial poison, no matter how much we are aware. I think that we do rather well, by and large, considering the extent and nature of our work. Those of us who have worked a long period of time in a mental hospital will know what I mean. The poisons of the soul infect the atmosphere to the extent that one can hardly tell patient from therapist in such institutions after a few years. Nor is this limited to the insane, in my opinion. The darkness of the psyche revealed every day in the newspaper and confronted on the freeways of social intercourse are compounded in our consulting rooms by perfectly decent people, including ourselves. The devils provoke our consciousness; our consciousness provokes the devils. The cure is in the process, but is never fully effected. When one speaks of the "wounded healer," I think of it as residing in my tense muscles, rather than in the unhealed complexes, and I think that I am not alone in this. Perhaps the muscles are where the complexes reside!

Mars, then, is insufficiently served in our work, since we can only accept him in the soul. We do not jump, fight, yell, run away; nor do we sit in a sweat box, sleep—or, most of all—turn off consciousness in those intense daily hours. Intensity without activity, and poison without antidote: those are the professional deformations that really count in this baleful work, a field more dismal, even, than economics.

I am still working on this problem which, for me, is to be even more aware of the body in my work and even more conscious of what is happening therein and to attend to it. I try to bring in my aggressive reactions, verbally, as much as possible, and to be "natural." I seek mutuality in the work with aggressive energies. Still, I search for new answers. I have weekly deep-tissue Ayurvedic massage, have experimented with bio-feedback. Colleagues do other things, such as Feldenkrais, as well as stretches (as I also do) and running.

Women therapists seem to have less of a problem with this matter than men do. Maybe they can relax better or are less aggressive by nature or by role. I would be glad to know why. Perhaps this is one compensation for them for the centuries of oppression by that same masculine aggression and why they have lived longer and, by and large, happier lives.

However we view the issue of "dealing with the poisons" on a personal, subjective basis, the implications of the transference and the resultant alchemical work with patients can not successfully be denied. Ultimately, we need to confront ourselves and our patients with the fact that these poisons are being extruded "into the room" and are shared as an alchemical "third" between the two partners. Jung recognized this dilemma in his book, *Psychology of the Transference*, and my own response has been to embrace what I call "mutual process"—the recognition that ultimately both partners are effected by the archetype and they work consciously and openly together to transform these poisons and gifts of Mercurius. The word used by Joe McNair for this process is "metabolize" and I think it is appropriate. This archetypal element arises from and goes into the very cells of the body, particularly since we are committed to a work of the soul and spirit and deal in image and word. The body gets it, and it is, in my opinion, only when we acknowledge and share these bodily reactions that there results a mutual "metabolization" of these transpersonal poisons and gifts.

Sexuality

When we turn from aggression to sexuality, we have to say "more of same" to all that we have already said about aggression. It seems that we male therapists suffer more from this general inhibition against acting-out than do our female colleagues. We are stimulated and restrained as well. We are seduced and become seducers. We are privy to all the sexual secrets and are challenged beyond wits end. If Mars is frustrated by analytic work and makes us pay the price in muscular tension, Aphrodite is both worshipped and denied. She is compelled to submit to being appreciated in the form of her son, Eros. We serve soul and spiritual union, not the flesh.

Furthermore, when we discover that we suffer more from the unexpressed, indirect form of aggression manifested by our patients than from open hostility, we also recognize that it is the silent seduction and stimulation that goes on in the therapeutic relation which clauses havoc. If I am "turned on," as they say, is it because I am feeling and experiencing something in the patient or in myself alone? And, if I acknowledge this openly, am I going to be misunderstood as making an overture to sexual acting-out, or am I being unconsciously seductive? And, if the patient opens up desire, lust, and love, may I react honestly and directly with what I experience—verbally, of course—or should I interpret, or merely acknowledge. Most of these possibilities (except interpretation) occur in non-analytic relationships, it is true, but in analysis they are heightened, carry more weight and implication.

My own resolution of the dilemma is to be open about not only the stimulation and arousal, but to present the accompanying fantasy, with the expressed intention of offering these as reactions, and inviting the patient to report his/her reactions and fantasies. With my viewpoint of mutual process, I believe that body reactions, including aggression and sexuality, are usually archetypal responses and, if I am open and show the way of dealing with them by example, I am aiding in the direction of integration, rather than repression, evasion or acting-out. I preface such self-revelation with a statement of the nature of analytic commitment to consciousness and enhancing the capacity to love—not to acting-out, nor to love affairs, etc. When the limitations of the work are mutually accepted, then both parties can open up to what the unconscious brings in when it is, indeed, mutual. It is in this way, in my experience, that the poison of the unexpressed, unresolved sexual and aggressive fantasies can be fruitfully worked on and transformed.

But one is always in danger of misunderstanding. I think, now, of a woman I worked with who had a very negative father problem. I liked her, but did not find her particularly attractive. After a time, however, I became aware of sexual feelings about and toward her. I hesitatingly told her so, and she was utterly startled, since she had no such feelings toward me. She reluctantly accepted these things, however, and, in time, I thought of this as a kind of ambivalent Eros coming through me which would repair the damage done by the father's disregard and rejection of this woman when she had reached adolescence. I was both bringing up the rejected and repressed and teaching her how to deal with it by listening to and expressing her own reactions. At times, however, I felt like a dirty old man.

One day, at the time of the notoriety of some child-abuse cases in our area, I had such feelings again, and then I said, "Perhaps I should open up a nursery school!" We both laughed uproariously. It was not long after that when a memory of her being abused as a child returned and the dissociated sexuality made perfect sense, both as a "return of the repressed" and as a healing of the wound (of rejection and invasion) of the father. This was a healing event. Would this have occurred if I had kept my mouth shut? I do not know. But that is our dilemma.

My own experience of the analytic work is that I am soon divided into my opposites by the patient and what he/she brings to the sessions. I often feel as if my "left hand" is open to the taboos of the soul, my own included, and my "right hand" maintains the protective, parenting, connecting energy, with both "hands" being necessary. My advantage is that I sit in the middle of these and can move toward or report either of these directions or fantasies, and not be possessed by nor identified with either of them. I continue until wholeness is achieved. I have to add, however, the word "usually" or one of Jung's favorite Latin quotations, *deo concedente*, for such is our need and trust when serving the healing god, the Self, as manifested in the analytic work.

What sort of life is this, for the analyst to talk about, stir up and express, although limitedly, this lustful and tabooed aspect of the psyche every day, with many people? Are we not secret Don Juans, or dirty old men? Yes, certainly, for these are "rejecta" of the psyche which intrude themselves into the work as the darker aspects of Eros, clamoring to be accepted, healed, integrated. And they must be included, but deprived of their destructive, violating aspects. Spirit and flesh, morality and desire are thereby re-united and the initial splitting effect of the patient, mirroring his/her own split, becomes healed in the relationship we call transference. Poison, once more, is included and dissolved through a healing connection.

This is strange work, is it not? Here we are, rather ordinary-looking men and women, engaged in a secret sex and aggressive life, like our brother and sister hustlers, prostitutes. Perhaps we are like the "enlightened one" in the last of the ten Zen Ox-herding pictures, consorting with wine-bibbers, butchers and other rejected ones. Perhaps then, as the commentary to the picture says, we and they are "all converted into Buddhas." No wonder we are secret heroes and heroines, as well as secret hustlers and "devils," because, indeed, we aim to be secret Buddhas, or at least to serve such divine images.

I find it difficult to understand how those colleagues of ours who do not have a religious attitude deal with these upsurges of lust, desire, and violence, as they bubble up in the vas, the vessel of the analytic work. If we did not have a religious attitude how could we (I) possibly do this work? Badly, I would imagine. But then, I don't know what other gods are being served, consciously or unconsciously, by colleagues. I am personally convinced that some god is being served, whether one is aware of it or not, and we are compelled, all of us, to find out which one and how.

Again, what strange work this is. Not even clergy are required to do this! Now, does it suit us? I think so, since we not only redeem the psyche in this work, we are ourselves continually redeemed thereby. But to whom but you, my colleagues, can I say this? It sounds so inflated. Yet it is clear that we are quite ordinary, all the same. Another paradox to accept.

Money

Money is a topic for us which may be even more charged and filled with taboo than sexuality and aggression. Everyone knows, of course, that we charge entirely too much for our time, that all we do is listen, that therapy has little effect. Besides that, are we not caretakers of the soul? Should we not be generous, loving and giving, a kind of Dr. Christian of the psyche? If not, we ought to be.

Now, such a collective image of what psychotherapists are or ought to be is bad enough for us, but if we add the suffering of patients about money, then we are in further trouble. How many of them feel cheated or deprived by unloving parents or a hostile world? And how many of these believe, somewhere deep down, that somebody—namely, the therapist—should make up for lacks and deprivations? To charge for our time is understandable, but we should be non-mercenary, non-materialistic, and self-sacrificing.

How is an analyst to deal with these images and expectations? First, we try to make them conscious. Even when they are made conscious, does that settle the matter? I remember working with a psychotherapist who told me that throughout his previous long Freudian analysis he had the mildly subliminal hope and belief that his analyst was saving up all his checks and would give them back to him at the end of the work. With me, his image was more that of an insurance policy. If he came and exposed his weaknesses and failings with me, then these would not destroy him in the outside world. The issue became, how much was he willing to pay for that service, and when would he get these things fulfilled elsewhere for less money? This financial attitude toward therapy came from a capable, generous, very conscious man—as much as I was. We, too, are just as generous, caring, socially responsible and devoted to service as was my analysand, but are also just as frightened, insecure, envious and greedy as the next man. We have worked at these things and are conscious, but money itself is such a charged and ambivalent symbol that one could construct a psychology with that as a center as much as with our more usual Eros and Thanatos psychologies.

We all share the consciousness of money as a symbol of security, value, prestige, personal worth, power, love, and even connected with the Self. But why do I become so enraged when patients not only do not pay me, but do not even apologize for not doing so? Why am I driven to murderous thoughts by such cheating, when with other losses I can be more philosophical? And why, too, do I worry when my practice drops, get chagrined when I hear that former students and colleagues have fuller practices or get more for their services than I do? Is this only the usual envy and competition? Am I alone in such emotional-financial intensity? I don't think so.

Surely, we analysts, like our patients and everybody else, suffer the usual problems of money, such as the need for security or power, that I mentioned above. We also suffer from the unreal expectations of patients and the collective. I am of the opinion, however, that we Jungians have an additional suffering this area, just because we believe that we are serving the Self. I have discovered that, in this belief of service, I welcome each new patient as, somehow, sent by God. I am there for his/her development as well as my own, and the problems that are presented are just the ones that I need to deal with at this time, even if I don't like it. That, of course, makes my working life and each patient quite meaningful for me. Jung thought that this was a good attitude for us to have. The other part of this belief, I have discovered, is that somewhere I have the expectation that the Self should take care of me. Since I am devoted to doing the work of the Self, both in my psyche and "in the world," then patients should be provided who can pay me enough for the livelihood of my family and myself. If the Self wants me to do this work, it should see to it, by golly, that I survive in it! If not, then I, like fallen-away priests and nuns, have lost my "vocation."

No wonder, then, that I am so enraged when patients do not pay, and don't even acknowledge that they owe me. They are denying the Self for me. The imagined penalty for that, in my mind, is death! Is it a wonder, then, when they—less conscious than I—expect me to work for nothing? Should I not be father and mother, even an agent of the Self for them, too? What to do, then, with this painful insight?

I am reminded of a dream I had some years ago, which still lies in the back of mind about many things, including money. In this dream, I was walking across a bridge to a futuristic city when a crippled beggar, bodiless and seated on a sort of skate board, comes to me and announces that he is God. I nod and offer to buy him a drink at the kiosk there. As I acknowledge him, this self-proclaimed God-figure grows a body and is quite whole. After we toast each other with wine, he holds out his palms to me, from which flow a huge number of gold and silver coins from every country and time. End of dream.

This, then, is how I understand the complexity about money: the Self is both beggar and a provider; it wants to incarnate into my life and needs my recognition. When I do so and share a relationship of spirit, then all the values and achievements of the ages—God expressing Himself/Herself through history and life—are vouchsafed me. But I can never forget that God is beggar as well as giver and that I, as a carrier of such an ever-incarnating content, am also beggar and giver. I can not escape this dilemma, but perhaps the insight can make me less murderous on the one hand, nor destroyed on the other.

A curious thing just happened. As I was writing the foregoing lines, a patient called and announced that she did owe me money, although in the last session she denied it. She was going to send the check by mail today. God does provide! But I also need to remember that one of the most common lies told is, "the check is in the mail"!

Alienation

This word, along with the concept of the "organization man," was more popular among intellectuals and students in the 1950's than it is today. Perhaps the reason it is less in vogue today is that alienation is more widespread. Movies and the arts no longer glorify and console the man who is different from the crowd, who goes against the pack. Instead, they look to virtues and values of the past, to the community of faithful farmers, to shared communion, ethnic solidarity. We are shown that communion because we lack it so much. Almost everybody feels alone in a hostile, uncaring world.

How does the analyst figure in this? We were always alienated and still are. We are "strangers in a strange land"; even the old word for our profession as healers of the mentally ill makes us "alienists." Jung told us the following, when he wrote about alchemy: the one who embarks on the individuation process finds himself alone, isolated, different from his surroundings and in possession of a secret which keeps him apart. He must work long and hard and deep to once again find his link with the collective world outside, and he must find it by going to equivalent lengths into the collective world inside.

We are, then, strangers, but friends to the patients who come to us, who themselves feel like strangers in the world. And how does this endless befriending of the stranger who comes to us effect us in the world? We are more strangers than ever, unable to engage in small talk. We often are rotten group participators, awkward and suspicious in social gatherings, guarded with our colleagues. Perhaps I paint too dark a picture and describe only myself and some others; but I venture to predict that not a few of those who see or hear these words will recognize themselves in the description.

Why is this so? Is it because of the individuation process? Or because our profession is a peculiar one and kept apart by projection and agreement?

Yes, this is true, but other people are embarked upon individuation and belong to peculiar professions without being especially alienated, such as astronauts, deep sea divers, and oil-well cappers. The reason, therefore, lies elsewhere. I believe, once more, that it lies in our concern with suffering and our play of self-disclosure. The person who is endlessly involved with hearing secrets, telling secrets, guarding secrets, being open and being closed, endlessly reflecting on what is going on in the background, is bound to be a peculiar fellow and one who is shunned as well as courted. Shamans have few friends.

How many times I remember going to parties and when the usual questions as to my occupation came up there were snorts and jokes, petitionings for advice, opening up of problems in a corner, or not-to-subtle hostility. That was years ago. Nowadays, along with the alienation of everybody, everyone has also been to a psychotherapist or is going to one, so the novelty has worn off. It is not the ordinary fellow in other fields who is alienated from us, it is we who are alienated from him. And this is just because we do this strange work of reveal-conceal, of suffering, and it effects us in the ways that I have mentioned. Since we serve the mentally ill, so are we seen as mentally ill. And, if our patients are not particularly mentally ill, still we are branded with the label. "Who can listen all day to such stuff?" they say. Or "Who listens?" We all know the jokes and stories, like these, and we all know how impossible it is to share what we really do and how we are, even amongst ourselves, let alone with other citizens.

What, then, are we to do? Jung's answer, of course, is that the deepening connection with the collective unconscious at first alienates us, but later finds us once more not only connected with our fellow humans but also to plants and animals and stones. Sometimes, however, we analysts are better connected to plants and stones than to social life, and are better nourished thereby. It was Jung, too, who said that after thirty-five every man is like a lonely ship who blinks to other ships, but goes about on his own voyage. He was connected deeply, but not too personally, I think, except with a very few. It is probably not different for us. Jung had his outer collective, however, as few of us have, and even our Swiss colleague, Adolf Guggenbühl, has addressed this isolation and alienation among us, espousing friendship as an answer to it.

For me, the answer lies partly in friendship, but also in being more open in the analytic work, in enjoying and appreciating family, in spending lots of time in nature. Many answers and no answer, because this alienation problem leads directly to the next item on our eight-fold path of the issue of the suffering of the analyst, namely Community.

Community

Carol Shahin has aptly described the Jungian community as a "village for people who could not remain in the village." That remark goes a long way to account for the fact that Jungian groups often split, that internecine squabbles and power plays are just as prevalent among us as in any political party. One might have thought that our penchant for integrating the shadow would have made us less quarrelsome or mutually rejecting. And for those of us who have even less invested in the Jungian or any collective, as such, there is apartness, "ships passing in the night." I have discovered that such a community-denigrating attitude is even built-in among Jungians generally.

Since I returned to membership in the Los Angeles Society a few years ago, I have found that almost every new graduate goes through a final darkness and frustration with the administration or some authority and comes out with the feeling that he or she would do just as well, or even better, by not being a member at all. Not only is this an unexpected outcome, but it seems to be even a desired one in some ways. In the background is the dictum, "Don't project the Self onto the Society," or any society for that matter.

Now, who can fault this advice? Certainly not I, who has had rough treatment from a Jungian collective in the past, and treats the current re-connection as an opportunity to work out my own shadow in relationship to social life. This distrust also exists for most of my colleagues. Many have expressed to me their frustration and disrespect for our Society life, yet all somehow try to do what they can. My own experience is that I can find some satisfactory mode of connection with almost any member of our group on an individual basis, but, as a collective, this is most difficult and frustrating. My chats with Jungians from other communities, by and large, reveal something similar.

What a paradox! All these individuation-pursuing and self-realization-promoting people have a difficult time being with each other, except on an individual basis! It would seem that we lack, on a group level, the kind of vessel that analysis itself provides, whereby consciousness, truthfulness, and relationship are deeply served. Nor are we likely to find it very readily. Group therapy will not do it, as attested by the experiments of analysts and trainees from various places and times. Nor is there much desire to find or create such a vessel, since Jung thought it hopeless, really. The Jung Club of Zürich, for example, was seen as a "battlefield," according to Franz Riklin, a place to encounter your shadow, but one goes home to work it out. I have been forced to conclude that he and Jung were right about groups, in general.

But what about community, and what do we analysts do about it? The answer is, not much. There are professional meetings and, as the number of Jungians increases, there is more variety and possibility of intellectual sharing, but kinship—such as it is—reduces still further. That is a fact, I believe, and one to further the suffering of the analyst. Where are the collective causes to serve, the parties to support, the truths to espouse? Mostly in the inner work, in the analytic structure, and in one's requirements of personal process. At best, we discover the *ecclesia spiritualis* of like-minded people apart from collectives. We discover our membership in the hidden community of seekers.

If we are lucky, we find our compensations in a more greatly appreciated marital, family and friendship life. Yet, we are deeply alone, making our link with the depths of the inner collective and looking for ways to manifest or connect in the world. Jung was both fortunate and capable in having sufficient depth and complexity to "give back" to the outer collective what he received from within, and to find, even in his lifetime, a sufficient resonance to enable him to go on. The rest of us have to do with less, although we also do not have to undergo the kind of hell he underwent, for example, in writing his *Answer to Job*.

Each of us carries his/her own process, but we do not have a communal vessel of equivalent value for further work in the transformation of our collective darkness. Yet the condition of the world obviously requires such a thing. If Jung is right, the only answer for collective darkness is for the individual to work on his own, inwardly, and to suffer the splits and lacks as incarnated by the Self in her/his own soul. That we must do anyway. In the future, however, with the increase in the number of extraverts who are attracted to Jungian psychology, there may be some creative contribution to our dilemma which will show a way of collective work which does not violate the individual, yet values group work, too. We who could not stay in the village find that the village we have joined is hardly a village at all!

Religion

The step from the issue of community to that of religion is a short one, indeed, and very much parallel to it. How many analysts are active members of a religious community? How many even attend services of any denomination with any regularity? About as many, I would suppose, as are active in community life! We are as introverted and atypical when it comes to religion as when we face community.

I used to think that this was a good thing; I shared the usual banalities about not being interested in "organized religion." By the time I had completed my training and had gone much deeper into the psyche, however, I changed and felt that it was important to have some connection with my religion of origin, that "the given"—as van der Leeuw had put it—was just as essential as "the possible." I had concluded that the chief transition events of human life—birth, initiation, marriage and death—were all social phenomena, requiring ritual and a link with the community and religion of my inheritance. I fulfilled this precept for myself, my wife and children. I even added further "observance" of ritual for the chief holidays of the year (national as well as religious), and treasured our regular Friday night prayers and family service ushering in the Sabbath. All this was important just because my personal myth was ecumenical and transcended the religion of my birth to include several others, as well as being a religion of the psyche. I suspect that most or my colleagues have felt something similar, since even those who were clergy to start with end up being more therapist than spiritual counselor.

Yet, since most of us are far from immersed in community religious life, just as we are estranged from general community life, we suffer this apartness. Our individuation offers us symbolic understanding, and even appreciation, but we are lacking, all the same. We do not, by and large, share the sacraments or behavioral laws which provide our fellow institutionally religious the succor and satisfaction of enactment and fulfillment. Our religious life comes from our relation to the Self, an ongoing dialogue within, which is sometimes shared in outer events with others, but it rarely can sustain the kind of mutual worship that is the rightful inheritance of humanity at large.

The loss is severe and causes a suffering which sets us apart from how humanity has always been. We are almost as non-observant as agnostics, yet we are at least as religious as the most intensely devoted practitioners. Few of us can abide being a member of a congregation. Our discrepancy militates against it. Some of us, for example Edward Eddinger and, before him, Esther Harding, think that Jungian psychology is itself a "new dispensation." And most of us think that Jung has indeed ushered in a new consciousness which is a "quantum" leap over the past. But we are not, luckily, like the members of a new sect who have found the "truth" and want to foist it on others. We are too well aware that we endlessly struggle to find and live our own truth and we respect others need and right to do the same. But the alienation from community, and particularly religious community, is a serious suffering for us.

For a number of years, I have been leading what I call a "psycho-ecumenical group", composed of clergy who are also therapists. They include rabbis, priests, nuns and ministers, all of whom have had Jungian analysis. We have met to give papers, to demonstrate rituals, to discuss issues, to share in religious holidays. Some in this group have even said that it is easier to share certain religious doubts and struggles with each other than with the clergy of their own community. I find this group, which meets about eight times a year, to be a very important one for me. It gives some outer form to my own inner ecumenical myth, as well as help me maintain connections with friends I might otherwise not see. This has been one resolution of my dilemma of lack of community.

Another resolution of this lack has been to attend High Holiday services at a local hospital, rituals led by a rabbi who is also a psychologist and good friend of mine. I thereby keep my connection with tradition and maintain an individual relationship. These, plus family observance, make me a most fortunate person, I believe. Yet I still feel that gap, that lack of organic connection with community and community religion which, I think, is part of the alienated condition of our time. M.L. von Franz has been of the opinion that the Self wants us to be strong enough to stand alone, and I think that she is right. Yet we suffer this deprivation, since the Self is also a deeply manifold being and process which yearns for kinship connection on an outer collective level as well.

In the section on Money, I related a dream I had in which the Self appeared as a crippled beggar, gradually taking on body as I acknowledged him and our relationship. During the same week that I had that dream, another one came to me in which I was informed that God's body constituted the entire universe, that it was like a worm biting its own tail, that its organs were composed of all the galactic systems and planets, and that all life constituted the cells of this Being. Furthermore, I was told that this Being breathed in and out in a vast harmony, and that those cells (or beings) lucky enough to be located at the places where this breathing occurred had mystical experiences.

My dream said nothing new about the apprehension of the divine. It has been frequently noted that we are all One, and that God is One in that multiplicity of existence. Yet the difference was that I dreamed it, it happened to me, personally, and it compensated that other image of God that I had, earlier in the week, which emphasized my particularity. I think the second dream, the more collective one, made a truth real for me, but did not indicate how this was to be lived. I also think that this is the problem of "the many," that of multiplicity of images, to be resolved in the next five hundred years, perhaps, the time that Jung told our colleague, Max Zeller, it would take to form the "new religion." That "new religion," I believe, will not replace any of the older ones, any more than Christianity has replaced Judaism, or Buddhism has replaced Hinduism. Yet one hopes that a balm will then be provided which our suffering souls need so badly. This will not happen for us, of course, who live now in that transition time, but we can still rejoice in having a glimpse of what is to come.

DISCUSSION

The foregoing reflections have revolved about two themes, as I mentioned at the outset. These have been self-disclosure and suffering. To round out our discussion, I think it valuable to see these issues from an archetypal perspective and for this purpose I have selected, from among other possible choices, the relation between Teiresias and the Goddess Athena for the theme of nakedness and self-disclosure.

Teiresias, you will recall, was a true prophet and visionary among the Greeks, being the one, for example, who warned about the violation of the incest taboo and prophesied several aspects of the Oedipus tale. He gained his prophetic capacity, it is related, as a consequence of inadvertently glimpsing Athena unclothed. This Goddess of culture and consciousness, born out of the head of Zeus, was deeply offended at being seen naked by Teiresias and blinded him. She recompensed him, afterwards, by giving him inner vision and the capacity to hear the gods. This same Teiresias had also been party to another event which he did not seek, when he chanced to see two snakes coupling. Attacked by them, he slew the female and was turned into a woman. After seven years, during which he lived as a harlot, he again saw snakes coupling and was attacked by them. This time, he slew the male and resumed his masculinity.

Our seer, the mythographer Kerenyi tells us, "saw things one does not normally see," and was both honored and punished thereby. He saw the nakedness of the Goddess, her secret Self, the naked truth that lies behind the bringing of culture and consciousness, I think. Athena, we remember, was the one who assisted Prometheus in achieving the divine fire. She is on the side of civilization, to be sure, yet to see her true nakedness—the secrets which lie behind the advancement of consciousness, as we see them in our consulting rooms—is to be blinded to the outer world as others know it. The recompense is to have increased powers of intuition and to see into the depths. We, like Teiresias, witness the breaking of taboos and the nakedness, not only of the human psyche, but also of the gods, as revealed in our work.

We also witness the union of the snakes—that symbol of divine healing—and more than most people, we are compelled to experience our inner contrasexual opposite, male and female. For this, too, we are handsomely paid. In all this, we are serving the divine in a feminine aspect, that of the expansion of consciousness and the advancement of civilization. We do this, I believe, like Teiresias, just because we happened to "be there" when the Goddess made her appearance. We surely do more than this—which is to say that other aspects of the divine principle, such as Aphrodite and Eros, are being manifested—but it is the nakedness which is of concern right now. I would add that even though the Goddess punishes Teiresias for the hubris of seeing her, she also desires this exposure, since she is so kind to him, giving him her best gift. Even Zeus and Hera look to him for authority, when they demand his expertise to resolve their quarrel as to who has more pleasure in sex, the male or female. I hope it is not disrespectful to suggest that here is even a root metaphor of marriage counseling!

I would conclude from the foregoing that the gods are ambivalent about us humans, both wanting us to see and punishing us for this. Here, perhaps, lies the deeper reason for the theme of self-disclosure, which is so central in our endeavors. I would say that what is disclosed in our work is the Self, both that of patient and therapist, but also transcending both. The Self is being incarnated and disclosed, and the aim, just as Athena supports, is the advancement of consciousness. We are honored and punished thereby.

This leads to our second theme, that of suffering. An archetypal basis behind this theme, one that I choose to discuss here, comes from a dream and vision that I had at Christmas time in 1950, a few months after beginning my first analysis. In it, a divine child was being born, and was attended by three new wise men, but these were a Jewish rabbi, a Christian priest, and a Buddhist priest. I did not know it then, fortunately, but this anticipated birth of the "anthropos" would be accompanied for me by these three fundamental images which are deeply related to the theme of suffering.

The Christian image, of course, that of the crucifixion of Christ, is centrally concerned with the suffering of God and man as the Self enters into the human condition. Jung has been his most profound, perhaps, in describing this event in *Answer to Job*. The central tenet in Buddhism, Duhka, the condition of suffering or dis-ease, is to be overcome by following the eightfold path of right living, leading to the experience of the Self. And it is no secret that Judaism, while not espousing the path of suffering as the way to the divine, has been a chief recipient of such agony during its entire history.

My dream and vision reported these attendants to the birth and now, thirty-five years later, I can acknowledge that this has been my fate—to cope with the suffering of my patients and myself as this ecumenical birth of the "anthropos" is ushered in at the end of the Piscean aeon. All three views—of the incarnation of the divine, of the endurance of transcendence of the opposites, and of the personal relationship with God as both an inner and outer fact—have permeated my own analytical work. I venture to suggest that some variant of these has affected my colleagues as well.

So, then, our suffering, perhaps, is not in vain and is itself the kind of penalty that Teiresias and Prometheus, to say nothing of Jesus and Buddha, paid with so dearly. In Judaism, there is a tradition that there are, at one time on the earth, a number of "just men"—Melamed Vovnikim—who suffer particularly because they carry the burden of the god-head. It is even greater suffering that some of them do not even know that they do this. I believe that the thirty-six men of that tradition are being added to in increasing numbers during the present generations and that we Jungian analysts are better off if we consciously realize that even to see the divine in manifestation is to be party to that suffering. The rewards are of greater consciousness and the realization of being co-creators in the vast evolutionary process which we glimpse with such awe. It is no wonder, then, that we are so burdened and uplifted by what goes on in the ordinary rooms in which we conduct our analytic work.

CHAPTER SIX

THE ONE AND THE MANY:
JUNG & THE POST JUNGIANS
(1989)

The present paper arose out of two experiences. The first one involved the writing for and editing a book called Jungian Analysts: Their Visions and Vulnerabilities (14), in which a dozen senior Jungian analysts, all of whom had contact with Jung, wrote personal documents in answer to a request to describe the evolution of their work. I and an advanced trainee, Joe McNair, commented upon these papers and elicited replies. The twelve major contributions—from three continents, five countries, seven cities—were remarkable in their candor, depth and individuality. I think Jung would have been pleased with them all.

The second experience came in the reading of a book by Andrew Samuels of London, called *Jung and the Post Jungians* (9). Samuels may be said to belong to the third generation of analysts since he says, in his response to my own paper in the Visions and Vulnerabilities book, that he was only twelve years old when Jung died in 1961. In his book, he carefully describes what he sees as three 'schools' of Jungian psychology—classical, developmental and archetypal—and compares them with each other and with branches of psychoanalysis.

Here are two books which consciously aim at eliciting and respecting a variety of viewpoints within analytical psychology, and here are two authors who consciously wish to perform a 'bridging' function among them; yet how different the approach and the outcome! The Post-Jungian book takes a classificatory approach, addresses ideological differences and similarities, and is almost wholly clinically oriented and objective, whereas the 'Visions' book is individual, subjective and depth-oriented.

At first glance, one might say that the difference is one of extraversion and introversion, or between a 'Developmental' person, as Samuels describes himself, and a 'Classical' one, as I would imagine he would describe me. Yet in the 'Visions' book there are several Archetypal psychologists (e.g., Güggenbuhl-Craig, Stein, Ziegler), two Developmental psychologists (Fordham, Jacoby), as well as Classical people (Vasavada, Dreifuss, Wheelwright, and Marjasch). I think that many of them, including most of the above, cannot be really be fitted into any of the classifications mentioned by Samuels. Beyme of Basle, for example, having had a traditional psychiatric training, Zürich analysis and Institute graduation, practices a kind of Behavioral Modification, although he seems to live his life from an archetypal viewpoint. And would Samuels place me firmly in his 'Classical' camp, as I imagine, since I, too, am Zürich trained and follow that tradition? I would be flattered to be classical in the sense of Bach and Maimonides, Jane Austen and Rembrandt, but what would Samuels do with the fact that I focus very heavily on transference and active interpretation as does the Developmental school, but am primarily archetypally and imaginally directed, as is the Archetypal school, and derive my fundamental orientation from the self, as does the Classical school? And to make matters even more difficult, I wonder how he would respond to the fact that I also had eight years of Reichian analysis, even practiced both Reichian therapy and its combination with Jungian work for several years, until I gave it up, largely because I felt I was not good at Reichian work and did not like the asymmetry of that type of analytical relationship.

In short, I am suggesting that the central Jungian focus has always been on individuality and depth, and those who opted for that path can be classified—or pigeon-holed, to use more opprobrious terminology—only with peril. But, in fairness to Samuels, his aim was the clarification of ideology and of difference, and not the assessing of individual styles or perspectives. From that point of view, Fordham is the only true 'Developmentalist' and Hillman the only true 'Archetypalist', since they are the originators of these views within the Jungian tradition, just as Jung was the only 'Jungian'. Hence I conclude that if any bridge-building is possible within the Jungian community, let alone the general depth psychological field, then an underlying theme is the problem of the one and the many. I shall address myself to this at the end, but first I want to respond more fully to the two books mentioned.

I will respond to Samuel's book first in my customary way, which is to give spontaneous emotional reactions followed by reflections. My style is to combine personal with impersonal, subjective with objective. I would also desire similar response from Samuels, both to my reactions and to the 'Visions' book, since I believe, like him, that truths emerge from both introspection and relationship, dialogue being the key word in both endeavors. Hence the following headlines serve as counters for discussion.

Astonishment

My first response to *Jung and the Post-Jungians* was astonishment that the chief feature of the Jungian viewpoint, as I understand it, the religious attitude toward the psyche, was practically non-existent. A few words reminding one of Jung's view of therapy and healing as deo concedente appear in Samuel's discussion of alchemy, but that is all. In my eight years of Jungian analysis with several analysts in Los Angeles and Zürich, I was always deeply aware of this attitude. It was this that united them and provided their distinctiveness from all other schools of depth-psychology. In Zürich, with all the differences and acrimony that existed among the analysts, what made us all—analysts and students, lay people and lecturers—part of one community was the respectful and reverent attitude toward the unconscious and a trust that the self of each person would indicate the path to be taken. Differences among analysts were sometimes so great as to evoke scorn and contempt, but I never heard any of them speak derogatorily of one another in regard to commitment and dedication to the analytic process as essentially a religious one.

Now the shadow of all that, to be sure, can be false piety, arrogance, pomposity, 'knowing better', and even evasion of personal and daily life problems. This latter neglect, I have been told by several younger analysts, is what led them to the Developmental school in the first place; their childhood and the transference were insufficiently analyzed in their classical Jungian analysis. I can also admit that I have lost more than one of my own patients to object-relations analysts since I did not deal adequately with their childhood, despite my own transference focus. Fordham has also said that the reason that he moved in the Developmental direction is that many of his early patients wanted their childhood analyzed and he did so, learning a lot in the process.

So I can see that there was a need on the part of many analysts to emphasize infancy and childhood. In attending to this need they were performing a useful return to psychoanalysis proper, connecting later developments from Klein, object-relations and so forth, and enacting a typically Jungian *reculer pour mieux sauter*. In point of fact this advance occurred in particular in the original work of Fordham. But why, one may reasonably ask, does this mean the abandonment, or at least the neglect, of the religious attitude? Fordham, at least, once even wrote about the 'dark night of the soul' of St. John of the Cross, but there is little of that sort of thing in the usual Developmental School's work. Rather, we hear endlessly about mother and father, about the infant and his 'omnipotence'. Are the Developmental Jungians not aware that the self in Jung's work referred, finally, to the image of God in the human soul? In the self as understood by Kohut and sometimes even as described by Fordham, it is surely revealed enough as an archetypal content but in it structural or personal aspects and not, as I see it, with its qualities of tremendum, mysterium and fascinans, the numinosum that is repeatedly referred to in Jung's works and has been the hallmark of that approach to the psyche.

The consequence of this viewpoint is that the divine images themselves now get centered on the parental imagos and even on the infant and child. We hear about the omnipotence of the infant without the realization that this quality belongs to the archetype of the self, played out in the infantile way of infants, to be sure, and, indeed, by others who have not got a personal relationship with this numinous image of the divine.

There is no reason, as far as I can tell, for Developmental analysts to have to give up the religious attitude while pursuing the myth of childhood in great earnestness. Indeed, if this were present there would be, I think, less likelihood of the frequent literalizing of the parental imagos, getting stuck in personalistic reduction, and the narrowing of the archetypal range to that of the great mother and father. They might even get help from the fact that it is the divine child and infant which is behind the fascination with those early events.

I am well aware that the continuing appeal of psychoanalysis is because of this same endless preoccupation with childhood, with parental images and with personal wounds of that period. Indeed, most of the people who seek analysis or therapy are so inclined to investigate their history in this way. And this need is what every therapist must in some way respond to sincerely if we are to perform our task. Yet one wonders how much this need is so all-important and how much is fostered by the very theories which focus so heavily upon it. The old saying that psychoanalysis is the spiritual disease which it aims to cure is certainly unfair, but the germ of truth it contains is that we may blind ourselves with our theories and that those ideas and experiences which help us transcend the personalistic (not *personal*) are in themselves healing and consciousness-raising.

I remember very well, in my first analysis, after endless months of working on my childhood, that the realization came to me—as a dream experience—that there was an archetype of the great mother behind my experiences of mother, that much of what I was undergoing belonged to that level rather than to the ordinary human being to whom I was born and by whom I was raised as lovingly as she could manage it. It was then that true relief occurred. I could then take up a dialogue with the inner figures, embark upon my own path and, finally, 'leave home' psychologically. I am perfectly well aware that Developmental Jungians are also so inclined to direct themselves, ultimately, else why by Jungians at all? Yet, I would offer that without that numinous experience, one gets stuck in childhood and the personal.

So, when one hears the complaints that one's childhood was insufficiently analyzed, one may also question whether those who remain fixed with that myth have ever experienced the self in its numinous forms. Perhaps we can be helped by the realization that, at bottom, Jung left Freud for this reason, and the two viewpoints are complementary in this regard. For the *recouler* of the Developmentalists to be also forward-looking, as Samuels and all of us desire, it would be of great value if this achievement of Jung, the religious attitude, were brought back to the regions and areas that he left behind.

I come now to the other half of my initial reaction to Samuel's excellent and stimulating book: *scorn*. The shadow to my astonishment at the lack of the religious attitude was the accompanying feeling of scorn. 'They haven't really dealt with the archetypal level of the psyche; they haven't struggled with the 'self (capital S); I am better than they are'. The pain of this admittedly inflated response led to deflation, and to the experience of chagrin and envy, which I shall take up next. If one invokes the name of God, inflation can readily ensue, as it did with me. But what I said I believe to true, also. The very wholeness which the self constitutes brought that painful dark half to me and the consequent depression. As a Developmental Jungian might put it, manic response was followed by a depressive reaction.

Chagrin and Envy

The emotions which followed my astonishment were those of envy and chagrin. I found myself envious that this young person, hardly beginning the second half of life, could already have produced such an excellent book and have it published by a prestigious house. How many years had I tried to get my books published! Only in the past few years have I had the good fortune to find a publisher to bring out my work. And, if the envy were not enough, I was further reduced to the chagrin of feeling neglected: none of my papers on the transference (e.g., 11), let alone my bridging books of Jungian psychology and the various religions (e.g., 15), were even mentioned. My old comrades from Zürich were given prominent attention, but not me. Poor me!

It helped to realize that my transference papers were probably not known by Samuels and that none of the mythological works of people like von Franz were mentioned either. If her work on fairy tales, myths, and so on was neglected, perhaps I was in good company. My psychomythology is in that area, too (e.g., 12). But still…

Then I had a night of dreams in which the self rubbed it in. First came a dream of desire for a tabooed, adulterous sexual encounter. This was followed by a dream of painful struggle with a manic entertainer who turned into a weeping four-year old boy. I understand these dreams as the validation of the importance given by the Developmental School to both the sexual taboo and childhood. I was reminded of my loneliness and depression from the ages of four to six, after my family had moved, and after my first important religious experience. It was as if the self was affirming that my own exhibitionistic shadow and manic need for recognition hid that lonely boy, despite my own years of work on myself, my childhood, and work with others along similar lines.

I then thought that I was required to take my own medicine, to apply that same religious attitude toward that little boy in myself who was touched by the divine and became lonely and depressed, later to be repressed by an exhibitionistic defense. And so I did, for the next two dreams of that night focused on an attempt to return home from a highly competitive city, and my need in my confusion to get direction from street-smart children and canny teenagers who were more generous and forbearing than I was. Following this came a dream of finding myself in a primitive land with my wife and several children, looking for ways of sustenance and survival.

I take these last two dreams as more forward-looking, in that they spoke of a chance to contact youthful sources who could, indeed, aid my woefully inadequate extraverted sensation function and help me find my 'orientation' afresh. Finally, it is in the more archaic and archetypal primitive land where the fundamentals can be worked with. For me, these dreams confirmed both Samuel's views and my own, and indicate the possibility of work on the 'fundamentals'. I marvel, once more, on the endless capacity of the psyche and the self for renewal.

One further insight came as a result of these dreams. I had often noted that I got depressed when reading many of the papers published by the Developmental Jungians. Fordham suggested that this reaction was that I was 'too high up' and needed to come down from my lofty, intuitive place. That seemed right, but I was further enlightened by Robert Bosnak's paper, 'The dirty needle' (1), in which he demonstrates, from the original dream of Freud, that analysts carry an image of being lustful, venal and incompetent, that our archetypal heritage from the 'founders' is partly an image of failure and inadequacy, hence depressing. But my present work showed me that part of the personal complex was triggered also. Reading about the reductive analysis of childhood touched that depressed little boy, insufficiently attended to. I had given ample attention to the earlier religious experience which 'took me up', but not enough to the subsequent depression which 'brought me down'. So personal and impersonal came together again.

Admiration

Followings my recognition and acceptance of my emotions of envy and chagrin, I was able to grasp more clearly the yeoman-like job that Samuels had accomplished. When I read his careful comparison of the work of Neumann and Fordham, I was especially aware of how he was able to simplify and inform in an objective way. Samuels' description of how both authors approached earliest states, the mother-infant relationship, the maturational process, and their common ground was impressive and helpful (9, pp. 154-161).

I was reminded of the time in Zürich, in 1958, when the first International Congress of Analytical Psychology took place, and we students at the Institute were agog when all the famous analysts showed up. The encounter between Fordham and Neumann was a brief though heated one, when suddenly there appeared the figure of Esther Harding, taking them both to task. My memory is uncertain at this point, but my fantasy includes a further heated addition by von Franz. Symbolically, it seems just about right: the

Developmental differences are mediated by a Classical person, but the final link is back to Jung's closest follower.

I wonder if the third generation of analysts can appreciate what it was like to be in such an environment as that Congress and Zürich itself, when Jung was alive. From the present tendencies towards debunking and reduction of what some see as 'idealization', I think not. That leads me to an archetypal perspective on such a development of the spirit. I remember the descriptions of a Zaddik in a school of Jewish mysticism, the Ba'al Shem Tov. It was said that the Ba'al Shem personally saw the divine fire in the forest and was able to show his immediate followers how to see it. The second generation was taught to experience that fire, but as time went on, only stories were told, and fewer and fewer of the subsequent generation could experience the fire for themselves.

It seems to me that the third generation, not so struck by those who 'have seen the fire', can be more objective and compare differences, as Samuels has done. They are also freer to find the 'fire' within themselves. I return, however, to my original point; the idea of Jungian psychology, finally, is to be connected with the divine flame. All else becomes partial if the religious experience is not included.

Appreciation

Following the roller-coaster emotional reactions, I arrived at a more differentiated feeling response of 'appreciation'. I much appreciated Samuel's presentation of the archetypal perspective of Hillman and the views of various psychoanalysts such as Bion. The Developmental School has certainly been deeply affected by the psychoanalytic variations, but it seems to me that this has been a rather one-sided love affair. We have yet to hear much appreciation of the Jungian field from the Freudians. But that does not detract from Samuels' integrative efforts.

He is both positive and gentle toward Hillman's work, although the latter was much less tender toward the Developmentalists. For me, Archetypal psychology is more comfortable, since I, too, am focused upon imagination and fantasy, the depth perspective, the play of metaphor and the multiple images of the divine. That Hillman's is an 'anima psychology' is all to the good, in my opinion; the world needs more of soul and flexibility and imagination, including the world of psychology. But why the hostility toward the self psychology of Jung, Samuels does not ask. Sure enough, one can be skeptical of new theologies, of authoritarian enforcements, of the rigidity of fundamentalisms, all of which are shadow aspects of the self in its monotheistic representation; but it does not follow that a fantasy (monotheism) which is ages old and underpins the psyches of the bulk of humanity should be merely be set aside as 'one among many'.

A similar cavil can be made with regard to the questions of sex and gender. As Samuels points out, Jung was remarkably early in his affirmation of the feminine principle. His enthusiastic appreciation of the Assumptio Mariae is not only a case in point, but his depth of detailed discussion of the importance of the elevation of the feminine principle into the monotheistic God image is one of the chief prophetic insights in his remarkable book, *Answer to Job* (6). How Developmentalists and Archetypalists can pass that great work by is hard for me to understand.

Much of the argument about feminism, it seems to me, is more political than psychological. That one supports full freedom and equality for women, as well as the specific encouragement to realize their particular potential, and that one not only embraces such views but asserts their concrete realization in practice in, for instance, equal pay for equal work, and freedom to enter any field for which one can qualify, is a natural outcome for a person who has looked deeply into his or her own soul. If one cannot the support the inner feminine—or masculine—there is no depth at all. Sure enough, unconscious prejudices can result in bad politics, but that is not the same as sexism. Something similar can be said about the anima and animus concepts. Either these have validity or they do not, or they may be only partially valid. But enough people, men and women, have undertaken that inner journey in such a way as to confirm, phenomenologically, the findings of Jung, Emma Jung, and others as to how these archetypal entities behave. Clearly, the dialogue with the psyche opens up every possibility of the masculine and feminine for both sexes, and it remains for us to become conscious of these qualities and develop them. Yet differences emerge, no doubt, which is an empirical matter, not a legal one. A central theme of our age is the elevation of the feminine, and the consequent freeing of us all from oppression. That Jung was also affected by this emerging archetypal condition is perfectly clear. It is also clear that all three schools of analytical psychology share in this consciousness.

In his conclusions, Samuels rightly affirms that 'to experience another from inside that other takes us into the imaginal and metaphorical'. Not only are these 'shades of a Klein-Hillman hybrid', it is a core realization. Samuels' second conclusion that 'We can place the interaction of the patient and analyst firmly within the imaginal realm without forgetting that there are two people present', is equally valuable and pithy. The two-person meeting is our datum. That the archetypes are evoked and experienced is discovered. What we do about this becomes an individual matter. Samuels is to be congratulated for picking out he 'main thing', as Freud said to Jung when the latter remarked that the transference was the alpha and omega of the work.

Similarities and Differences

Appreciation leads naturally into a consideration of differences and similarities. First of all, it was a good thing, I think, that Samuels included one of his own cases as an example of how one works analytically. That this was a supervised case, as he points out, suggests that he did this work while he was still in training, which makes it even more remarkable. He emerges as a sensitive, intelligent, informed and effecting healer, humanly making mistakes, as he acknowledges. His is a classical Developmental analysis, if I may make such a statement, and his results are clear. The crucial point for me is that the dream of the patient when she terminates her analysis could indicate the possibility of there now beginning a more classical Jungian analysis. It is not that the work was unfinished, I hasten to add. No, it was quite sufficient for the purposes of this patient at this time. But I would submit that the difference now shows itself: were the patient to continue, the analytic work would be likely to become more archetypal.

With this realization, I think that we can further clarify our differences. Analysts, confronted with the psyches of patients who come to them, work on the basis of training and experience. We are often challenged to venture on new paths, but it is our experience which determines this. It may be too idealistic to assert that each therapist gets the patients that he or she needs, but is clear that we all have to cope with the psychic reality that each patient brings. Samuels notes with surprise that Jung reported that two-thirds of his patients were in the second half of life and practically all of them had previous analysis. No wonder he needed to be more involved with meaning, with archetypal issues, with individuation. Psychoanalysis was founded on work with younger people with hysterical and obsessive-compulsive symptoms, hence the theory. Samuels, understandably, has also dealt mostly with younger persons and first-timers

I understand this all too well. When I first came back from Switzerland, age thirty-three, I was ready to embark on deep, Jungian-style analyses. Reality proved otherwise and most of my patients during my first two years were more like those I saw in clinics in the Veterans Administration and the army years before. I would come home exhausted until I realized that I was trying to sustain a traditional, somewhat detached and objective, analytic stance. Holding back my reactions is what exhausted me. Remembering that Jung was quite spontaneous and reactive, I undertook to do the same, and the exhaustion vanished. That resulted, of course, in the ever-extending need to deal with transference-counter transference reactions all the time. It also led to a change in clientele. My patients were now more frequently therapy professionals, clergy, and students embarked upon similar paths. Many of them had also had previous therapy or analysis. Perhaps that is why my own experience is more similar to that of Jung and the Classical School, but also why I fully understand the need to be archetypal in perspective but embroiled in transference-counter transference issues.

Another similarity: Samuels sees himself as performing a bridging function. So do I. But mine has been to link up Jungian psychology with the various religions. This was based on a dream in which a divine child was being born and attended by three new wise men or magicians, a rabbi, a Christian priest, and a Buddhist monk. That child, I think, carries a psychological function as a basis of unity. Therefore, my attempts, unlike those of Samuels or Hillman, is to bridge these traditional realms of the spirit, via the soul and psychology. I also once dreamt that I was crossing a bridge, part-Renaissance, part-modern, into a futuristic city. On the way, I encountered a divine figure who placed coins of every nation and time in my hands. So, my 'bridging' requires such particular honoring of tradition. I wonder if Samuels has had bridge dreams, too.

Finally, as the book blurb states, I think that Samuel's work is the first comprehensive attempt to survey the extraordinarily fruitful developments in Jungian psychology that have taken place since Jung's death in 1961'. He is to be congratulated.

I turn now, to the book I mentioned earlier, *Jungian Analysts: Their Visions and Vulnerabilities* (14). In order to get the flavor of what these dozen remarkable people have written about themselves and their work, I shall give snippets of descriptions and quotations.

I begin with Fritz Beyme, a Swiss psychiatrist from Basle, fully trained at the C.G. Jung Institute, Zürich, who tells of thirty years' work as a physician, behavioral modifier and researcher, while nominally practicing as an analyst. Faced with the demands of patients not suitable for analysis, and the limits of treatment given by insurance companies, Dr. Beyme has seen some 9,000 patients and describes his work day as one in which the teaching of groups, the use of tapes, advice and behavioral methods are common, with only five per cent of analysis. Yet with all this he has the attitude of a Jungian: he declined to accept a prestigious position with Eysenk of London and a future professorship as well, on the basis of a dream which warned him about ambition; he also treasured a black pearl, given in a dream, which showed his healing from an anima bout and from tuberculosis. His account is touching and astonishing. I went to Switzerland and Jung to get away from American Behaviorism; Beyme, a Swiss, became a Jungian and only then had to embrace 'American methods.' But we both rely on the movements of the soul.

A second presentation, from Gustav Dreifuss of Israel, reveals a gentle, empathetic men who works and writes from his own feeling place. As a therapist of Holocaust victims, among others, he says, 'the main healing for me is modesty, humility in what I can achieve, and I hope for help from the beyond'.

Adolf Güggenbuhl of Zürich says, 'It seems that I was born a Jungian psychologist,' but he also says that he never liked Jung personally and was put off by the people around him. He says that most outside influences on Jungian psychology, such as Klein and Kohut, 'seem to me to be a betrayal of the way Jung showed us to confront the wonderful and frightening world of the psyche'. Yet he does work other than analysis, including psychiatric evaluation with courts and criminals. 'I often feel very tired,' he confides, 'tired of seeing patients, angry and discouraged and overwhelmed by a hopeless ness'. Yet, 'After all these years, I am still a staunch and passionate Jungian psychiatrist and still no admirer of Jung himself.'

Vera von der Heydt of London, at eighty-six finds her career is 'in the past'. She 'watched and observed...accepting limitations with good humor' As a Catholic, she could view dreams of crumbling churches which caused her to question: 'What was crumbling, belief or faith?' What emerged was a precision particularly suited for people who love and need their religious tradition, yet need to develop individually as well.

Mario Jacoby, also of Zürich, saw his analyst clearly, warts and all. Yet when his dreams showed her as a goddess, he says, 'Our psyche makes use of a real person for the sake of its own unconscious purposes'. In Zürich, he 'absorbed much of what is considered a Jungian way of being, living in touch with the unconscious and ready to read its signals', but he was also attracted to the London group who 'had developed skills to reach the child within the adult patient by using transference/counter transference interpretations in most refined way. In time, he had a new dream of Jung as a little boy, and they played together, imaginatively.

Sonja Marjasch's first Zürich office was felt as a 'mere branch of the paternal enterprise' of her father, a Freudian analyst, and also of her Jungian training analyst. Later she had an office of her own with 'light, air, nature and animals,' in the country. 'I started to photograph again... I literally devel oped my own point of view and image of the world.' When her plumbing pipes corroded, she noted: '...Water pipes do not last forever...one canno rely on traditions forever. After a few generations...the sources of life have t be revised and partly renewed. Yet I also believe in continuity in the midst o change, and this expresses itself in the way in which each analyst remains true to himself.'

Arwind Vasavada, of India, after graduating from the Institute in Zürich says: 'As a fresh graduate, working in mental hospitals in Jaipur and Jodh pur, successes and failures with patients made me feel I was doing therapy.. Later, I began to feel that therapy was happening. Success and failure do no affect me...' 'It seems to be my fate to speak about Jung through Eastern eye and also speak about Eastern tradition through Jung's eyes. I am here an there and nowhere'. 'I follow...two different paths...following either one the journey ends and the doors of the Divine open and a new journey begin of which no one can speak. It is unspeakable'.

Joe Wheelwright of San Francisco focused on the earlier part of Jung work, which I found quite compatible with Frieda Fromm-Reichman an Erik Erikson. Psychological types are his specialty, but he says, quoting Jung

"Freud and Adler and I are not exceptions to this rule [that you must not generalize your own psychology, but everybody does] so our concepts are really personal confessions. We have generalized them, we have abstracted them, and we produce lots of documentation so it will appear that we based these notions upon an overwhelming body of evidence we had amassed through the years of clinical practice. Do not let that fool you a minute. What surprised me is not so much that none of us has the whole truth, but that there are so many people who find our value systems and our attitudes and our truths congenial to them."

Alfred Ziegler, of Zürich, has inaugurated an 'archetypal medicine', and can report: 'We might say that in the first half of life people see the psychologist and psychiatrist with the same problems they submit to the internist in the second half, whereby they demonstrate yet again the existence of a mercurial spirit'.

Michael Fordham of London took his path because 'patients were trying to get me to analyze their childhood'. He discovered that 'analytic practice involves introjecting parts of various people and it may not be possible to find the means of digesting and projecting these parts back... When that predominates, my identity may become threatened, boundaries become insecure, and I may be put in the position of 'fighting for my life!' ...Thus analysis is 'a precarious operation for any analyst who opens himself to patients so as to individualize his analytic endeavors'.

Robert Stein of Los Angeles revealed: 'I believe that I have become much more connected to and accepting of my true self, and that my capacity to relate empathetically and deeply has become highly developed. But I also feel that the analyst's habitually reflective and emotionally detached attitude has, in many respects, diminished my capacity for intimacy ... If I am an example of what happens to a Jungian analyst who has been dedicated to working on his own individuation process for almost forty years and working to help others for thirty years, it would be a sad commentary on our profession.'

Stein's antidote for this lamentable situation: change our focus to being and spontaneity.

And finally, Marvin Spiegelman: 'My own experience of analytic work is that I am soon divided into my opposites by the patient... I often feel as if my 'left hand' is open to the taboos of the soul, my own included, and my 'right hand' maintains the protective, parenting, connecting energy, and both hands' are necessary... I sit in the middle... I continue (left and right) until wholeness is achieved... I have to add *deo concedente*, for such is our need and trust when we serve the healing god, the self, as manifested in analytic work'.

The One and the Many

We come, now, to the underlying theme which I mentioned at the out set of this examination of contemporary Jungian psychology, 'The One and the Many'. Is there a unified depth psychology, or even a Jungian psychol ogy, or are we faced with the situation that our work produces analysts who are artists of the soul, each unique, and not scientists of the soul, wherein gen eral principles are discovered?

The them of the one versus the many underlies the history of depth psy chology, does it not, right from the days when Freud demanded total loyalty and gave rings to his disciples, despite—or perhaps because of—the defec tions of Adler and Jung? And it was not just these outstandingly creative geniuses who needed to go their own way and form new 'schools'; the mos original of the later followers were also forced out. If one reads the biogra phies of Otto Rank (8) and Wilhelm Reich (10), one sees in depth psychology the intolerance, cruelty, and lack of appreciation of differences which give the lie to the oft-spoken claim that diversity is welcomed and individuality treasured. Rather, we see the competitive struggles, the repeat of a kind o Chief Ape exercise which makes Freud's fantasy of totem and taboo a truth of his own psyche as well that of his followers, rather than of our primitive ancestors.

In our own Jungian psychology, we are all familiar with the work o James Hillman, fierce proponent of polytheism (4), since he rightly experi enced the rigidity and fundamentalism of the monotheistic archetype in ou own field. Yet those of us who are more 'classical' can hardly understand that he simply ignores all that we know of the self, of Jung's *Answer to Job*—in my view, the outstanding psychological document of the twentieth century. Ye this emphasis upon anima and upon soul, is all to the good.

As we have seen from *Visions and Vulnerabilities*, this struggle between the expression of individuality and the consequent multiplicity of those indi vidualities is matched by the battle between the artistic vision of creation and the striving to adduce scientific regularity. In short, the one and the many is fundamental to our field.

The theme of the one and the many is also fundamental in biology, when we see the passion of the female egg to join with only one of the many sper matozoic suitors who seek to mate with her. And each new being itself becomes the union of the one land the many, destined to differentiate and integrate biologically and psychologically for the rest of its existence. The same is seen in social life and history, in the conflict of nations, of classes, o religious groups, to say nothing of families and clans.

What does Jung say of this obviously archetypal theme, which has also occupied some religious thinkers? When one realizes that all Jung's work i concerned with the opposites, and that the theme of integration and multi plicity is primary in this, it is surprising that there are only two references in the Index where Jung explicitly takes this up; Volume 11, par. 798 (Jung 7) and Volume 13, par. 280, on Mercurius. In the latter Jung quotes the spirit Mercurius saying of himself: "I am One and the same time Many in myself" (Jung 5). The treatise quoted also says that the "center of the circle, man, is the earth, the 'salt' to which Christ referred when he said: 'Ye are the salt of the earth'".

A fuller discussion is to be found in Jung's *Commentary on The Tibetan Book of the Great Liberation*. In discussing the Tibetan and alchemical view that, finally, 'there being no duality, pluralism is untrue', Jung comes up with the view that the oneness is in the psychic matrix, the unconscious, but that multiplicity, including duality, comes with consciousness, and that this is as true or real as unity. At-one-ment, as we know, is as much 'given' in potential, as it is achieved through spiritual disciplines. The Mercurial solution that the one appears as the many leads Jung to the question of:

"Why should the One appear as the Many, when ultimately reality is All-One? What is the cause of pluralisms, or of the illusion of pluralism? If the One is pleased with itself, why should it mirror itself in the Many? Which, after all, is the more real, the one that mirrors itself, or the mirror it uses? Probably we should not ask such questions, seeing there is no answer to them (Jung 7, par. 798)."

Marie-Louise von Franz has been more explicit on this issue of the one and the many in her paper, 'Jung and Society' (3). She points out that all human relatedness is based on the archetype of the anthropos, who is a personification of Eros and simultaneously carries the image of the self for people who have delved sufficiently into their own psyche, but is also represented in all religions and myths as a totem of mankind. One might then say that the self is both one in the individual and multiple in mankind, but also one in mankind and multiple in individuals.

Von Franz concludes that, 'in practical terms, this means that the more we individuate, that is, truly become conscious of our unique self, the better related and the closer we come to our fellow men'. She shows that the development of this archetype, from Adam to the Adam Qadmon in Jewish mysticism and in the figures of Christ, Buddha and Mohammed, who have been the best representatives, has carried this content of relatedness. With the breakdown of the religions, this image is to be found within, and those who carefully pursue their individuation and cease to project their shadow, she says, are the forerunners of a new anthropos, yet to reveal itself.

I find von Franz's discussion both enlightening and comforting, particularly as we see the dreadful disintegration of modern life of which she, too, is acutely aware. I am less sanguine, however, about her affirmation, along with Jung, that it is only those who so devote themselves to individuation, in some form, can help bring about a newer, better era of relatedness and avoid the final catastrophe. The reason for my disquiet is that one sees all too little relatedness and group cohesion among those who, presumably, are the most devoted and committed to the individuation process, namely Jungian analysts. Not only do we see the fragmentation apparent in Jungian societies in England and Italy, but I understand from representatives of all countries that the bickering, hate, and power drive of a not inconsiderable number of Jungians is no less than that of 'collective man'. Struggle with the shadow does not seem to mean that we cease to project it, or that we are better related.

Does this mean that we can just work on our own process, be as conscious as possible, and let the rest of the world, including Jungians, do what they need to do? That is largely what I have concluded and, in my own talks with von Franz, have found that this is the best attitude. After all, tribes consist historically of no more than fifty to a hundred individuals at a time, and if we can be related to that many people, on whatever level of depth, we are doing fairly well. But I also think that this is our typical introverted way of dealing with things and that we seem also to need some extraverted methods. As Jungian psychology grows more popular we may attract those extraverts who are also capable of introverted depth who can show us a way to work with group life as well, not in the ways that are so far known to us, but in a way in which both the individual is treasured as well as the group. Perhaps one may employ a kind of group active imagination which touches a common anthropos. However, until this is invented or discovered. I think that we simply have to carry the conflict, both individually and collectively, of being both artist and scientist, 'classical' Jungian, depth psychologist and 'revisionist'. The one and many means that each of us is alone, yet also a member of multiple groups of family, friends, associations, and so on, and that these overlap.

There are a number of forms of the myth of the one and the many, which I discussed in *Jungian Psychology and the Passions of the Soul* (13), but as to our professional affiliations, I can only see a continuing and—I hope—fruitful conflict. In this, we are still alchemists after all, since we abide with a 'warring peace' and a 'sweet wound'.

SUMMARY

The author raises the following questions: Is there a unified depth psychology, or even Jungian psychology, or are we faced with the situation that our work produces analysts who are artists of the soul, each unique, and not scientists of the soul, wherein general principles are discovered?

The answer is based on two experiences: (1) editing and writing for a book called *Jungian Analysts: Their Visions and Vulnerabilities* in which a dozen senior analysts describe the evolution of their work; (2) reading Andrew Samuel's book *Jung and the Post-Jungians*. He also draws on Jung and on von

Franz, linking it up to the myth of the one and the many.

He concludes that struggle with the shadow does not seem to mean that we cease to project it or that we are better related to each other and that the best we can do individually is to work on our own development. For collective solutions, we have to await extraverts who are also capable of introverted depth and can show us a new way to work with group life in which both individual and group are treasured.

EPILOGUE

'The divine suzerainty has a secret and it is *thou—this thou* is the being to whom one speaks; if [this *thou*] should disappear this suzerainty would also cease to be.'   — Sahl Tustari, quoted by Ibn 'Arabi

'I was a hidden Treasure, I longed to be known.'   — Ibn 'Arabi

A few months after completing the foregoing reflections on the problem of 'The One and the Many', I happened upon a solution to this issue in the thought of a thirteenth-century mystic of Islam, the Sufi Master, Ibn 'Arabi. In an outstanding monograph by the French Islamicist, Henry Corbin, entitled *Creative Imagination in the Sufism of Ibn 'Arabi* (2), we learn that one can distinguish between God in general (Allah) and each person's particular Lord (rabb). The former, in Ibn 'Arabi's view, is fundamentally transcendent and not to be grasped by any single individual or even any organized religion (the 'God in the faiths'). We can all have an intimate dialogue with our own Lord, that aspect of the divine which comes into existence with us. Furthermore, our very longing for God is actually the divine within us which yearns to be recognized and realized (see the above quotation). Each aspect of being, including persons, is a particular divine name, waiting to be manifested. The totality of divine names is the God who transcends us but is continually being created in us, as we realize his being. And this very creativity comes under a feminine aspect of the divine in the form of love. Creation is theophany, and is a product of the imagination, both human and divine. Parts of the foregoing will be familiar to some of us from Jewish mysticism and other theosophical systems. Its similarity to Jungian concepts of the individual self as a fragment of the divine is quite clear. [There are a number of other similarities which I discuss in a paper entitled "Active Imagination in Ibn 'Arabi and C.G. Jung", which appears in a book I edited with Pir Vilayat Khan entitled *Sufism, Islam and Jungian Psychology,* New Falcon Publications, 1991].

Particularly relevant to our present discussion is how the many names and the one are connected. All the names manifesting in existence refer to the one and the same named one. But each name refers to a unique aspect, different from all others. The totality of Names refers to the One God who reveals Himself to Himself to and by the theophanic imagination, which is also human imagination. To confine oneself to the plurality of names is to be with the multiplicity of the world, past, present and future. To confine oneself to the unity of the named one is to be with the Divine Being in the aspect of his Self (*dhat*) independent of the world and relationships.

What is of especial interest is Ibn 'Arabi's view that both are necessary. To reject the first is to forget that the divine being reveals Himself to us only in the numberless configurations of the theophanic imagination, and it is this which gives effective reality to those Divine Names. And it is these Divine Names who, in their sadness, yearned for concrete beings in whom to manifest. To miss the second is to fail to perceive the unity in the plurality.

Now it is here that Ibn 'Arabi provides us with a new solution: to occupy both simultaneously is to be equidistant from polytheism and also from monolithic, abstract and unilateral monotheism. The servant of his own Lord and of the larger God of the totality recognizes his task as that of realizing the particular divine name that he/she was meant to bring into being. 'I am the hearing by which he hears, his eyesight by which he sees'. By so doing, the servant of God helps to make the particular name increasingly transparent and serves both the particular and the universal.

REFERENCES

1. Bosnak, R. (1984). 'The dirty needle: images of the inferior analyst'. *Spring*, pp. 105-115.

2. Corbin, H. (1969). *Creative Imagination in the Sufism of Ibn 'Arabi*. Princeton. Princeton University Press.

3. Franz, M-L von, (1983). 'Jung and Society' in M. Tuby (Ed.) *In the Wake of Jung*. London. Coventure.

4. Hillman, J. (1971). 'Psychology: monotheistic or polytheistic?' *Spring*, pp. 193-232.

5. Jung, C.G. (1948). 'The Spirit Mercurius'. *Coll. Wks.* 13.

6. Jung, C.G. (1952). 'Answer to Job'. *Coll. Wks.* 11

7. Jung, C.G. (1954). 'Psychological Commentary on the *Tibetan Book of the Great Liberation. Coll. Wks.* 11

8. Lieberman, E. (1985). *Acts of Will: the Life and Work of Otto Rank*. New York. Free Press.

9. Samuels, A. (1985). *Jung and the Post-Jungians*. London. Routledge & Kegan Paul.

10. Sharaf, J. (1983). *Fury on Earth:: A Biography of Wilhelm Reich*. New York. St. Martin's Press.

11. Spiegelman, J. Marvin (1980). 'The image of the Jungian analyst and the problem of authority'. *Spring*, pp. 101-116.

12. Spiegelman, J. Marvin (1982). *The Tree: Tales in Psychomythology*. Phoenix. Falcon Press. [Now *The Tree of Life: Paths in Jungian Individuation*, New Falcon Publications, 1993].

13. Spiegelman, J. Marvin (1988). *Jungian Psychology and the Passions of the Soul*. Phoenix. Falcon Press.

14. Spiegelman, J. Marvin (Ed.) (988). *Jungian Analysts: Their Visions and Vulnerabilities*. Phoenix. Falcon Press.

15. Spiegelman, J. Marvin and Miyuki, Mokusen. (1984) *Buddhism and Jungian Psychology*. Phoenix. Falcon Press.

CHAPTER SEVEN

THE INTERACTIVE FIELD IN ANALYSIS: AGREEMENTS AND DISAGREEMENTS (1991)

The following (a shortened version of lectures given to the Chicago Society of Jungian Analysts and to the Independent Group in London in the spring and summer of 1989) is a discussion of four areas each of agreement and disagreement among analysts, particularly Jungians, regarding our common understanding of the transference. I include, as a special consideration, the issue of self-disclosure and, therefore, I make use of personal examples.

Areas Of Agreement

Therapeutic Situation as a Field

We Jungians often refer to the therapeutic situation as an analytic "field," without realizing, perhaps, that this term has some history to it in physics, mathematics and even academic psychology. For our present purposes, however, I want to focus on the pragmatics and experience of this field in our daily work.

For example, I very often get "symptoms" when a patient begins a session, or after some moments of work. These are usually bodily reactions of various kinds, such as headaches, stomach aches, heartaches, shortness of breath, sphincter tension, fatigue, etc. They do not usually have a direct connection with what is being said, but whenever I reveal these reactions, I almost always discover that the patient is having, or had in the recent past, the same symptom or one related to it. Most of the time, an underlying symbolic parallel is associated to the psychological content being discussed. When this occurs, I am relieved and take it as a fact that the "therapeutic field" is now operating; there has been a constellation of complexes and an energy exchange so that both the patient and myself are embedded in that field. The work of awareness, interpretation, and integration of content can now proceed in a harmonious, therapeutically useful fashion. It is my task, now, to be alert to what is happening in myself and in the patient, as always, but to share that awareness and understand what it means. This generally results in a clearing up of the symptom.

My second kind of apparently unconnected reaction has to do with feelings. After a session begins, I may become quite sad or dreamy, so that my energy level seems to be depressed, as well as my mood. When I mention this condition, particularly sadness, to the patient, a similar awareness usually emerges, or they seem to fall into that condition and some repressed content emerges.

The loss of energy is more complicated. There I may mention the fact that I feel listless or without energy or even bored, am drawn into the unconscious, and wonder what is happening to my therapeutic partner. When a parallel condition is reported, I suggest that we both "drop" into the unconscious at that point, into fantasy or aloneness for a few moments, and then return to share the content. This, too, has useful consequences and confirms that not only is there a therapeutic field in which we are embedded, but there is a concrete movement of psychic energy that also takes place.

These kinds of experience, I think, are not uncommon among psychotherapists, although my way of revealing these reactions is not likely to be typical. Some analysts, particularly Freudians, suggest that this loss of energy, for example, is because the patient is sucking our vitality out of us, or because, via projective identification, a content is being thrust into us. I cannot fully agree with the interpretation that the patient is doing such things to us, consciously or unconsciously, although at times this is certainly the case. The patient often experiences us as doing something to him or her which we do not think we are doing at all, we need to remember, and we are likely to chalk this up to projection. What makes our judgment of who is doing what to whom so certain?

I think is more useful to suggest that a field is set up, whereby some content of the patient, usually, sets off something is us, consciously or unconsciously, and the interchange takes place. Reactions of both patient and therapist are connected with the archetypal forms in the background, and the admixture of psyches includes the personal and transpersonal on both sides. The analyst's advantage is that he or she is more experienced in dealing with these unconscious invasions or reactions, has tools of understanding, and is committed to helping the partner.

Even if one agrees with the foregoing understanding, there remains the question, why are the analyst's response just those of sensations or feelings? Is this typical or typological? My answer is that it is both. I happen to be an introverted intuitive/thinking type, so when the unconscious is mobilized in the work, the content that emerges will understandably have a lot of feeling and sensation in it. I would imagine that sensation and feeling types would get the reactions of intuitions and thoughts. But, since so many Jungian analysts tend to be intuitives, I would not be surprised that reactions of many colleagues are often similar to mine. The sensations and feelings, arising from our unconsciously evoked third and fourth functions, can then be combined with our differentiated intuition and thinking to produce useful interpretations or comments. In any case, the unconscious first strikes us with emotion, so we would all encounter that first.

But we must not pass too quickly over this experience of real energy exchange going on in the analytic process. Few of us have the sensitivity or skill to read auras or energy fields but it is precisely in this area that we are treading. We think that our interpretations of behavior or dreams or fantasies is what has effect, but it is obvious to many of us that the energy exchange going on in the room is profound and is just as healing—or disturbing—as the exchange of words. Indeed, it has long been apparent to me that many of my dream interpretations get their power and significance from the fact that I am in tune with patient and thus all my knowledge and experience comes to use in the service of that connection. I shall later give an example of the attunement in connection with bodily symptoms.

Openness to the Patient

All therapists are agreed that we are open and receptive to each patient or analysand who comes into our office and psyches, attentive to what they say and do and, very soon, also their impact upon us. The field eventually created is dependent, first of all, upon what they are and what they bring. This is as it should be, since the purpose of the relationship is healing and enlightenment of the paying customer, after all, and whatever benefit the therapist gets from this process is merely included as a fringe benefit. Yet, in reality, things are more complicated: the patient reacts, too, to the office and person of the therapist. He or she selects and responds to all of that, consciously or unconsciously, and we all know that to think of ourselves as a blank screen for analysands is inaccurate and even merely defensive. But we do need to protect ourselves from patients, also, do we not? From the abuse and passing on of toxic conditions, even poisons? Yet we also know that our capacity to contain and transform these noxious processes is crucial to the healing process.

We recall that the original meaning of the German word for transference, *übertragung*, referred to the ancient Teutonic practice of applying a bandage to a wounded area of a person and then putting this same bandage on a healthy tree. The idea, of course, is that the healthy tree could absorb this "transferring" of the wound to itself and thereby cure. Psychologically, we might see this as an act whereby the analyst is open to the poisons of the patient—as a consequence of wounds—and allows these to enter into himself or herself and be absorbed by one's own "tree", the Self, as manifested in this relationship, accomplishing healing thereby. Or rather, it is the Self that does the healing, evoked by the patient, carried by the therapist, and experienced jointly in the process: damaged Self evokes healthy Self, followed by the awakening of healthy Self in the process and in the patient.

The foregoing is, perhaps, a bit idealized, since we often do various things to avoid such exposure, even unconsciously. One can make a case, for example, that the traditional analyst's stance of objectivity and interpretative "throwing back" of the projections is, in truth, a defensive maneuvering to ward off impact. Yet, as Jung told us repeatedly in his therapeutic papers, our effect on patients is proportional to their effect upon us, and to ward off the impact is to reduce the possibility of healing. Once more, we are brought to the concept of the "field."

I am reminded of C. A. Meier's paper (1959), in which he discusses the "totalistic" character of the analytical situation and concludes that not a few analysts "go under," so to speak, as a consequence. The high suicide rate among therapists, plus the folk fantasy that they do not possess a lot of mental health are hints at the partial validity of this point (Spiegelman 1988).

An example that graphically illuminates the foregoing is unusual in that it is not from a traditional analytical situation, but from a kind of marriage counseling, one that had been going on for three years at the time of the illustrative event. I hasten to add that this is a unique situation for me; I have often worked with couples for some sessions or months, finding it a valuable task in the holding of opposites and enhancing the capacity to empathize with divergent positions, but this case expanded into years, since both the love and the difficulties went deep, indeed. Briefly, the couple, well into middle age, foundered on the belief of the wife that her husband, a retired executive, was unfaithful and even had attempted to poison her. This—to him, false—accusation drove him to both rage and despair. The unraveling of the relationship and the antecedents in youth and childhood took a lot of time, including work with dreams. At the time in question, the man had been suffering from extreme depression for some months, reactivated from years past. His dreams were positive, reminding of a happy time in his youth, but he was split and bitter. My own attempts were to attend to him, connect with him as best I could. At the time in question, I had done so and found that I was ineffective, failing and sinking back into despair myself. After I said this, the man reported that he was feeling much better, uplifted. It was noteworthy that the dark mood, transferred to me, allowed his positive condition in the unconscious to emerge. This process repeated itself, but then we shifted to the fact of the wife's suspicion and our hopelessness in convincing her that this was not a concrete fact, but a psychological one (his rage, during the earlier years of their marriage, and her fears, had "poisoned" her).

At that moment, I experienced a sharp pain in the stomach and nausea, as if I had been literally poisoned. When I reported this experience to the woman, she was astonished and said this was exactly what was happening to her at that moment. This simultaneous, field-connected, link-up with both spouses provided a kind of turning point in the process, permitting a more rapid transformation of the toxic conditions damaging to both of them.

Analysis, interpretation of dreams, work on the relationship, all had been insufficient to this point and the depth of the disturbance required not only the openness to the unconscious on my part, but a concrete participation. Thus we experience not only a *participation mystique* that Jung so often spoke of, but one that includes a consciousness of that mutual immersion. This leads us to the third area of agreement, that of the analyst being touched by the process.

Analyst Effected by the Process

My previous example, that of the depressed husband and suspicious wife, is unusual only in the sense that it is couple's therapy and therefore includes more in the analytic field, triangularity particularly. We are immediately reminded of Jung's use of the alchemical metaphor of the Royal Couple and their transformation. The famous "axiom of Maria Prophetissa," of the sequence of stages in the transformations process from one to two to three, with the fourth arising out of the third, is mentioned frequently by him. Both he and others have illustrated that the interplay of analyst and patient implies at least a foursome: analyst and his anima or her animus, the patient and his or her anima or animus. Freud always felt that at least three people were present, psychologically, in the sexual act—referring to the presence in the psyches of the couple of the primal scene and the Oedipus complex—and Jung was at his most profound in referring to the alchemical imagery arising in the transference. For us inheritors of the pioneering efforts of our founders, it has been important to convince ourselves of these facts by experience. Advance in understanding has been more uncertain.

My own experience has been that the unconscious usually appears and effects me as a "third", between analysand and analyst, rather than as a fourth. For example, a shadow figure or content is projected onto me, which evokes a shadowy reaction. The patient dreams of me as licentious or money-grubbing. My feelings are hurt at this projection, like it or not, even if I am aware of the projective character and the fact that I provide hooks for this, both consciously and unconsciously. The feeling of being "misunderstood," for example, arises when I have contributed to this projection by reporting a sexual fantasy. I know that I have done so, but I also know that my motive is that of honesty, or making conscious, it hurts to be adversely labeled, even by the patient's unconscious. My shadow is apparent, but the hurt is that I am only partially seen and judged. But the hurt induces the archetype of the "wounded healer," leading to further awareness and healing.

The "fourth," in such conditions, usually emerges only later on. I am thinking now of a patient I had seen for over a year who dreamed of being married to an "older man," with certain characteristics similar to me, but she also had a lover in this dream. The "older man" had a "housekeeper" with whom he had a previous liaison who did not like the new marriage. This dream came after a session wherein I had gone over the hour; boundaries were transgressed, so to speak, and the deeper transference, in the alchemical sense, was finally achieved. A foursome resulted.

But these foursomes are not always what Jung reported. I recall a very early case I had, only a couple of years after becoming an analyst, in which the patient dreamed that she and I were at the seashore observing two strange fish. One was a "harem-fish" and the other was a "cat-fish." The harem-fish entered into her vagina while the cat-fish suckled my penis. Both fish then went into the ocean and united with each other. I thought immediately of the famous anima/animus foursome of alchemy, but my patient said that the harem-fish was female and the cat-fish was male, so we were in for long shadow-integration work, rather than the anima/animus sharing that I had anticipated.

In any case, the analyst is ultimately touched in his own soul by any work which goes beyond superficial counseling, and this demands increased consciousness on his or her part. We continually get affected and infected and thus have to work on ourselves, as well as with the patient. This is supposed to be good for us, and I suppose it is, in the long run, since it helps us realize our myth as healers: we continually are re-wounded and have to be healed in deeper fashion. In our being affected, however, there arises the issue of whether one communicates this effect or contains it, the "reveal versus conceal" dilemma I referred to in an earlier paper (1988). Since this brings up an area of disagreement, I shall defer its discussion, and briefly speak of the final area of agreement, in Jungian circles, about the transference, that of the archetypal dimension.

Archetypal Basis

Jungians agree that the ultimate basis of psychic functioning is archetypal in nature and that the complexes evoked and treated in the work have such a root foundation. It is this foundation that both provides the similarity between analyst and analysand and also serves as the healing source. Whether this archetypal basis is dealt with on a conscious level or not depends, of course, on the necessities of the patient, but normally these occur with increasing frequency as the work progresses, in time and depth. Where disagreement occurs, it has to do with the nature and importance of the myths that arise and how to handle these.

Areas of Disagreement

Mutual Process versus Asymmetry

Ever since the early 1960's, I have been arguing in favor of the approach to analysis and the transference as one in which a "mutual process" takes place, ultimately, if not from the very outset (Spiegelman 1965, 1972, 1980). The interplay of psyches, the evocation of the analyst's complexes, leads to the archetypal level of connection and the two parties are then embroiled in an alchemical stew. This requires the analyst to leave his perch of authority and defensive objectivity and relate to the unconscious as a participant in that process. In various papers, I have spelled this out and have invoked Jung as one who shares my conviction (Jung 1946). Interest leads to involvement, which leads to being affected, which leads to embroilment, which results in a mutual process and equality.

The opposition to this view has said that my mutual process idea is exaggerated, that the very nature of the relationship is unequal: the patient comes to the therapist, pays for sessions, relies on the knowledge and control of the analyst, holds us as ultimately responsible. The analytical relationship, therefore, is asymmetrical rather than symmetrical.

I have responded that the process indeed begins in this asymmetrical fashion, but as the unconscious enters into the relationship, the two parties are so affected that now the connection is symmetrical. The analyst, I have said, has to give up his or her claim to authority and, using one's knowledge and greater experience with the unconscious, apply oneself to the discovery and service of the authority of the Self as it manifests in both patient and therapist. Both are equal, I have claimed, in the sense of the American Declaration of Independence: we are equal under God. To translate that into psychological terms, patient and analyst are equal under the authority of the Self which emerges in an alchemical transformation to which both are submitting.

To prove that the money exchanged is not the crucial issue, I have worked with a number of people where there was no fee and the process was not so terribly different. Furthermore, I have been in what might be called "mutual process" with friends, at various periods and for varying lengths of time, in which my therapeutic responsibility was abdicated and these, too, were not terribly different.

More recently, however, I have come to see that my "proofs" were far from adequate. In those cases where no money was exchanged, there was either an implied "gift" on my part, as one does in a free-clinic situation, or the partner was a former patient. With friends, furthermore, I found that mutual process work was usually only for brief periods, in which something particular was accomplished, rather than a long-term alchemical seeking of the gold of the Self. I have been fortunate to have friends where my psychological experience has been of use in the relationship, such as supervision or sharing of life, and who have been, in turn, equally benefiting of me in various ways, so that I have not been "the authority." Yet these experiences have not proved that mutual process, in the sense of equality, does exist characteristically. I have to admit, therefore, that I was wrong.

Inequality does pertain in the analytic relationship, as my critics have maintained, not only with money, seeking for service, and expertise, but in the difference in psychological consciousness. We are equal under God, of course, but not in the world, including the world of therapy. It is obvious that we are all created unequal in abilities, station in life, etc. Our equality occurs only in the belief that we are all fragments of the divine, and no fragment is less divine than another. The sharing of divinity does not presume equality, however, and I was mistaken.

Where I am right, I believe, is in the fact that one can face this inequality and make an *individual* relationship to it, decided *mutually*, which, paradoxically, increases the *equality*! This joint decision, repeated at different times in the process, enhances the Self of each partner. In this process, inequality (on both sides!) is accepted, but the fundamental and equal meeting of Self with Self is acknowledged. I can think of several examples of this, but the ones that come to mind all entail some violation of social custom or general expectation of therapists which I am loathe to report, both because of my respect for these customs and my fear of opprobrium. But I shall mention two anyway, since I feel obliged to give evidence for my view.

The first example is that of a clergyman with whom I worked in analysis for the first time more than twenty years ago. We worked for several years, off and on, and then completed an analytic process in an intense two-year period. Some time after termination, we became friends, in another context, and participated together in an on-going group of therapists and clergy on the problems of psychology and religion. Periodically, he returned to work with me for a time, and we needed to discuss this changing relationship and mixing-up of roles. We decided to continue. Later on, there were more connections of friendship between us, in a variety of ways, and still later, he came to for supervision for therapy work he did himself. At times, I also was his pupil in both other areas of therapy, in which he was expert, and in friendship exchanges of a religious character. The relationship has continued; its flourishing has depended, I believe, on the consciousness of both parties and making ourselves aware of the risks and values of individualizing of our relationship. This relationship, although unique, is not the only one where analysis has shifted to friendship and to other ways of connection.

A second example that comes to mind is that of a friend since my early teens, one with whom I went to school, served in the Merchant Marine, and shared deeply in life. Some time ago, some marital counseling was needed by him and his wife, and the situation was such that they did not trust anyone else. After discussing this with them at length, I agreed to attempt the counseling, noting the confusion of roles, the possibility of my being prejudiced in favor of my friend over his wife, etc. I also noted the possible threat to our friendship. We tried it, anyway, with my friend giving me works of his art in exchange for my time and effort. The result was quite positive: I am particularly proud of the fact that the wife found me to be as supportive and understanding of her as of him. Surprisingly, the friendship itself proved to be of particular value, since I was compelled to be honest about my personal reactions and values in their relationship. When it became possible for them to make use of another therapist, for a time, I was pleased that this was accomplished easily and effectively. They were not dependent upon me in a destructive way. The friendship has not only continued, but has deepened and developed with both parties.

I could give other examples of this nature, as well. In so doing, however, I in no way want to imply that the general ethic warning against such confusion of roles on the part of therapists is erroneous. On the contrary, I think that, in general, modalities of ethics are the result of collective experience and values and should be regarded highly. Their abrogation should take place with prudence and circumspection and only in connection with the value equal and opposite to collective truths, namely individuation. Individuation and the collective are worthy opposites, and need each other. It is this very struggle that is involved in analytic work, is it not?

An awareness of this antinomy can assist us in understanding the successful outcomes of the above two relationships. If I ask myself why these thrived in spite of the ethical dangers involved, I can readily see that they did so because my friends had their own Self well in hand; it was not—or no longer—projected onto me. They were either religious persons who had their authority from the outset, or had discovered it in the course of their development, with me or with others. I conclude, therefore, that I was both wrong and right about "mutual process" and equality. It really only is achieved when both parties have their inner authority, have an independent Self that can be and is effected by the other, but remains solidly within. This, in the end, is what we seek generally in analytic work. We help each person, we hope, to come to and unite with his or her own inner authority, the Self. On the way, we rely on our own connection with the Self to enhance this possibility. As the process continues, furthermore, this Self-to-Self relationship becomes more conscious. Equality, therefore, is a *result*, more than a given.

My opponents are right and I, too, am right. To resolve this paradox, suggest that we are dealing here with both an archetypal potential and an actualization. Equality "under God" (read Self) is there, archetypally, at the outset of the analysis, but it has to be made conscious and, therefore, it is achieved.

Analyze versus Connect

A second area of disagreement about analytical work has to do with the nature of the analyst's response to the patient, rather than the nature of the work itself. Should one analyze the communications of the patient, including behavior, questions, comments, etc. or connect with him or her? Sometimes this is expressed as a conflict between the work conceived as that in which the discovery of the roots of complexes and symptoms is at issue versus the patient's need of "re-parenting" as required for healing. Every analyst engages in both activities, of course, but the conflict as to which attitude should be the primary one is great enough as to suggest that the difference between analysis and psychotherapy rests on this distinction. I recently heard a psychoanalyst, for example, admit that she made a grave error with a patient when she responded to a compliment of his by saying "thank you" instead of analyzing it. I imagine that one could just as well say "thank you," if one felt like that, and only afterwards raise the question as to whether the patient had some motive in mind in making such a compliment. If the warm, appreciative comment is not accepted, then what might be the chap's nice overture toward a healing eros is unnecessarily turned into a problem to be dissected. We are all familiar with the fun made of our professions' question, "What did he mean by that?"

Extremes certainly exist in this field, with the psychoanalysts usually occupying one end of the continuum and "re-parenting" psychotherapists occupying the other end. Michael Fordham once said, after reading my contribution to *Jungian Analysts* (Spiegelman 1988), that I did "confrontation therapy" rather than analysis. I responded that I analyze dreams and the relationship rather than the person. "Analyzing" everything can prove to be merely a defense against the natural embroilment in the process; pure "responsiveness" can turn the situation into a chat fest or friendly exchange rather than analysis. Probably, one needs to "connect" as deeply as possible in order to make meaningful analytic interpretations, whether of content or person. Equally, one needs to interpret what is taking place in the relationship in order to bring about consciousness. Healing needs both.

The foregoing analysis of the situation seems rather obvious, so we might do better by asking ourselves why there needs to be a conflict between two necessary components of the analyst's activity, response and analysis. Is it a typological difference, say, between thinking and feeling? Or a fundamental difference as to what really heals, consciousness or empathy? One suspects that both are true. My own typology, as I have said, is introverted intuitive/thinking with extroverted feeling, finds the Freudian extroverted thinking analysis of the person as both distancing and existentially inaccurate. Philosophically, I can only know how I experience the other person, not how he or she really is. I therefore can speak of what I feel, think, observe, intuit, etc., rather than say that Mr. A is doing such and such because of a particular motivation. Both the Freudians and I can agree to interpret dreams (objective evidence), but the accuracy of our interpretation, from a scientific point of view, is subject to the agreement or disagreement of the patient. The impactful effect is what really matters. Differences in analytic viewpoint arise, for example, when we choose to focus on behavior or experience. When I say that to interpret a person is both a presumption and unscientific, they might say that I am derelict in not analyzing behavior and thus missing the point of the work. So it is a typological matter.

Yet it is also an even more fundamental one, when we think of the therapeutic relation as a field of psyches interacting, as most analysts agree. I can recall discussions with a classical Freudian colleague in London, during my study years in Zürich, in which we both agreed that the central aim of analysis was to "make the unconscious conscious," allowing maximum freedom of choice for the patient, and not to attempt to "heal" at all! In this, a classical Freudian and a classical Jungian were more attuned than either one was with the "neo" variants based on healing rather than awareness. For Jungians, generally, however, the crucial difference, I think, is that of the archetypal basis of the psyche. I will address this issue later on. Here, we need to acknowledge that both modes of response, analyzing and connecting, are necessary, depending on the particular needs of the analytical relationship at the moment.

Self-Disclosure versus "Use" of the Transference

This same pair of opposites continues to polarize when we consider the role of self-disclosure versus the "use" of the transference for one's own therapeutic aim. For some classical Freudians, even the idea of self-disclosure of the analyst is a bizarre one: the point is to keep one's self as much of blank screen as possible in order to facilitate projections and the working through of these for the sake of increased consciousness. Who can fault this lofty aim?

Yet the reality of the field condition of the process and the requirements of scientific veracity (mentioned earlier), suggest to me that I should report to the analysand what is happening with me, for comparison's sake, rather than merely attribute my reaction to what the latter is "doing" to me. The use of the transference, on the other hand, smacks of manipulation, and this something clearly to be avoided, as both classical Freudians and Jungians are strongly agreed.

But even if one assents to self-disclosure by the analyst in the therapeutic process, what is it that should be disclosed? Facts about one's life or experiences are usually unnecessary or even evasions, although judicious presentation of such facts can provide a humanizing effect on the work, or else add to the "re-parenting" effect sometimes needed. What generally needs to be disclosed, I think, is one's apprehension of the unconscious impact of what is happening, without there being a sense of attribution or blame of the patient.

As I mentioned earlier, I often report bodily symptoms to the patient such as sleepiness or impulses, carefully stating them as possibly meaningful contents connecting with the patient, rather than attributing these as caused by the latter. I invite the patient to report the same also, or tell me the impact of my reportage on them. We are both thereby attuned to the unconscious field between us and ready to work jointly on the conscious understanding of what is happening. This applies even more to the reporting of fantasies, for now there is the possibility of embroiling the patient in one's own counter transference or even one's own complexes, without the constellation of a field at all! Yet the mistake is also useful, in that the therapist is seen as humanly in error and ready to abandon preconceived ideas or clinging to authority. As we all know, sometimes these fantasies are indeed accurate, so to speak, but premature.

I am reminded of a woman with whom I worked; early on, I had the strong fantasy of being a kind of Prince Charming who was going to "awaken" her, even though she was middle-aged, happily married, and mother of two! Although this was smilingly disparaged at the time, two years later it proved to be the compelling myth of the analytic work! So, it behooves us to attend to our fantasies, although we may be "out of time." Yet that is just what is expected of us, as Jungians: if we are attuned to the collective unconscious, we will be touched by its timelessness and will often be archetypally linked rather than immediately or superficially so.

The disadvantage of self-disclosure is that an opportunity is lost for the patient to experience these things in himself or herself first. If I "hold" my sexual fantasy for a time, even months or years, the theory is that the corresponding content will ultimately appear in the patient and will have a more compelling effect. When to hold and when not, when to reveal and when to conceal, these are a pair of opposites which are ever in our minds. There is no compelling rule of thumb as to how to choose, but my own guideline is to try to ascertain when the field is clearly activated in the two parties, such as by the presence of synchronistic or parapsychological events.

An example that occurs to me is not one in therapy, but from a Jungian meeting. I had presented a paper on self-disclosure, among other things, to a large group and a discussant was disagreeing with my views, presenting an alternative approach to dealing with transference. While she was speaking, I was increasingly aware of a need to urinate and recalled that this theme, urination, had popped up repeatedly during the previous hours among different speakers. When my discussant unexpectedly used an expression involving urination also, I spoke up and told the large assembled group what was going on. It seemed to me that we, the discussant and myself, if not the entire group, were embedded in a field in which the need to relieve one's self and even to express one's self (the interpretation of this instinctive activity by von Franz) was a key issue. Should one express or hold, risk being wrong or even humiliated by such revelation or expression? The group as a whole very much responded to what I said and got a clear understanding of both "mutual process" and what I meant when I suggested self-disclosure. My discussant, however, remained outside this sharing, although I was convinced that there was a heavy transference condition between us. I was able to confirm it later that night, when we were dancing at a post-conference celebration.

Another clue as to when to reveal rather than conceal is when the symptom or impulse or fantasy is so strong that it demands attention. The pressure is such that one cannot fully attend to what the patient is saying or doing. The conflict engendered between staying connected and being pressed by one's own inner content can only be resolved, as I see it, by reporting the content and saying that it has been forcing itself. Does the analysand connect with it or not?

So, keep aware of reactions is my counsel and be prepared to share these with analysands. Even if these reactions are "wrong" or out of sync, it is likely—because of the field conditions—that they have some link with truth or with healing. In any case, it generally proves to be valuable, particularly if one is not identified with or attached to these reactions as "truth," but sees them as useful indicators of possible connecting stories or myths.

As I have reported elsewhere (Spiegelman 1988), my own stance is to be present in the analytic work with both a "left hand" and a "right hand": one hand is connected with the unconscious, its taboos, impulses, imagery, while the other is related to the care-taking, responsible, connecting, parenting energies which "mind the store." I do not identify with either, but try to sit in the middle, going both left and right until wholeness is achieved.

Roots in Childhood or in Myth

This leads us to the final area of disagreement I wish to address in the present discussion: whether the practical basis of the patient's difficulties lie in the wounds of infancy and childhood, or whether one's personal myth, its discovery and enhancement, is the focus of our work. At first blush, this sounds like a difference of opinion which would arise between Freudians and Jungians, but there have been enough newcomers to Jungian psychology, over the last generation or so, to indicate that at least the developmentalist branch of the latter is as focused upon the events of infancy and childhood and how these are played out in the transference as is any psychoanalyst (Samuels 1985). The impact of Klein upon our London colleagues has been immense; so much so that there is a large group of Jungians, both in England and elsewhere, who are very much at home with this viewpoint.

The archetypalists and the classical Jungians, however, to continue with Samuels' differentiation, are rather of a different mind. Jung's psychology is archetypal, after all, they would say, and what the preoccupation with childhood is about is likely to be a fixation, with the myth of the divine child in the background.

Now we might ask, is this conflict in Jungian circles part of a general attempt at a reintegration among analytic schools, split endlessly since those of Freud and Adler and Jung? It might seem so, since people such as Kohut

mong the Freudians speak about "self psychology" in almost archetypal
erms. Yet the differences, primarily connected with the religious attitude
owards the psyche on the part of Jungians, remains profound.

Is this, then, typology once more, or school-centered conflict? I do not
now, but it seems rather obvious that such differences are based on what one
ctually experiences in analysis, one's own or with patients. All of us know
nat most patients are much involved with their childhood, but we do not
now if this is partially culturally conditioned, what one is expected to deal
vith in analysis, or is "the real thing." And, even it is the real thing, we do
ot know if this is founded on the myth of childhood, which lies behind all
nese real experiences, the time when the archetypes were first unleashed in
ll power, or if the reported woundings were indeed the product of parent-
hild interaction. Surely, both are true, as well as the importance of one's
wn experience.

As a classical Jungian, one whose first analysis as a young man had
nuch focus on childhood, and whose second training analysis in Zürich
roved to be much more archetypal and myth-discovering, I can say yea to
oth. Furthermore, as a Jungian highly disposed to working with archetypal
epths with patients, I have been compelled, by their need, to spend lots of
me on their childhood. As a matter of fact, it is only the rare person, in my
xperience, who goes through the entire process described by Jung in "The
elations Between the Ego and the Unconscious" (1928) wherein the arche-
ʳpal figures of anima/animus, old wise man/woman, mana personality, and
elf are confronted and internalized, and the ego is relativized to the point
ʳhere an ongoing ego-Self axis is arrived at and maintained. Yet parts of this
rocess, even including an experience of and connection with the Self, are
ndergone by almost every patient. How to resolve this seeming paradox?

It is apparent to me, and to us all, I presume, that the structure of the
syche is archetypal, and that one or more myths underlie each of our dramas
f existence. The myths of our patients and ourselves may be discovered,
layed out, and dealt with, particularly in our highly extraverted American
ociety, in ways different from those investigated deeply by Jung. But it is
so the same psyche, we must assume, and it is probably like that famous
dian elephant who was grasped by several blind wise men at various places
d thus understood differently by each of them as consisting of trunk or tail,
hallus or rump, depending upon which part was touched. The psyche is
erily like a Freudian or Adlerian or Reichian or Jungian, indeed!

For Jungians, therefore, it is probably best for us to undergo the kind
f deep process that he described, so that we can be helpful in this matter
ʳr those who need this from us (Jung 1946). It is also important, I think, to
alize that those who are convinced that their particular handle on the psy-
ne is "the true one" are probably basing this on their own experience. It is
uch like the general condition in the world today: we are faced with fun-

damentalists of all sorts, some of whom are even fanatic. Others are pluralis
tically inclined.

It is a sad paradox, in the general psychotherapeutic field, that the mos
committed analysts are likely to get best results, whereas the bland relativist
are less likely to be effective. Ideally, it would be nice to be committed and
connected with our own experience of the Self, like the fundamentalists, and
flexibly open to other understandings, like the relativists. According to the
great thirteenth century Sufi mystic of Islam, Ibn 'Arabi, it is incumbent upon
us all to discover or own Rabb (or Lord), yet realize that the Lord of all (Allah
includes all of these particular lords, yet transcends them all also, even the
god revealed in each of the great faiths. The more we can experience and
comprehend the varying manifestations of the divine in all of these forms, the
more we can approach the God who transcends us all.

To translate this task for our ordinary therapeutic work: the more we can
help our patients to find their own myth, their own selves, the more we, too
can comprehend and relate to the greater Self which both includes and tran
scends us all. In this work, then, we are indeed doing a valuable thing: repair
ing the world (to use a Jewish mystical expression) by helping the soul and
the sparks of the divine to reunite with the godhead. Maybe that is why our
endless preoccupation with transference seems strange to others, yet so
important to us.

REFERENCES

1. Jung, C.G. 1928. 'The relations between the ego and the uncon
scious'. *CW* 7: 121-241. Princeton, N.J. Princeton University Press, 1953.

2. Jung, C.G. 1946. 'The Psychology of the Transference'. *CW* 16:163
323. Princeton N.J.: Princeton University Press, 1954.

3. Meier, C.A. 1959. 'Projection, Transference and the Subject-Objec
Relation in Psychology'. *Journal of Analytical Psychology* 4:21-34.

4. Samuels, Andrew. 1985. *Jung and the Post-Jungians*. London: Rout
ledge and Kegan Paul.

5. Spiegelman, J. Marvin. 1965. 'Some Implications of the Transference
In *Spectrum Psychologiae: Festschrift für C.A. Meier*, C.T. Frey, ed. Zürich
Rascher Verlag.

6. Spiegelman, J. Marvin. 1972. 'Transference, Individuation an
Mutual Process'. A talk for the San Diego Jungian group, privately printed.

7. Spiegelman, J. Marvin. 1980. 'The Image of the Jungian Analyst an
The Problem of Authority'. *Spring* (1980): 101-116.

8. Spiegelman, J. Marvin. 1988. 'The Impact of Suffering and Self-Dis
closure on the Life of the Analyst'. In *Jungian Analysts: Their Visions and Vu
nerabilities*. J.M. Spiegelman, ed. Phoenix: Falcon Press.

CHAPTER EIGHT

THE UNHEALED HEALER AND THE UNPUBLISHED WRITER:
Thirty-plus Year Report to Alma Mater
(1991)

In the spring of 1959, after three-plus years of intensive work at the C.G. Jung Institute in Zürich, Switzerland, and nine years after I had begun analysis in Los Angeles, I completed my studies, was awarded the Analyst's Diploma, and returned to California. Now, in the spring of 1991, more than thirty years later, a month before my 65th birthday, I am returning to my alma mater and have decided to give a report, so-so-speak, about these many years of life and work since then, so that current students and fellow graduates might have a glimpse of the experiences of one such alumnus.

The titles for these two lectures—"The Unhealed Healer" and "The Unpublished Writer"—sound rather unpromising, I admit, but I hurry to inform you that the results are not so grim as it may appear. I employ this heading since two books of mine with these titles are being published soon, written twenty years ago but appearing only now, synchronistic with my return to Zürich and certainly bearing on the theme of what can transpire for a dedicated psychologist and psychotherapist, deeply immersed in Jungian analysis, when he returns to the land of his birth, tries to practice his craft and live the symbolic life.

I will begin, as most Jungians would, with a dream. This dream summarized my experience and rather uncannily predicted some important aspects of my future work. I had it at the end of my analysis in Zürich. Here it is:

> I am in the consulting room of my analyst, C.A. Meier. We are deeply engaged in conversation and then begin to roll about the room together, in a kind of ball. We wrestle and generate both light and heat. At last, we stop and my analyst kneels at my feet, recognizing me with a bow, but also with a touch of scorn. I shake his hand and leave the office. As I do so, I also see the Institute secretary, my friend, Alice Maurer, standing there and I bid her farewell also.
>
> Outside the office, I encounter my maternal grandmother, who points, with great significance, to a bricked-in room which has no windows or doors, but is open to the sky. It is a sunny day, but above the room appears

a night sky, filled with myriad stars. Inside the room is a dark and intense man, writing passionately and occasionally looking up to have a conversation with an non-visible divinity. I see this man through the walls. I then nod to my grandmother and proceed onward.

Now I find myself on a ship where I serve as first officer (chief mate), to a captain who is as much a luminous presence as an actual person. The ship has a circular deck where we stand, which rotates slowly in relation to the sun. The ship somehow manages to go across Switzerland and Italy to the Mediterranean and from thence sails around South America to California. At the port of Los Angeles, it changes into a truck, drops off a young sailor in Pasadena, and then proceeds to the beach at Santa Monica. The captain and I now stand on the beach. A Greek temple is nearby, in which a red-haired woman has experienced a near-fatal fire. We now look toward Asia and are astounded to see the sun rising in the west. End of dream.

This dream, as I have said, was strangely predictive of certain qualities or events in my work as a therapist and writer. In these two lectures, I will be speaking about these events, concerning my therapeutic work in the first meeting and writing in the second. Before I do so, however, I wish to comment briefly about some of the symbols in the dream.

First off, there is the presentation of my analysis with Professor Meier as a sort of wrestle, rolling in a circle and generating heat and light. This, I think, was an accurate portrayal of what my psyche underwent during this formidable three-year period of intense analysis and I am deeply grateful both to him and to Zürich, to the Institute and to colleagues, for such a profound and fulfilling experience. At another level, this struggle with my Analytic Self was to continue as a wrestle long afterward, rather like Jacob with his Angel, but also like that of Japanese Sumo wrestler. My therapeutic Self has indeed embraced me and challenged me, as we shall see.

Secondly, I did not know it at the time, but that wild-eyed and intense writer in that bricked-in room was to break out in earnest some seven years later and has embroiled me with his passion and intensity ever since.

Thirdly, the small detail of the young sailor getting off in Pasadena upon my arrival back in Southern California was humorously accurate. When my wife and I returned from Zürich, penniless and pregnant, I needed to get a job of some sort while building up a practice. Well, I did so—in Pasadena! I took a position as a psychologist with a management-consulting firm, thanks to a former student of mine. I had taught him Rorschach in my earlier days at the University and I had been known as a capable diagnostician, a skill which I was ready to abandon now that I was an analyst. They hired me, though, to assess executives in connection with jobs which were offered, something for which I was very poorly equipped, being knowledgeable about psychodynamics and diagnosis, but not at all about business. I did the best I could for some months but ultimately resigned this position. Suffice to say, however, that this was indeed a youngish aspect of myself—a kind of side issue—that was engaged in Pasadena!

Finally, the astounding aspect of watching the sun rising in the west, coming from the Land of the Rising Sun, was concretely realized within two years of my return. While I was teaching once more at UCLA (Rorschach, largely), a visiting Fullbright scholar from Japan, Hayao Kawai, took, my class and soon embarked upon an analysis with me. After about eighteen months of work, he returned to Japan, ultimately came to study in Zürich as well, and has become a famous person, bringing Jungian psychology to his nation and serving as a model for many psychiatrists and psychologists. When he completed his work with me, he referred his friend, the Buddhist priest, Mokusen Miyuki, to me and this analysis lasted four years. Dr. Miyuki then also went to the Institute in Zürich to study, became an analyst, and returned to California. We have been friends and colleagues ever since. After Dr. Miyuki, a steady stream of psychologists and psychiatrists have come from Japan to work with me. I realized, after a wonderful visit there with Professor Miyuki, some years ago, how one can become a sort of admired grandfather under such conditions, an unmerited Wise Old Man. So the dream predicted that event also.

Sadly, the fearful fate of the red-haired woman in the Greek temple was also predictive. As it is with many analysts, one woman patient, in a life-and-death struggle and producing very rich dreams, was particularly challenging, and the emotional and passionate uproar it produced in me almost cost me my emotional balance. Before I tell about that however, I want to suggest to students who are near graduation to pay particular attention to your final dreams, since you are indeed living in a kind of special place and condition, conducive to predictive dreams, I think.

Resuming life in California was rather mixed, at best. I missed the introversion and ordered life of Zürich and felt the stress of driving long distances on the freeways with our Volkswagen, pretending to be a psychologist to business. I did as best I could, however, and, earning a rather good income, established a practice in Beverly Hills, slowly building it up. I continued the consulting job for some ten months until I had the following dream:

> I am in my office in Beverly Hills, talking to the wife of a colleague from Switzerland. She is very attractive and well-dressed, showing every inch of her wealthy background and personal security. The telephone rings and I answer it. Apparently, my job is to provide membership cards in resorts and country clubs. I speak for a time and hang up, returning to speak with my friend. She now looks haggard and ill. I ask her what is the matter? Speechless, she points to the telephone, obviously agonized as to how I was on it. "But I was only being natural," I say. She then nods significantly. End of dream.

And end of job! The next day, I resigned from the consulting job and spent full time in my practice, although I was soon to resume teaching at the University, as well. As all of you will readily recognize, it was all right for me to do this industrial psychological work, even coming home sick and crying pathetically in the bathroom, as long as I was aware of the conflict and doing as best I could. As soon as it became "natural," I was lost. I am grateful to this "wealthy" anima, not seduced by money, who knew when the time was up.

How, then, did this practice go? Was I inundated with interesting, Jungian-type clients eager to do active imagination and actively pursue individuation? Unfortunately, no. Although I had a few such patients, most of them were much like those suffering individuals I had worked with in the Veterans Administration and the army, years before, more interested in symptom-reduction or improving their lives rather than in the psyche itself. Besides, an economic recession was on and my desire to be on a par with my financially more successful Freudian colleagues had to be abandoned. I continued to work deeply on my own dreams and fantasies, however, and enjoyed being a husband, father and friend. The *I Ching* gave the message of "Difficulty at the Beginning", so I was comforted.

Alas, after a time, my family happiness was impaired by my often coming home after work in a state of exhaustion, hardly able to enjoy these very relationships I treasured. I worked mightily on trying to figure out why I was so tired, since I had always been a rather energetic person. At last, I realized that this fatigue was not so much that I was drained by patients or the work— although this, too, did take place—but that I was exhausted by the endless efforts to maintain "analytic objectivity." I labored to be reflective, to contain my emotions and reactions, to provide a safe and non-threatening vessel for my patients. In short, I modeled myself on many Freudian and some Jungian colleagues. This was killing me. I then remembered that Jung had been quite spontaneous during my one interview with him; indeed after an initial period of openness to me, he talked most of the time. If Jung could be spontaneous, why not I? Indeed, why not? So, I changed and was much more reactive, natural and myself. Result? Exhaustion vanished. I gave full attention and energy to each analytic hour, but was able, then, to come home and have lots of stuff left to be with my family.

This increase in spontaneity had an immediate effect on my practice: I started to get many more "Jungian-type" patients. Giving up being "the analyst" and being myself, paradoxically resulted in more analytical-type work. It also compelled me to deal with the transference much more. Embroilment in the process required much more sorting out with the patient as partner. So, after about four years home and a reasonably successful practice, I was ready to go back to Zürich for some weeks and undergo what an American might describe as a 100,000 mile check-up.

I am amazed that I was able to save enough money to go to Europe and provide for my wife and two children for a month or more! But I did. Luckily, neither family nor patients felt abandoned. Looking forward to a period of intense introversion in Zürich, I found, instead, that my dreams and fantasies lead me to a true termination of my analyses with Drs. C.A. Meier and Liliane Frey. My earlier ending had more to do with finishing training than with finishing analysis, actually. I had continued analysis with some senior analysts after I was back in Los Angeles for about two years. Now, however, I could conclude my work with a very satisfying series of paintings and dreams which found me at one with my Self. So, off I went, back to America, ready now to "be my own man."

This sense of wholeness and well-being was challenged before long—as it is for many analysts approaching middle age—by an intense transference/counter transference situation with a woman who was in a life and death struggle. I can recall, even now, the moment when the transference had changed its character. We had worked with great intensity on her difficult personal situation for a couple of years, in which much archetypal material had been revealed. In this, I had been essentially in a rather caring, interested and objective position, compassionate—even life-saving on more than one occasion—but still not "embroiled." Then, one day, this person transformed before my eyes into someone with a full body and power, perhaps both goddess and witch. Undaunted by this experience, I welcomed the archetypal transference, but the vicissitudes of that relationship did echo my dream of the woman threatened by fire in the Greek temple. I will mention two images which were crucial in this challenge.

The first image involved her need—nay, demand—that I be more fully in the relationship with all of my feelings and reactions, rather than remaining "analytical." Knowing nothing of alchemy, she had the image of a divine bird present in our relationship, with a fine thread which it wrapped around us. When the relationship was going well, this thread was harmonious and healing. When, however, I retreated or became objective, she experienced the bird continuing to wrap the thread about herself, now choking her. A dream of hers also pushed me deeper into what I later began to call, a "mutual process," with this analysand. In the dream, the woman saw both of us at the seashore, watching two fish come up from the deep. One, a "harem fish," entered into her genital, while the other, a "cat fish," latched on to my genital. The two fish then went back into the sea and united with each other. As I have said, she knew nothing of alchemy and I assumed, following Jung, that the harem fish was male (her animus) and the cat fish was female (my anima). I was surprised to find out that the reverse was true. Perhaps needless to say, a long period of intense mutual shadow work took place, the analysis finally ending successfully, but I felt in danger rather often.

This case, however, was crucial in my embrace of the idea of mutual process and I have written a number of papers on this theme (1,3,4,7). Almost all of these have been published, but it is also synchronistic that these papers will be appearing shortly in a book being published in Japanese, more than a year before it will be printed in English!

I did not realize it at the time, but my espousal of the idea of mutual process, plus my own emotional upheaval at this period, was propelling me toward a course different from that of many colleagues, particularly some senior ones. In retrospect—but not at the time—it is not surprising that when a close friend and fellow Zürich graduate and I came up for appointment as training analysts, we were both advised to wait for six months, since we were not considered to have a sufficiently tutorial persona. This came on the heels of a visit to our area by Laurens van der Post. My colleague and I were rather forthright in our comments at a public meeting, thus producing opprobrium from senior colleagues. We were both deeply chagrined by their rejection, which followed. He was furious because this appointment was supposed to be automatic after five years, unless there were serious doubts, and his view was that the current Board had an unrecognized image of how a Jungian analyst and training analyst ought to be, but were unwilling to discuss it.

My own chagrin was more connected with justice and reason. I had been Director of Studies for several years, had just got off this very Certifying Board itself, and was actively engaged in both teaching and treating professional therapists. It seemed bizarre to me that they should reject me because I was not only already a training analyst in function, but also had just been among those who decided who and when people were to become training analysts!

Our desire for dialogue on the issues was rejected, so my friend and I felt it necessary to retreat. At first, I merely withdrew, hoping that someone from the Society would interpose themselves as mediator, but no one did so. We both then withdrew from our local Society and maintained membership in the International via our status as Graduates of the C.G. Jung Institute Zürich.

This separation from colleagues proved to be both painful and fruitful. First of all, it led to my fictional writing, or "psycho-mythology," as I call it, and I will talk about that in my second lecture. It also led to a deeper confrontation with my individuality, as both a healer and as a man. In a moment, I shall try and describe the results of this many-year confrontation, but first I must mention another deep encounter which occurred five years later, when I was forty-five.

During the preceding years, a colleague and I had been interested in the western occult tradition, often known by the name of "magic"—an unfortunate appellation linking this honorable study with both a parlor amusement and with primitive kinds of thinking, but in actuality including a long history of concepts and methods of a spiritual path which included alchemy, astrology, meditation and kindred topics known to Jungians as fields but less known by them as developed disciplines. My colleague discovered that a world-famous practitioner in this area, Francis Israel Regardie, although of British origin and a leading figure in the Golden Dawn Order, lived not only in the Los Angeles area, but even in our local part of it, Studio City! We telephoned him for an interview, which he granted. When we expressed the desire to study with him in his area, he said that the energies released in magical study and work were quite profound and that it would be wise to undertake, along with that study, a course of Reichian therapy.

I knew of an interesting book Regardie had written on the Middle Pillar meditation and its relation to Jungian psychology (he had undergone both an extensive Freudian analysis in England, as well as a two-year Jungian one), but we did not know that he was also a qualified practitioner of the methods of Wilhelm Reich. We were both a little skeptical about such an undertaking, since each of us had undergone many years of Jungian work, but I was intrigued since, when I had been informed of my Jungian colleagues rejection of me, I had experienced a deep pain in my back, which had responded to treatment only minimally. I had accepted this pain as both a symbolic statement of my feeling "stabbed in the back," and a dubious reward for years of poor posture, as well as a consequence of an athletic injury. Dr. Regardie, however, felt that more could be accomplished with this condition, let alone the deeper relaxation and opening up to be achieved with such a body therapy. My colleague and I both agreed to undertake this work and did so, for the next eight years! My eight years of Jungian analysis were now matched by eight years of Reichian work.

This was an enormously impactful experience, as one might imagine. I took notes and did active imagination in connection with this work during the first four years of it and produced a book, at the time, called *The Unhealed Healer*. I did it for my own edification, largely, but my publisher saw it last year and offered to bring it out. This spring, once more in synchronistic connection with these lectures, the book is being published, some twenty years after beginning to write it.

It seems incumbent upon me, in this *Report to Alma Mater*, to describe some of the effects of such experiences and how it has impacted my therapeutic work. I should say at the outset that I never had the remotest intention of abandoning my Jungian orientation and work—indeed, the body work seemed a reasonable extension of my Jungian process. This was true even though I also took some training in Reichian therapy during the latter four years of my own work. My therapist was reasonably friendly to Jung's orientation but he held "Jungians"—those he knew—in rather low esteem as being "too much in the head." I knew what he meant, from having attended some Jungian congresses of various kinds, but I also had my own experience, later on, of attending Reichian congresses. These, I often found, were like experiencing a convention of physical education teachers—perhaps not reflective enough about what they were doing. In any case, my actual therapeutic work was relatively free from polemics, even of interpretations, luckily, because the therapist both wanted me to have my own experiences and because he trusted my knowledge and grasp of the symbolic domain.

So, the bulk of my time was spent on the couch, undergoing the special kinds of breathing and body work characteristic of this field. Such work would routinely bring about increased relaxation, often clonisms of various kinds and an upsurge of energy which one can characterize as orgone or subtle body, depending upon one's orientation. Early in the work, there was quite a bit of emotion released and also some vivid memories from childhood. I did not, however, experience these emotions and memories as qualitatively different from my earlier Jungian work. They did have a more intense or "whole body" aspect, however, in line with the inclusion of muscle, blood and bone, so to speak. The psyche not only took on more body, it also seemed to arise from the body. I began to feel, in time, the validity of the *chakras* in Kundalini Yoga and the *sephiroth* in Kabbalah in Jewish mysticism. That experience and belief has increased over the years.

I sometimes even had mystical experiences on that Reichian couch—profound feelings of oneness with the universe, the benevolence of God, the unity of life. When I asked Regardie why this was not generally experienced by people undergoing Reichian therapy—they are not a particularly religious group—he said that they did indeed have similar experiences but put them in a different rubric, rather like that of the oneness of Nature. Just as one can readily experience the archetypes in Jungian work, although not everybody does, Reichian work enhances this experience of cosmic energy, with or without specific content or imagery.

You might ask whether I experienced the kind of "end-state" that one expects from successful Reichian work, namely the orgasmic reflex. This is the kind of full relaxation, similar to that following a total orgasm or what undergoes when shaking in total shedding of muscular tension. This is equivalent in value, in Reichian work—in goal rather than content—to the importance of the working through of the Oedipus complex and achievement of genitality in Freudian work. The goal of comparable importance in Jungian work is the experience of the Self, wherein the ego fundamentally shifts its orientation to an internalization of the symbol of totality and is in ongoing relation to it. Well, I both did and did not experience this orgasmic reflex. That is to say, I sometimes did, but the effects were always temporary and I soon returned to a condition of some kind of muscular armor or tension. My therapist informed me—as I also discovered in my reading—that the orgasmic reflex was not the *sine qua non* of the work—since it could even be experienced by schizophrenics—but, like the relativization of the ego to the Self in Jungian work, was an important end-state for formal therapy. But, I am deficient along those lines.

I see myself as still "in process" in this area, although I believe that there are structural limits to my capacity to achieve this desirable state. These limits come from postural defects since childhood, athletic injury in youth, and the effect of age itself.

During those eight years of Reichian work, I was also actively engaged in what had brought my colleague and me to our Reichian therapist in the first place, namely the work with "magick" or, more precisely expressed, the attention and devotion to those methods of spiritual transformation which belong to the occult field. These include various kinds of meditation, including Buddhist and Kabbalistic, as well as a course in working with images in an evocative or directed way, such as guided imagery. Working with Tarot card images is an example, as well the daily practice of the Kabbalistic meditative method of the Middle Pillar. The latter involves the circulation of a form of light through various "centers" or sephiroth in the body, while invoking and chanting names of the divine. Another is the "mindfulness" method of Buddhism, wherein one focuses upon and describes the sequential sensations of the body, leading to relaxation and, perhaps, to a mystical state.

Along with all of these "magical" practices, I continued, with religious devotion, my many-year practice of Jungian active imagination, even though the latter is opposite in character. In active imagination, as we know, we let the unconscious speak for itself and let it provide direction for our work, whereas the former attempts to specify forms and goals.

Unlike what I was led to believe about such combining of practices in my earlier education on the spiritual path of individuation, I did not find these diverse ways of approaching the psyche to cause undue disharmony or damage, just as I was able to do Reichian therapy with some patients along with Jungian work. Ultimately, I gave up doing Reichian therapy because it did not suit me temperamentally and also because it required an asymmetrical approach to the therapeutic relationship which was at odds with my continuing belief in the analytic process as fundamentally a mutual one, the processes of which could or should be discussed.

In addition to these activities, I also continued my writing of both fiction and articles. So, it was obviously a busy time, even though primarily introverted. The energy for all that, I believe, came partly from that withdrawn from my deep involvement with Jungian collectives, and partly from what was released in the Reichian and magical work itself.

It remains, now, for me to describe to you—as I promised earlier—just how all this study and work effected my efforts as a Jungian Analyst, for that is what I remained, throughout this "hegira." Not only did I remain true to the Jungian viewpoint, I have continued to see myself as a "classical" Jungian, as I have described both in my paper commenting on the multiplicity of positions in the international community at this time (5), and in my book, *Jungian Analysts: Their Visions and Vulnerabilities* (4). I am "classical" in the sense that I am archetypally oriented, as is Hillman's archetypal psychology, but am convinced of the fundamental importance of the Self, as both center and circumference of the psyche, as he is not. Nor am I so impressed with the centrality of childhood, as are the Developmental Jungians. I am of the opinion that much of that involvement constitutes an excessive preoccupation with the child archetype, often at the expense of the religious attitude. I also believe that the active relationship with the psyche, with such methods as active imagination, are of central importance for those who would like to prove empirically, for themselves, just what it was that Jung discovered. The Developmentalists and Archetypalists seem less so inclined.

Where, then, you might ask, does my individuality, as an analyst, reside? I would answer that it resides in my own preoccupation with the transference all these years, as my papers attest (1,2,4,5,6). From the outset of my analytical practice, I have been impressed with what might be called the "field" character of the psychotherapeutic encounter. As Jung remarked long ago, the psyches of therapist and patient are ultimately enmeshed, if they are not so at the outset, and the impact upon each other is proportional. Indeed, he felt that the therapist could only have an effect on the patient to the degree that the analyst was open to the latter's psyche.

Over the years, I have written a number of papers on this "mutual process" theme, detailing how I see it working, the conditions under which it appears and its limits. I would like to briefly summarize what this approach to analysis is like by means of examples.

I can think of my analytic practice as divisible into four categories, when it comes to the question of the degree of personal involvement in the transference. These four categories, therefore, are really division points on a continuum of mutual process, and each constitutes about one-fourth of the people I see in long-term analytic work. In addition to these, I, like others in our field, see a fair number of people for relatively brief periods—usually less than a year—for traditional psychotherapy. In those cases, the transference may or may not be present to any appreciable degree, but it is largely in the background, and interpreted only when there is some sort of interference or blockage; the focus is on problem-solution, goal orientation, etc. At any time, in such work, even in the very earliest sessions, the psychotherapy can turn into analysis proper, which I understand as following a process whereby the analysand develops a relationship with his/her psyche and gradually becomes united with the soul, following its peregrinations, deepening and developing the particular *religio* we come to expect in analytic work. Many patients, coming for counseling, never do this. These, however, constitute a small portion of my work, even though such work can also be interesting, exciting, even deep.

To illustrate how psychotherapy can change into analysis, I think of the example of a neuroscientist who came to me because of his interest in dreams, wanting to understand them better and develop his capacity for lucid dreaming. We worked happily for about a year, systematically interpreting dreams, but also dealing with his sense that people did not enter deeply into relationship with him, not seeing his soul and hurting him thereby. After these many months of good but not particularly deep connection between us, he dreamt of being stung by a scorpion, his sun sign and my moon sign. My psyche was then mobilized more profoundly than it had been with him and I said so. The next session, he spoke about his desire to terminate, to my amazement and hurt, and I called his attention to what had transpired between us in the previous session. He saw the validity of my interpretation, but also said that he had been thinking of stopping for a couple of months—therapy was expensive, he had other things to do, was not sure it was worth it. "Yes," I said. "Let's wait for some more dreams and decide whether we stop or not."

In the next session, he told a dream in which he had been wanting to buy a special tool so that he could sharpen his ax with it, one that he used to chop wood for his fireplace. It was expensive and he didn't know if it was worth it. In the next part of his dream, he was experiencing a terrible loneliness. I interpreted this as his coming to therapy in order to learn techniques of dream interpretation, ones that he could use in the privacy of his own hearth (fireplace), but that this was, indeed, now too expensive. If we went on, we would have to deal more deeply with his loneliness, also in the context of our relationship. We could no longer approach this as a learning technique. He agreed. So, now the issue was: do we terminate the therapy altogether or do we begin a true analytic work? Here, as in the analytic cases, the transference/counter transference situation is the dramatic, unexpected quality which decides the course of further direction. He decided to stop for the time being.

I now move to my four categories of analytic process, in terms of increasing consciousness of mutuality in the transference field. The first category is rather traditional analysis, of the type that M-L von Franz called, when she supervised me here in Zürich, a "womb analysis." In this situation, the analysis is a cave or womb, a vessel in which the analysand can safely explore and relate to the unconscious and the analyst provides a protective and supportive environment for it. The example that comes to mind is that of a highly creative writer I worked with, one who had much analysis, was professionally well-placed, had many rich dreams, and worked quite well by himself. I provided dream comments or interpretations, only occasionally having to remark about what was transpiring in the relationship between us. Nor is this merely intellectual; the one image the sustained itself as transference one for a long time was that of a giant lingam of light between us! Otherwise, however, the process proceeded without much discussion of our interaction.

The second category might be called "womb-interaction," perhaps, indicating that there is, indeed, more conscious attention to the relationship. The example that comes to mind is a former priest, who had suffered from serious depression and anxiety for years. After many months of work and our mutual experience of inability to change his condition, despite interesting dreams which referred back to his initial vocation and loss of connection with the divine, I finally revealed to him a fantasy I had. This involved us praying together before a Dürer print I had in the room, of Christ crowned with thorns. He immediately expressed a desire to do this concretely and we both knelt and prayed. As we knelt there, shoulder to shoulder, I felt a Christ-like presence, with an arm on each of our shoulders. I reported this and he responded that he, too, felt this. He was amazed. I then had the strong impression that my analysand was much larger than I was, even though we were physically about the same size. When I mentioned this, he was startled, since had the same impression. Right away, he knelt lower, feeling that he was too inflated, and touched his forehead to the ground. I strongly said, "No, not at all!" He, after all, was indeed far larger than I in relation to a Christian manifestation of the divine, and it was exactly right that he acknowledge this. He wept with relief and joy and we embraced. This was a turning point in his analysis and subsequent sessions presented a great influx of energy, content and direction, which was experienced as rather miraculous.

The third category, which one can call "mutual process" proper, has a wide variety of conditions and examples, characterized by frequent and sometimes intense reference to what is happening in the analytic relationship. This can be the typical parent-child situation, many archetypal relations, the kind we are familiar with from Jung's diagram, but in which I differ by being much more explicit about it. It can range all the way, in my experience, to the use of mutual active imagination. I am thinking, now, of a very intense sexual transference with an older woman, in which the sharing and working through of these images led to a tremendous sense of wholeness.

The fourth category includes all of the regular mutual process I have written about, but added to this is the experience of actual subtle-body energies and effects on the various chakras or sephiroth—head, chest, diaphragm, etc. One woman I am thinking of, who had done much analytical and body work, experienced, with me, an intense period of work with sexual and other energies, leading to a revelation of a goddess figure in the background which was highly numinous and conveyed a priestess-type of vocation to this professional woman. Synchronicity seems to be characteristic in such encounters and exchanges.

All of these varieties of mutual process are of interest, of course, and often change back and forth from one category to another. My own desire to include subtle-body energies makes the last category particularly salient at this time. Whenever the numinous manifests, however, whatever the "category" or type of analysand, one realizes that this work is truly alchemical, as Jung discovered. I also realized, partly as a consequence of my Reichian body work and magical practice, that alchemy does indeed have an apparent material dimension, best characterized as subtle body, I think, and this is of continuing promise in our field.

Also of promise, I think, is what I have called "joint active imagination"—a natural outgrowth of mutual process. This arises when the transference situation presents a mutually constellated content. As an example, what comes to mind is the incident reported by Jo Wheelwright, when he was supervising someone in training. The latter's patient dreamt of him as a lascivious, sex-seeking person and the person in training was overwhelmed and apologized. He was no doubt correct in this and he was surely more honest and therapeutic than the usual analyst's interpretation that this was a projection on the part of the patient onto the analyst. But one might also suggest that the content in question, the dark sexual figure, belonged to both parties and could be jointly addressed. I have done such joint fantasy work frequently and find it valuable, particularly when the content is archetypal in nature. I shall discuss another development in active imagination in my second lecture.

In conclusion, I want to reiterate my thanks to all my analysts and teachers, as well as to the continuingly present spirit of Jung. This has truly supported me in the work when little else did so.

SOME PAPERS ON THERAPY AND MUTUAL PROCESS

1. "Some Implications of the Transference," in *Festschrift für C.A. Meier*, edited by C.T Frey, Rascher Verlag, Zürich, 1965, pp.163-175.

2. "Notes from the Underground: A View of Religion and Love From a Psycho-therapist's Cave." *Spring*, 1970, pp. 196-211.

3. "Transference, Individuation, Mutual Process." A lecture presented to the Jung Group of San Diego and privately printed, April 1972.

4. "The Image of the Jungian Analyst and the Problem of Authority," *Spring, An Annual of Archetypal Psychology*, 1980, pp. 101-117.

5. Editor/contributor, *Jungian Analysts: Their Visions and Vulnerabilities*. Falcon Press, Arizona, 1988. 181ff.

6. "The One and the Many: Jung and the Post-Jungians," *Journal of Analytical Psychology*, 1989, Vol;. 34, #1, pp. 53-73.

7. "The Interactive Field in Analysis: Agreements and Disagreements," Chiron Publications, Illinois, 1991, pp. 133-150.

CHAPTER NINE

THE SELF IN PSYCHOTHERAPY AND ANALYSIS:
Present and Future
(1994)

Trends and Typology

The field of psychotherapy seems to be suffering a great success. The United States is likely to accept, at last, that health programs include psychotherapy among its recognized modes of treatment. Research has demonstrated that brief psychotherapy, behavioral and cognitive, has been effective with a variety of conditions, including depression, phobias, addictions, etc. As a result, insured health plans will no doubt include not only inpatient treatment (traditionally the province of psychiatry, but lately including non-medical people as therapists, particularly serving those suffering from drug abuse), but also outpatient sessions as well—as much as thirty or more per year.

When I recall how eager clinical psychologists were to be licensed and included in such insurance-reimbursed programs when I was a newly minted Ph.D., more than forty years ago, I should, perhaps, rejoice. I am sorry to say, however, that I do not. In between, I have become an analyst, one committed to work with the unconscious, to dialogue between analyst and analysand, and between conscious and unconscious, as a "mutual process" (as I have called it), and not with the medical model of therapy as a symptom-removing, goal-oriented procedure which has a very different aim and path. As we already discover in the healing professions' encounter with insurance companies, the therapist is required to make a treatment plan, to set goals and methods, to join a health group accepting limited fees, to make periodic reports for approval from a referee, as well as to accept a particular statistical manual's psychiatric diagnosis for what ails the person. Behavior modification and cognitive restructuring are the models. Good-bye individuality, good-bye unconscious! Good-bye, finally, to following the spontaneous promptings of the psyche and the unique demands of the Self. What we see, now, is the victory of American pragmatism and practicality, of extraversion and "results" over introversion and psychological process. Depth psychology, both Freudian and Jungian, will probably have to find another home outside that system.

Perhaps that is how things should be. In my own practice, I tend to see

142

people who are oriented towards dealing with "problems in living," such as relationships and love, meaning of one's life, consciousness enhancement, and spiritual growth, none of which can be subsumed under the diagnostic categories of the approved system. Even when symptoms exist, they are hardly ever the "main thing," so to speak; the unconscious speaks about other matters. When clients do have insurance which helps pay for their therapy, it is at best partial, anyway, and does not last for the longish time that such people need to pursue the path that their soul leads them along. Furthermore, even the current state of the analytic climate, as reflected in Training Institutes, is also not very friendly to Aphrodite or Eros and less supportive of the individual path than it used to be, but is caught up in building ethical codes and institutional requirements. Even Jungians tend to be fascinated, as is the outer culture, with the archetype of the divine child, projected, once more, onto the literal child of memory and fantasy. A surprising number are strongly attracted to the Kleinian school and to Object Relations.

Meanwhile, the larger society in general is taken with an image of women being abused by predatory men while children are seen as victims of incest and lascivious priests. No doubt the fantasy has some basis in reality and is part of the overall rejection of the older, patriarchal attitude, manifested, however, in anger toward men in positions of power. Often this anger is well-deserved, but sometimes victims become victimizers and concern about abuse can be readily turned into further injustice under the guise of correction of previous injustice. The true necessity of the liberation of the feminine is sometimes corrupted by the continuation of the dominating patriarchy in both women and men. Surely freedom from both the inner and outer tyrant needs to take place, and is at issue for all persecuted minorities, whether ethnic, religious, gender or within us.

Where is the Self in all this, in our psychotherapeutic enterprise? And where or how is the meaningful path of openness to the psyche and "making the unconscious conscious"—adumbrated initially by Freud and extended in depth by Jung—leading? In order to answer this question, I would like to recall some classificatory systems which tried to bring order into our multiply-directed psychotherapeutic field. To do so, I shall begin with the system initiated by Professor Bruno Klopfer and me, about thirty years ago, followed by one given by Jung fifty years ago, and then another one I used to describe my own work three years ago. I trust that this extraverted-thinking method of using classification systems will help us prepare the way for a deeper examination of the issue of our topic, The Self in Psychotherapy and Analysis: Present and Future.

Professor Klopfer and I presented a typology of therapists' attitudes or standpoint toward patients' therapeutic process and reality (Klopfer and Spiegelman, 1965). We devised a four-fold system of opposites in the form of a cross (see Figure 1, a revision of our earlier one), which included two axes: the standpoint of the therapist with respect to the outer and inner reality of the patient, client or analysand; second the standpoint of the therapist toward the psychotherapeutic movement, whether he is "in" it or part of it, or completely outside it. As a result, the four attitudes which emerged were: (1) the directive approach, in which the therapist focuses on the outer reality of the patient and keeps himself/herself apart in an advisory, tutorial and authoritative position—the method of behavioral modification, symptom removal, etc., paying no attention to the inner reality of the patient or the unconscious; (2) the non-directive approach, as with Carl Rogers, in which the therapist finds himself "in" the process with the patient, reflecting feelings, attitudes, plans, but not psycho dynamics, and also pays no attention to the unconscious; (3) the psychoanalytic approach, which pays attention to the unconscious, with the analyst objective, outside observer; (4) the Jungian approach, in which the analyst participates "in" the process and focuses on the unconscious itself. This system, a variant of Jung's, adds that one can examine "inner" issues from an extraverted analytic viewpoint.

Roger's Non-directive therapy is no longer as popular as it was thirty years ago, but a somewhat similar viewpoint can be found today among cognitive therapists, who pay attention to the inner life of clients, e.g., beliefs and feelings, but stay with consciousness and work in the directive fashion with techniques of changing troublesome contents. One can also notice that the

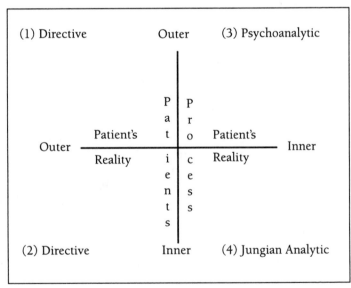

Figure 1

raditional psychoanalytic approach of interpretative reflection has been mod-
fied by the Object-Relations and Kleinian views which are much more active
and participatory. Yet the system can still be seen as a rough differentiation
between problem solution (outer or inner objects in behavioral modification
and cognitive therapy), versus focus upon process, with inclusion of the
unconscious (Freudian extraverted and Jungian introverted attitudes to inner
objects).

From the above, we can see that our American viewpoint will support
the materialistic, directive approach with insurance payments, etc. and incorporate it into the medical model, including psyche (cognitive) when it also
leads in a pragmatic, problem-solution direction. The participatory approach,
which involves the unconscious, will still find some place (the Division of
Psychoanalysis is still an important one in the American Psychological Association), but the truly spiritual approach of many Jungians will probably
enjoy a quiet life outside all of that, even though the professionalization and
popularity of Jungian societies increases greatly throughout the world. Willing adaptation, by these societies, to institutional demands, will change Jungian psychology in a collective fashion and leave the individuation-attend-
ing and spiritually-oriented therapists outside, I am afraid. This seems to be
the direction in the United States, certainly, but I am aware that the European Union, with its demand for the collectivization of psychotherapy standards and of licensure, is going in the same direction. During my last visit to
Switzerland, a few years ago, I learned of the state demand for proof that
psychotherapy works at all! One has heard this cry in the United States for
many years, with lamentably conflicting results, since we do not even agree as
to what it is that works! The West has defeated Russian bureaucracy and
communism, only to face our own collectivization.

We now turn to the classification of Jung, wherein he discusses when
any psychological treatment can come to an end, temporarily or permanently.
Strikingly, he takes up this theme in the introduction to *Psychology and
Alchemy* (Jung 1953), the profound work which itself introduces the significance of the transformation of matter into spirit as a psychological task. I shall
quote that meaty little paragraph in full (p. 4):

> There is in the analytical process, that is to say in the dialectical dis-
> cussion between the conscious mind and the unconscious, a development
> or an advance toward some goal or end the perplexing nature of which has
> engaged my attention for many years. Psychological treatment may come
> to an end at any stage in the development without one's always or neces-
> sarily having the feeling that a goal has been reached. Typical and temporary
> termination may occur (1) after receiving a piece of good advice; (2) after
> making a more or less complete but still satisfactory confession; (3) after
> having recognized some hitherto unconscious but essential psychic con-

tent whose realization gives a new impetus to one's life and activity; (4) after a hard-won separation from the childhood psyche; (5) after having worked out a new and rational mode of adaptation to perhaps difficult or unusual circumstances and surroundings; (6) after the disappearance of painful neurotic symptoms; (7) after some positive turn of fortune such as an examination, engagement, marriage, divorce, change of profession, etc.; (8) after having found one's way back to the church to which one previously belonged or after a conversion; and finally, (9) after having begun to build up a practical philosophy of life (a 'philosophy' in the classical sense of the word).

One can see that each of these terminations can be especially found in the various schemas I mentioned earlier. For example, (1) and (6) can be found in the directive methods; (2) and (3) and especially (4) in Freudian psychoanalysis; (5) and (7) in the non-directive methods; (8) and (9) customarily in Jungian work. Yet most therapists have surely found themselves working and terminating in all of the other conditions as well. In our paper Professor Klopfer and I felt that it would be worth-while for all of us therapists to recognize this diversity and either refer patients to other modes, when this became necessary or valuable, or become sufficiently broad ourselves to work with more than one attitude.

But where is the Self in all of this? Jung found it useful to speak of his classification in the context of a book which took up the profound issue of the transformation of our images of the divine and one's self as a spiritual quest emerging out of his life-long work with the unconscious with patients and himself. Is the Self only in this deeper work, as shown by Jung? Or is it, as Jung also wrote, the most powerful archetype in the psyche, and always present whether "summoned" or not? We shall defer discussion of this issue until we have taken up yet another classification scheme, one that I used in a lecture to my alma mater, the C.G. Jung Institute of Zürich, a couple of years ago, when I tried to describe what my practice was like (Spiegelman 1992, pp. 205-208).

After addressing examples of brief psychotherapy, such as the problems noted in Jung's categories from (1) through (7), except (5), I noted four categories of analytic process, in terms of increasing consciousness of mutuality in the transference work. The first category was that of traditional analysis, the type that Marie-Louise von Franz described, when she supervised me, as "womb-analysis." In this situation, the analysis is a cave or womb, a vessel in which the analysand can safely explore and relate to the unconscious. The analyst provides a protective and supportive environment for this. An example of such a process was that of a very creative and successful writer: he presented his dreams and active imaginations, including interpretations, and provided comments. The transference was hardly discussed, although we sustained an image of a lingam of light between us.

The second category I called "womb-interaction," a kind of safe vessel, but with much more interchange, even an appearance of the Self in the relationship. This is the kind of work familiar to analysts of all persuasions, in which all sorts of archetypal relations, such as parent-child, teacher-pupil, etc. take place and are interpreted at either the level of the personal unconscious or, in Jungian perspective, archetypally. This typical way of working can be distinguished from the third category, that of mutual process proper, in which there is explicit reference to the mutuality of the transference, the presence— "in the room" and in the relationship—of a third factor, namely the archetype itself.

The fourth category is similar to the third, but includes what we can call subtle-body interaction, energies noted in Reichian therapy and the various Eastern religions such as Kundalini Yoga and also by Jung when he speaks of the somatic unconscious (Jung 1934). Here are experienced archetypal manifestations and synchronistic events which include body and matter. Joint active-imagination can occur in such conditions. Here, too, one can speak of the alchemy of the relationship in the transformation of instincts and affects, as well as the manifestation of powerful symbols of union and division.

An example is that of a former Catholic priest who had been seriously depressed for years and despite several years of treatment, with others and myself, was hardly helped. At last, I suggested that he and I pray together, before a Dürer print on my wall, of *Jesus Crowned with Thorns*. He agreed and we both knelt. After a time, I experienced a presence above and between us, as if Jesus were placing a hand on each of our shoulders. My patient, startled, said he experienced the same thing. Then, feeling that my patient was much larger than myself, even though we were physically about the same size, I told him so and he responded that he felt that also and promptly bent his forehead to the floor to avoid inflation. I said that this was nonsense, since he, as a former Priest and Catholic scholar, was certainly far larger than I in relation to a Christian image of the Self, and that this was certainly how he ought to see himself. This experience changed his condition profoundly, brought back his sense of priestly vocation, and thereafter we worked on this process as an inner event.

Naturally, all the four categories can shift back and forth during any particular analytic work and the results are relative to each individual condition and constellation. But one can see that all of these four categories are a far cry from the medical model of treatment for a condition or symptom. Yet I do not want to denigrate the treatment model or the asymmetrical condition. I have worked with physicians and analysts who conduct therapy in that mode in a tremendously sensitive and deep way, helping to bring about profound changes without the patient having even a clue that the doctor is working deeply within himself/herself but keeping quiet.

Such a mode is a natural one for Japan, I believe, where there is tremendous concern for privacy and non-intrusion. A Japanese specialist in psychosomatic medicine, one that I have supervised, comes to mind. I know that this person's work inwardly, with dreams and fantasy, is no less than that of Jungian analysts, yet the work with patients is in this traditional mode. Sandplay methods with children and adults also comes to mind. I have myself worked this way with children long ago and have noted profound effects on the part of other analysts with children and adults, allowing the patient to work and create as he or she wishes and producing their own, hardly verbalized, process of change.

Who is to say that this method is less valuable than the highly articulate, interpretative, interactive process? But the attitude of religious respect for the unconscious, I am afraid, is not found among most of the medical model or asymmetrically-oriented people and, therefore, the work tends to remain at the practical level I spoke about earlier. I must also add that I have worked in a category (3) and (4) manner with Japanese therapists as well, so that this mode, with its introverted orientation, is not so strange either, when there has been sufficient time to build up a deep trust.

What are we to conclude about all this for our issue of the manifestation of the Self in psychotherapy? Well, for starters I think that the field of psychotherapy will, as I noted at the outset, begin to break up into three broad classifications: (1) that of brief therapy using the medical model; (2) longer term therapy focussing upon childhood processes or pathological conditions, perhaps including work with the unconscious but with diagnostic categories in mind; (3) spiritually based process analysis, focussing on work with the unconscious, both in the analysand and in the analytic relationship. Category (1) will be supported by the collective and health plans, as will some of category (2), but within limits, while category (3) will once more be outside the system, as it was originally. Psychoanalysis, particularly the Jungian variety, was originally sought after by people who knew that their malaise had spiritual components. I would not be surprised to find that the tendency toward break-up among Jungian Institutes would advance apace, leading to clearer demarcations. On the other hand—and this forces me to admit my poor prognostic ability—the reverse may take place and there will be integration on an even higher level, with all the analytic schools gathered together in one sort of union, differentiating itself, in a friendly way, from the briefer therapies, but with a common connection, such as currently exists in the American Psychological Association. I think, though, that Jung's discoveries and basic orientation will be in full use only by a small minority, just as he suspected long ago, and even affirmed as natural.

But what about the Self as it appears in the dreams and fantasies of people, no matter how the therapeutic process is seen?

Changing Images of the Self in Analytic Work

My own experience is that the Self appears in some form in every work, even the briefest, yet often is disguised or, rather, presents itself under some other condition or archetype. Very common, for example, is the persistent appearance of a highly critical figure, usually male but sometimes a witch-like female, who endlessly debunks, puts down or otherwise denigrates the person. This can be seen as the traditional superego, formulated by Freud as the opposite of the id, or by a negative animus in women or shadow in men, as conceived of by Jung. This figure, I think, manifests in our culture as a surviving power of the negative patriarchy. He is playing his role in a destructive manner as a symbol of the Old King, the Self as portrayed in fairy tales (see the work of von Franz, e.g., 1970).

The King is too heavily weighted with sons, in some of these tales, and there is a need for the union with the feminine principle. This is similarly pointed out by Jung, at the ultimate archetypal level, as the necessity of the western Judeo-Christian image of the divine to incorporate a feminine "fourth" (Jung 1958). In another connection, the same element is demonstrated in Jewish mysticism where evil is seen as the consequence of one aspect of a pair of opposites, such as Justice versus Mercy, being unbalanced. Too much justice or power, for example, at the expense of its opposite, brings evil. When that side of the Sephiroth, as they are called, breaks off altogether from its opposite of Mercy and Love, then total Evil is present. So, this very common struggle in analytical work is mirroring the ongoing change in our culture. One can see, alas, that the dark, vengeful masculine figure may also dominate some women's psyches as seeming to support women and their legitimate issues of equality and respect, but it sometimes loses all feminine connection with eros, with mercy and with individuality, leading to the same injustice it seeks to remedy. Hence the complexity of our changing times.

In analytic work, it seems incumbent that the analysand, male or female, develops a true self-respect, a capacity to stand up to this critic, inner and outer, and to differentiate the critical function in a helpful way. The result, at last, is another connection with the Self, so that an individual conscience is achieved, based on one's own being and wholeness, and not the machine-like, automatic and conventional superego, which treats the person like an object.

The concern with an inner collective, impersonal psychic content in analysands leads one to note that there is a definite increase in what is a relatively new diagnosis, namely Multiple Personality Disorder. This condition, characterized by many distinct sub-personalities often not in communication with each other, was a rare, almost unheard-of diagnosis when brought to the attention of the psychiatric world by Morton Prince almost a century ago (Prince 1957). Nowadays, it is a more popular illness, sometimes connected with a condition which also seemed relatively unheard of in the early psychoanalytic days, namely concrete parental incest with children. From a symbolic point-of-view, the breakdown of the ancient patriarchal incest taboo can be seen as a continuation of the disintegration of the King myth, with multiplicity of perspectives as a consequence and the appearance of surprising sexual pathologies.

In some ways, one wonders why there is not even more Multiple Personality Disorder, when we consider the relatively easy dissociability of the psyche. Freud's tripartite division of the psyche—into ego, superego and id—still makes good sense, as does Jung's more differentiated division into persona, ego, shadow, anima-animus, old wise-man and woman, and Self. Dreams readily demonstrate this differentiation. There is less disorder, one thinks, because the ego itself maintains continuity and repression does not take the total form noted by Morton Prince. Yet psychic contents do irrupt from the unconscious, as Jung showed us, and he was able to formulate a method whereby a person can use this dissociability to good advantage, namely the use of active imagination, in which the person dialogues with his various sub-parts, leading to greater consciousness and integration.

This break-up of psyche into many parts can be paralleled at the societal level by the multiplicity of sects and movements, both within the churches and in political parties. It may be a case of individualism—not individuation—run rampant. Our excessive individualism in the West, leading to disregard of group needs and the "commons", as it is called, needs compensation. The presence, in the East, such as in Japan, of a tendency to value the group over the individual, is a necessary corrective. Perhaps the growing interpenetration of East and West on a global level will result in the integration of more group values in the West and a greater valuing of the individual in the East. After all, Jung pointed out that individuation requires both sides—relation to the inner authority as well as to the outer society—and is incomplete otherwise. He showed that when one goes deeply into one's self there is a connection with the collective unconscious and, thereby, a more profound union with humankind, and even with animals and plants. One can see this in psychotherapy, as well as in the great attraction people have for the environmental movement.

So there are a number of issues manifesting in analytic work which show the changes in both American society and psyche and, presumably, in other parts of the world: namely, the end of the patriarchate and the building up of something other, hopefully not just a regression to the matriarchy (which had its own severe limitations), but a consciousness which will incorporate feminine as well as masculine, individual as well as collective values

Can we see this happening? Let me quote from a letter of Jung to Sir Herbert Read, dated 2 September 1960 (Jung 1976, p. 590):

> The great problem of our time is that we don't understand what is happening to the world. We are confronted with the darkness of our soul, the unconscious. It sends up its dark and unrecognizable urges. It hollows out and hacks up the shapes of our culture and its historical dominants. We have no dominants any more, they are in the future. Our values are shifting, everything loses its certainty, even sanctissima causalitas has descended from the throne of the axioma and has become a mere field of probability. Who is the awe-inspiring guest who knocks at our door portentously? Fear precedes him, showing that ultimate values already flow toward him. Our hitherto believed values decay accordingly and our only certainty is that the new world will be something different from what we are used to.

This impressive observation of more than thirty years ago applies to us now with even greater force. From my understanding and discussion with many Japanese analysands over this same period, I think that the East is undergoing the same degree of change that we in the West are experiencing. Can we see traces of this "awe-inspiring guest" in our dreams? Before we try to assess that, I wish to give some examples of how the psyche is dealing with various of the significant problems of our time in our American society. As everyone knows, these can be readily observed as our struggle with drug addiction, with violence and, underlying both of these and, perhaps, causal to all of it, the breakdown of our several-thousand year-old value system associated with patriarchy.

Case 1:

As an example of the first problem, that of drug addiction, I wish to present four dreams of a man in his late thirties, an actor, who was addicted in his youth but who has been "sober," as they say, for almost fifteen years. Here is the first dream (names changed):

> Joe, Maude and I are in an apartment we are all sharing in New York City. Joe just smoked pot (marijuana), something I haven't done for fourteen years. "Why shouldn't I try it? No one will know," I think. The ambiance of the apartment is very decadent, the western version of an opium den. Maude and I are discussing whether we should move to LA or stay in New York. I go outside alone into the streets of Manhattan and spy a cappuccino place in an unlikely setting, an alley. I decide to go to it.

The second dream occurs the same night:

> My wife and I are in a car coming down a very steep hill in San Francisco. I tell her the hill is too steep to drive, so I pull over and cut my own path through vacant lots that line the road.

These dreams clearly reveal the temptation to return to a practice that once gave this man a "high," a sense of ecstasy and freedom which is hard come by in ordinary life. His shadow is already at it, and the former lover (from that same period) is willing. LA means, for him, contemporary life and New York is the past attitude. He decides to defer the decision, in the dream, accepting a lesser and legal "drug," cappuccino, in the out-of-the-way place. In the second dream he is shown in danger of a terrible regression, a fall into similar behavior, but decides to "cut my own path through vacant lots," an apt symbol for the path of individuation, also hinted at in the out-of-the way place in the cappuccino dream. Much later on, this man had two other dreams which address the need for ecstatic experience and the transformation of drug addiction. The first dream:

> At a Ferbrungen, (a Jewish religious celebration with dancing and singing). I go into a levitation trance, spinning, eyes closed, balanced on one foot, arms extended but bent at the elbow in a 90 degree angle. I close my eyes and ask myself if God exists and answer, "I believe so." Opening my eyes, I've traveled a quarter length along the circumference of the circle we are dancing in. I bring my hands together in gassho (prayer) and bow to the circle of people, half of whom respond by bowing back; the others are passive.

In this dream, the actor, who was born and raised as a Catholic but has been actively Buddhist for many years, achieves an ecstatic experience at a Jewish religious celebration, in a dance which has Muslim influence (the spinning and trance of the dervishes) and, after acknowledging his belief in God, comes to a Buddhist experience, bowing in the circle of the Self. This ecumenical kind of dream appears to be an answer to this man's need for the ecstasy which the drugs brought to him long ago. In the next dream, occurring the same night, there is a reappearance of the addict shadow figure:

Joe is transformed into a poet/troubadour type in a madrigal costume playing a lute and leading a group of people in song.

The addicted shadow is transformed into a poet/troubadour, an apt symbol for our dreamer, who has become a writer as well as an actor. I am struck that this transformation is in line with the previous ecumenical kind of material, in that the ancient form of the God of wine and ecstasy was Dionysus, who, among the Greeks, was also Lord of the Theater and of Music. In this case, an individual is following his own path, redeeming himself and, in the process, encountering and integrating other religious orientations, including those extant and those apparently "dead" but still alive in the psyche.

Case 2:

I now want to shift to the more underlying issue in our contemporary situation, namely the coming to an end of our long period of patriarchal consciousness, whose dying is mirrored not only in the world-wide protest of women, but also in some aspects of that protest which appear very much like the tyrant-male himself. One aspect is shown in some dreams of a professor of natural science in the eastern United States, one who has pursued a spiritual path for much of his life but has undergone rather little analysis. He had journeyed to India, seeking to have a darshan with the famous Indian saint, Shankara, but that worthy died during his visit. Our dreamer had a powerful dream two nights afterward. In the first part of the dream, he is trying to have breakfast at a little coffee shop, but the proprietor is a fat, European male who is proud of his "castle" but serves poor food. After various amounts of frustration, the dreamer gets angry and leaves. The dream goes on:

I now go to the West entrance to my grandmother's house (this was the site of many early childhood family experiences with my grandparents and extended family). The cellar was amazingly clean and refurbished. I thought how I would enjoy telling my cousin B. (my closest male childhood relative) how good it looks since I fixed it up. I went upstairs to the kitchen and turned the light on, thinking I might find a coffee cup. The old house was unoccupied, but clean. I thought the kitchen would seem smaller than I remembered it—it was not. It was open, light, and airy. My mother, grandmother and aunt appeared in the kitchen. I could not tell if my grandmother was just an older version of my mother or they were distinct beings. They were looking over the old kitchen too. I asked my mother if she had eaten breakfast. She says that she cannot eat with her health. She is trying to play upon my sympathies, make me feel sorry for her as she often does.

I sit in a chair in the corner. The three of them look through the West windows that have flowing white lace curtains blown by the wind. I do not know what they are looking for. Maybe they are just looking over the old back yard. They had to bow slightly forward to look out the windows. The light illuminating them from the windows is cool, blue, lunar. They seem so real, so substantial. I wonder whether they are ghosts or real or what they are. I think that they certainly cannot be dream figures, because they seem so real, so substantial, so three-dimensional. I get up and embrace all three of them. I break into deep and powerful sobbing. The sobs ripple from my feet to my head like labor contractions. I awake feeling a deep love for the simple, earthy women in my family and for the whole feminine principle.

This impressive dream is noteworthy, particularly since it is dreamt by a very masculine, spiritual man. At the outset, he, too, like the previous dreamer, is looking for coffee, something of the spiritual principle which gives a "high" but is legal. The pompous male owner, however, is disappointing and non-nourishing, leaving the dreamer to return to the home of his female relatives. The women are uncannily real, representing both their simple selves and a larger feminine principle. Their situation is clear, open, light and airy, unlike the previous "king." The scientist notes and accepts the shadow aspect of his mother's bid for sympathy. Then the atmosphere turns truly archetypal. The lace curtains, symbol of the delicately feminine, is blown by the wind, a new spirit which the women are looking toward, from the West. The dreamer embraces them all and is deeply moved, finally experiencing his own emotion as if he, too, were giving birth. Indeed, the feminine is profoundly at work in him and he awakens with love and sincere devotion. What that spirit, the wind, coming through the delicate lace curtains, is, we do not yet know, just as Jung did now yet know what the "awe-inspiring guest" would be like. I do know, however, that there is a great difference between this gentle, luminous quality and the love for the feminine, as contrasted with the rough, tough spirit, found these days among both women and men, which can be seen in the next dream of this natural scientist.

> It is the end of a season, a time to put away all the traveling gear-boxes, big storage units. C., (a very masculine, lesbian friend) is driving a tractor or fork lift and moving the boxes around, putting them in storage. I am inside this old wooden house and the wind is starting to blow cold. My dog, L, runs outside to bark at passing strangers. I let him do his thing. We are sitting at a large, wooden rectangular table. There is an ominous air about everything. The moaning wind is coming through an old wooden window that I try to secure more tightly. A big commotion occurs outside because a great woman saint is coming. People are rushing about in excitement and preparation. I follow the crowd along to see what is happening. Some nuns who are part of her entourage are going to arrange for an audience for me in a windowless, dark room with a square table. I think she is an older, dark, slightly heavy Indian woman with real spiritual power—perhaps like Ananda Mayi Ma (perhaps the greatest Indian woman saint of the century). Although she is mysterious, I have no doubt that I want to ask for her help. The nun-attendant shows me a sculpture of several elephants in a row with raised trunks. (Elephants are definitely associated with India and my visits to Shankara. They have appeared in some very powerful dreams about him.) They are old with greenish copper patina (malachite), but she thinks that they are not important for the interview. I decide to ask the great woman for help and advice on how to combine religious devotion with understanding, how to combine the heart with the head, yearning for God with intel-

lectual study of Buddhism, Hinduism and ancient Greek philosophy. My wife is worried because I am not being properly prepared for the interview. I do not know the proper protocol to use, and so on. I think that it does not matter, my sincerity will make everything OK. I might even kneel before her and pray for her help.

This dream, an obvious sequel to the more personal and gentle one earlier, shows that a dark spirit is accompanying the feminine as well. It is the end of an era, and the masculinized feminine, both positive and negative, is fully at work. The male instinct barks, as is its wont, but the now moaning wind howls, too. Our dreamer attempts measures for security, but the female saint is coming. Is she like those of the past or not? It is not clear. But it is clear that his attachment to the male principle, like the elephants—hints at the great story-teller Ganesha?—is not necessary, just his yearning, intellect, devotion, and readiness to kneel are what are required.

That the old masculine spirit, positive or negative, dies easily and readily is too optimistic also, vide the next dream of this scientist:

Shankara died and the people at the sanctuary ask me to carry this huge altar stone used by him in his worship to a small village a few miles down the road toward the hotels. An outpost there would use the stone now that Shankara had died. The stone is a large, gray, rectangle and it has sacred writing imbedded inside, in its very grain. Because it is so sacred I ask if it is OK that I carry it on my shoulder rather than in some ceremonial way. I realize that it will be too heavy to carry in an elegant way. It is OK. I could barely lift the stone, but I put it on my left shoulder and went off with it. At times I got so tired from the effort I had to put it down and rest. My wife was worried about the exertion. At one point I laid on the ground next to it and put my head on it and went to sleep. I laid on my left side with the left side of my face resting on the altar stone. There was never a doubt or a complaint about the task. At one point I carried it inside a stone or concrete block tunnel which opened out into a larger room. Here there were all sorts of very large snakes and even more primitive black, flat, snake-like creatures. They were shiny black, flat on their bottom surface, and they may have had legs like salamanders, but they were very primitive and slug-like. These people used the snakes and creatures in some ritual. There was an attractive, pregnant Western woman there who used these extremely primitive snakes and lizard-like beasts in her ritual.

We left and started out into the open. A young boy was being pesky as kids are in India. I saw another of the black beasts on the road, flat, crawly, and unappealing. I was surprised the boy was not interested in it, since it seemed so unusual to me. I guess he had seen lots of them and lost interest in them. The beast was crawling toward a lake-river on our left. We were getting closer to our destination. I switched the stone to my right shoulder to ease the pain and weariness. We then saw what looked like a big and a small elephant. It turned out that the big one was actually more like a rhino or primitive, blunt-nosed beast. The little elephant was very beautiful and light on its feet. They were moving toward the river, perhaps to get a drink.

With this dream, we see that the end of the father principle, even in the form of the great saint, Shankara, involves that one carry the symbol of the Self, the stone, as it has been achieved, in all its realization, however painful and heavy. The dreamer does so without complaint, but now comes upon the very primitive animals that are associated with the feminine principle, who are also in need of the water of life. A Western woman is also there pregnant—his western anima, no doubt—as well as the pesky youthfulness which will demand attention. A new version of the elephant, suggesting continuing historical creativity, is also present. It is likely that our dreamer is one of those who will carry the spirit of the coming aeon.

Case 3:

I turn, now, to the dreams of some women, whose souls seem to reflect at least some of the change that is happening among those who are able to devote themselves to their own spirit without becoming possessed by the internal masculine. One sees many dreams in which women are being assaulted and dominated. I think of one young woman who dreamt that a wild young man held her hostage with a gun to her head. Our work, in which she admitted her incapacity to flee him (in active imagination), led to his becoming gentle; he just wanted a hearing! Some women's spirits are indeed aggressive, judgmental and persecutory of men, which reflects what is going on inside them as well. Their own spirit, in part a version of that same patriarchy they hate, oppresses them. If they can turn toward that inner negative spirit and find a better way of relating to it, then union becomes possible. I am reminded of a film I saw recently, in which Marie-Louis von Franz is interviewed. She mentions—this interview was in 1977, I think—that women's liberation should indeed be directed toward the inner animus. If this is done creativity and a broadening consciousness emerges. If men also work on their inner feminine—at least as I see it—then the desired mutuality and equality can take place.

What seems to be emerging in this struggle, at least when the animus is no longer the inner tyrant, is an attitude toward nature, toward sexuality, toward all those aspects of the feminine which are both sacred and profound. The first dream, from a woman living on the east coast of the United States who had undertaken much spiritual work but little analysis, was given to me after a seminar and workshop I conducted there. It followed several dreams in which she had experienced ecstasy of various kinds. I chose this one since it has an atmosphere which is somewhat Japanese in character, at least it is so for westerners who experience the Japanese spirit in this way. The dreamer is a Caucasian woman in her forties:

> I am sitting at dusk on a large rock near a pond. The pond is to my left and I must turn my head in that direction to see the rock garden at the pond's edge. Nature has arranged this garden in the way that the Japanese do, almost as if deliberate choices were made about where to place the rocks, and where to place the aquatic plants so as to create a delicate asymmetry. I know that if I am patient and quiet a numinous event will occur. The world is beautifully silent in cooperation, and I am enjoying the silence with every fiber in me. Very shortly thereafter, in a slow motion manner, with no noise whatsoever, a trout leaps up, travels for a few feet just above the water, and resubmerges effortlessly. By now, the dusk has nearly turned to darkness, but I am able to recognize the darker form of the fish in the dark night. Next there is a powerful humming or buzzing in the bushes on the bank of the pond. I can feel the urge to be frightened—to worry about the evil import of this energy in the bushes, but I remind myself to remain calm and to have faith. This contained bundle of humming energy moves out of the bushes and towards me. Now I feel the little gnat-like energy surrounding my head and bumping pleasantly into my face. I feel serene and blissful, not an ecstatic bliss, but rather a sweet and gentle bliss.

A nature-sensitive awareness is present, as well as a full appreciation of the divine, the numinous. The trout, a symbol, perhaps, of the Piscean age which is now passing, with its close connection with Christ as a fish, is very beautiful and holy, but a new energy, even frightening, is at hand. In it are hints of both Hindu symbolism (the "buzzing," as in Kundalini Yoga), and the connection with the collective insect energy. Is this not just what Jung was referring to in his letter, as the new image of the divine, at the gate, just beyond us, powerfully spiritual, collective, yet present to the individual? In my case, there is serenity and bliss, not ecstasy, which may be just as well, since too much ecstasy has the nasty habit of going painfully into its opposite.

Case 4:

Related, but also in contrast, is a dream of a woman nearing sixty, married, a therapist with many years of her own analysis:

> Standing in what appears to be a living-room of a large, grand old home, built by a fine architect in the 20's. Many of my friends and colleagues are there. M., an artist and translator of folk tales, comes up to me. She is very fat. I notice this and get very analytical on the spot. I have given

M. too much food lately; I mean psychological food. M is an endlessly caring individual. She spent the week prior to this dream tending to her sick sister in the hospital even though she should have been getting prepared for her book-signing party. She is overly caring and tending to her physician husband. She cares for newborns, helps out friends, is always kind, etc. Seeing her so fat there in the living room, I leave almost without saying goodbye. I go down the steps to a circular driveway. I see another building, looks like it might be a mobile home. I walk in unhesitatingly. Through the living-room I see a room with a large, king-size bed in it. It is covered only with one bottom, king-size, fitted sheet. There are levers on the right hand side. I push one, thinking I can get in it by stepping up one step. But that doesn't work, so I leap into the bed and lie down, sort of near the center. I stretch out, do some yoga stretches and relax. I love how my body feels in the bed. I don't seem perturbed that I'm all alone in this bed. Then, almost like lightening, I feel Dionysus' presence behind me and bending over my head, neck and shoulder areas. He strokes my hair and neck. I feel overpowering ecstasy. I can't describe how wonderful the feeling is. It's not a happy feeling, it's more of an exquisite gorgeous flow that streams down my body and all around me. It is so intense that I wake up.

This dream is self-explanatory. The "mothering" impulse has been overfed and the dreamer needs to be with the great Greek god of wine, ecstasy, music and theater. The dreamer has experienced him several times in her life. In a dream some ten years earlier, he led her to a hospital where she did clinical work. This woman has had several ecumenical dreams which, she feels, prepare her for a coming change in consciousness.

Case 5:

Among many such dreams, here is one from a woman who had very little analysis, and none at the time of the dream. She is approaching middle age, is married, a mother and interested in Buddhism. She dreamt that the Dalai Lama, whom she reveres very much, came to her and wanted to make love. He said, in her dream, that he is rather in a kind of "fish bowl" all the time and has little time for privacy or love. He needed a more personal and intimate relationship. The resulting love-making was ecstatic. It is notable, I think, that these divine figures (the Dalai Lama, after all, is an incarnation of the Boddhisattva) are uniting with women, ecstatically, on an inner level and this is a harbinger, I believe, for some new births in the feminine spirit.

Case 6:

That this connection with ecstasy, joy and Nature is not limited to Americans who have had some analysis, I want to show by bringing dreams from an Israeli woman and, later, from a Japanese woman which are related, but somewhat different. The Israeli woman, also professional, married, a mother, with many years of psychological work, dreams:

> We were sitting in a beautiful place on the Kinneret (in Galilee). It was almost evening. There were shadows on the water. Everyone sat on a rock in the water. There was a group of soldiers, among them a commander who talked to each one in a most understanding way. They were full of hardships, "kshei yom." I sat there, too, on the rock. Somebody started to sing a beautiful song, the melody and words were magnificent. The refrain of the song was "Elda, Elda," meaning "God knows" or "Know God." But this was also the name of the commander, which is a masculine form that can be also the name of a woman. Everyone joined in. The song was new. I felt tears streaming down my face, and everyone else did, too, including the commander. His shoulders were shaking as if he was crying. It was a kind of "thank you" in the form of a song, full of emotion, for his understanding. Then as the song ended, they started to sing it again. I joined in.

This touching dream suggests the dreamer's contact with what a Jungian would understand as a symbol of the Self, a higher inner authority who connects with the divine. Characteristically, the figure combines male and female in some manner and is both deeply affecting and affected by the dreamer. It of course gave her great solace in her suffering and the sense that "God knows," or "Know God." Noteworthy also, is the presence of Nature and of great joy, as was the case with the American dreamer.

Case 7:

A Japanese woman, also a professional, married and a mother, with a long history of treasuring her dreams, often comes in contact with numinous events. In one dream, however, which brings us all closer to our current world-wide concern with environmental devastation, she is walking in a beautiful desert, enjoying the dusk and the abundant life in the midst of the apparent bareness and then sees some very modern, fast-food restaurants. She is horrified, naturally. In another dream, she is aware of a revolutionary figure in the Philippines who is arising powerfully, while one does not know if he is criminal or presages something positive. But she notices that he is nostalgic for the type of gaslight on the streets which was common in the nineteenth century. I think that such a forthcoming spirit, in a country she sees as poor but vital and happy, is still uncertain, but there is nostalgia for the kind of consciousness ("gas light") as existed in the world more than a century ago, with its more leisurely pace. The patriarchy was still positive then, of course.

Return to Case 4:

I want to close this discussion, at this point, by reference to several dreams, from three women, which hint at what is happening in the deeper psyche in at least some women. The first dream is from the professional therapist, mentioned earlier, who has outgrown the maternal role.

> I am in the room of my office I use to lead dream groups. Members of the dream group, all women, are seated around in a circle. Instead of the oval-shaped wicker coffee table in the center, there is something larger, also oval. At first I think it has an aura of death. I look again. It looks like a human is wrapped like a mummy, but the wrapping seems to be starting to fall off.
>
> All the members of the group help me. They tug and pull and finally help me to get the person out of what now appears to be a transparent sack. It is an old woman with very long straight white hair. Her skin is aged and wrinkled. We all help her to stand up. It takes all of us to do it. As she stands, she turns into a black woman, about 45 or 50 years old, short black curly hair, very nice figure, wearing a black leotard, long sleeves, a gauze skirt in black, white and brown tones, looks like from India, and leather sandals. She wears no jewelry. She is greeting each member of the group. She goes around to everyone, asking them about themselves, making very individual connections with each person. She tells them she will be leading the dream group. In the last scene of the dream, I am in my leader's chair, exhausted. I am sunk way back into it, too tired from my efforts to get the old Crone out of the sack. I wonder how I am going to get along with the group with her taking over.

This dream seems quite clear: the dreamer and her group, all of whom are women with advanced consciousness, have been actively working on achieving a new image of the feminine Self, in mind and in action. The fruits of their labor are now beginning to manifest. Out of the Crone, there emerges an attractive, related, black woman—to whom the dreamer associates the Black Madonna, a figure with whom she has had both inner and outer connections in such places as Einsiedeln in Switzerland, for example—who is going to "take over," now. The ego is exhausted, and now a larger Self image will lead. The behavior of this feminine image, oriented to each individual, yet collectively connected, is quite attractive. It reminded me of the writer, Anaïs Nin, who went her own way in a masculine society but maintained her feminine values of relatedness, kindness, subjectivity, etc. Such a Black Madonna, if that is what she is, seems eminently more attractive than some of the current models of radical feminism. Perhaps an animus-dominated image is temporarily necessary, facilitating the empowerment of women before a more whole, even divine, figure makes its appearance. As Jung said, we are waiting for the new image of the Self, both male and female, to make itself known, and our dreams are hinting at it.

Case 8:

Another woman, struggling with the guilt and passion of an infidelity, the same person who dreamt of uniting with the Dalai Lama, dreams that she and her very sensual eight-year old daughter need to get into the body of a large cat. The head of the girl does not fit in, however, and the entrance is delayed. Here, too, the union of head and heart, mind and body, sensuality and conscience, is leading one woman, at least, towards a new image of the female godhead, as represented by the cat. This animal has a great history, belonging to at least two Egyptian goddesses. For us, I think that this union in the feminine principle is essential for our next advance of the spirit.

Case 9:

Finally, I want to present the dream of another woman, fairly well into middle age, who has also worked deeply on the spiritual life, without benefit of much analysis. Six months earlier, she had a dream in which she unsuccessfully tried to connect with the Dalai Lama, an extremely important spiritual figure for her. After awakening from that dream with "much sadness, tears and a sense of defeat," she labored hard, these many months, and then dreamt:

At a large meeting with the Dalai Lama. Lots of activity and excitement. I think I will try to talk with him, but know I can't ask for a private interview. Later, in a quieter setting with the Dalai Lama talking with my spiritual group. He looks directly at me and asks if I have a question. I say, "No," and feel shy and unworthy. Then I say, "Yes, I do." It's embarrassing to say in public but I will do it. It doesn't matter. "I've been meditating twenty years. I have had a few glimpses, but I really can't concentrate." He asks if I practice regularly. I say, "Almost every day." He is very sweet and kind and patient. He says some things. Great feeling of inner bliss. I think, "I'm too blissed out to remember this. I'm so glad someone is making a tape I can listen to." The comments are positive and reassuring. Then he says, "I offer the Divine Bliss of my Overself to God." He is offering this to me as a practice. I think, "I don't have any divine bliss to offer," but I try to put away my thoughts and listen to him. He is divine, compassionate, and overwhelming.

The scene changes and the Dalai Lama is now a beautiful, middle-aged Tibetan woman with long dark hair and clothes that are fanciful Arabic (as in Kismet—long, loose, silky sleeves and pants, tight waist band, bare midriff). She is very sensuous. I am awed by this woman and very much in love with her. We are in a large gymnasium with students in high school jackets around. She does a dance. I am the focus of the dance. My husband is on my right side. On my left and slightly behind my left shoulder is a negative female complaining constantly about the woman teacher and what she is doing. The negative woman gets quieter when she realizes I am the focus of the dance. The dance is exotic and contains some tumbling. My feet are the focus of two large circular patterns through which she moves. The whole pattern makes an infinity symbol with my outstretched feet as the focus. I know this is an initiation for me. I am overwhelmed.

A woman organizer of the Dalai Lama's visit is talking to P. She is a straight-looking woman in her fifties. She tells P how nice it is to deal with people from our Group. We all come on time and behave perfectly—in essence, we have our worldly act together. P. suggests we work together with this woman's group at a future time.

The dreamer does lead a women's group and is a member, together with her husband, of a thriving spiritual center. Her dream, like the previous ones, suggest a coming-to-be of a new image of the feminine Self, growing out of the woman's union with the positive, spiritual masculine figure. The Self's symbols are there in abundance. Very interestingly, however, is the lysis of this dream, wherein there is plenty of "women's work" to be done, both alone and collectively, suggesting that the new image of the Self will also find a home in meaningful group life, as well.

SUMMARY

A description of the current state of psychotherapy in the United States is presented, focussing upon the effect of insurance disbursements and legal requirements which will tend to rule out analytical methods and support directive procedures and asymmetrical models. Categorizations of the field, by Jung, Klopfer and the author, support this description of the relativization of the field. A further description of the Self as currently portrayed in dreams of men and women suggests a contrary movement away from such patriarchal models to more alchemical and democratic ones, suggesting continued polarization between the viewpoints of Jungian therapists and those with an institutional perspective.

REFERENCES

1. von Franz, M.L., (1970) Introduction to the Interpretation of Fairy Tales, *Spring* Publications, 1970.

2. Jung, C.G. (1953) *Psychology and Alchemy, Collected Works*, Vol. 12, Bollingen, Pantheon Books, New York, 1953.

3. Jung, C.G. (1934) Zarathustra Seminars, Unpublished seminar notes, 1934-1939, recorded and edited by Mary Foote.

4. Jung, C.G. (1958) *Answer to Job, Collected Works*, Vol. 11, Bollingen, Pantheon Books, New York, 1958.

5. Jung, C.G. (1976) *Letters*, Vol. 2, Gerhard Adler, Editor, Routledge and Kegan Paul, London, 1976.

6. Klopfer, Bruno and Spiegelman, J. Marvin. (1965) "Some Dimensions in Psycho-therapy," in *Speculum Psychologiae, Festschrift für C.A. Meier*, edited by C.T Frey, Rascher Verlag, Zürich, 1965, pp. 177-184.

7. Prince, Morton, (1957)*The Dissociation of Personality*, Meridian Books, New York, 1957. Original, 1905.

8. Spiegelman, J. Marvin, (1992)*Reich, Jung, Regardie and Me: The Unhealed Healer*, New Falcon Publications, Scottsdale, AZ, 1992, 208pp.

CHAPTER TEN

TRANSFERENCE AS MUTUAL PROCESS AND INTERACTIVE FIELD (1995)

Ever since the early days of psychoanalysis, until the present, both founders and followers in that branch of psychotherapy have experienced something similar to what Jung famously responded to Freud, at their first meeting in the early 1900's, when the latter asked him about what he thought of the transference: "It is the alpha and omega of analysis." And Freud's reply, that Jung had grasped the main thing, is what practically all depth psychologists have also concluded when they have become immersed in the particular and peculiar kind of intimacy that our vocation demands. That Jung subsequently stated that the transference is not so central in every case, that it is a poison for some, as well as a panacea, is also a common experience, but this by no means diminishes the importance of the effects of that relationship upon both analyst and analysand.

Freud's initial solution to the fact of the transference—which he understood as the projecting onto the analyst those experiences of one's parents and other significant figures of the analysand's childhood—was to stay apart and neutral as much he was able. The reason for this kind of objectivity was to enable the patient to clearly see these images as projections, thereby permitting the reliving and reclaiming of them, thus freeing him/her from infantile repressions and neurosis (Freud, 1927, p. 257):

> For it is not greatly to the advantage of patients if their physician's therapeutic interest has too marked an emotional emphasis. They are best helped if he carries out his task coolly and keeping as closely as possible to the rules.

Freud discovered that transference engendered counter-transference, but felt that this was to be worked out privately by the analyst, either alone or with his/her own analyst or supervisor, thus freeing the patient from anything "not quite right" in the analyst's condition. We know that the later Freud relented on this austerity, somewhat, but he maintained the necessity for separateness, neutrality and objectivity until the end. This insistence on objectivity, in a relationship which is clearly heavily mutually subjective, is not foolish. Given the inescapable subjective involvement, there remains a necessary condition of the analyst's task—and ultimately the patient, as well—to discover the natural objectivity of the deeper unconscious itself. This insight of Anson Levine (personal communication), enabled me to understand why the obvious existence of the collective unconscious, objective in nature, seems to evade our Freudian colleagues. It seems to me that they are often likely to identify with the objectivity of the logos principle or a particular archetypal constellation, such as the parent-child.

Freud's later followers, such as Melanie Klein and the Object Relations analysts, felt that such strictures requiring non-participation were counter-productive and they were inclined to "make use" of the counter-transference to understand what the patient was projecting and to get clues as to what was happening in the relationship. For them, the dynamics of "projective identification" were of central interest and they allowed themselves to be much more participatory and interactive. In this, they were not totally original (Ferenczi, for example, did this early on), but their view has garnered extensive support.

It was Jung, however, who first saw that the analytic relationship ultimately, although not at the outset, attained a kind of mutuality which was "chemical" in nature, and which he, in his master work on the transference (Jung, 1946), used a 16th century alchemical model to explain. His observations regarding mutuality, however, which constituted the "fourth" stage of the therapeutic process—after catharsis, elucidation and education, that of transformation—are profound and of special relevance, even today, sixty-five years since he made these remarks (Jung, 1929, p. 71 ff).

> For, twist and turn the matter as we may, the relation between doctor and patient remains a personal one within the impersonal framework of the professional treatment. By no device can the treatment be anything but the product of mutual influence, in which the whole being of the doctor, as well as that of his patient plays its part ... For two personalities to meet is like mixing two different substances: if there is any combination at all, both are transformed ...

> One of the best known symptoms of this kind is the counter transference evoked by the transference. But the effects are often much more subtle, and their nature can best be conveyed by the old idea of the demon of sickness. According to this, a sufferer can transmit his disease to a healthy person whose powers then subdue the demon—but not without impairing the well-being of the subduer.

> What does this mean [the necessity, as Jung recognized, that the analyst be analyzed]? Nothing less than the doctor is as much "in the analysis" as is the patient ... Indeed, to the extent that the doctor shows himself impervious to this influence, he forfeits influence over the patient; and if he is influenced only unconsciously, there is a gap in his field of conscious-

ness which makes it impossible for him to see the patient in true perspective. In either case the result of the treatment is compromised.

C.A. Meier has carried the discussion about mutual impact in the transference farther by suggesting that it is the very act of the analytic work, of carrying the "cut" of consciousness ever more deeply into the analysand, that produces a condition wherein one does not know where one's own consciousness ends and the other begins (Meier, 1959). Groesbeck has elaborated Jung's famous four-fold model into the myth of the wounded healer (Groesbeck, 1975). Healer and patient both connect with the source of wounding and healing (the healing "god" or archetype) within each and between them both as the process continues and this results in mutual transformation. He convincingly demonstrates (using his dreams, among others) that the analyst can not hide his own wounds and weakness, but must confront them anew with each patient. Only by keeping one's hand in the darkness—one's own and that of the patient—can one stay in touch with reality.

The present writer has had his own share of preoccupation with the implications of the transference for some thirty years and has tried to describe what this "mutual process," as he has called it, entails (e.g., Spiegelman 1965 and 1991). Over time, it has seemed a good idea to differentiate the degree to which mutual process occurs in the work and to see this as becoming an "interactive field." Nathan Schwartz-Salant has had similar experiences and has elaborated this conception as well (see Schwartz-Salant 1989, Ch. 5, and 1992).

Before presenting this differentiation, however, it is useful to add a third concept to those of mutual process and interactive field, namely, Jung's ideas of the "psychic unconscious" and the "somatic unconscious", which he presented in his Nietzsche seminars (Jung, C.G. 1934-39, especially 1935) and which Schwartz-Salant made use of in his work. By the former, one refers to the imagery and fantasy which appear when one attends to the psychic background, whereas the latter refers to the physical sensations and events which arise as one focuses upon the body and contacts the somatic background. The psychic background, or "psychic unconscious," which manifests when one attends to the patient's imagery, will be familiar to all depth psychologists, but the "somatic unconscious" may be less well known. I have suggested that symptoms, such as headache, stomach ache, tingling, etc., arising in the analyst during the course of a session, represent an activation of the somatic unconscious and is often in parallel with what is going on in the analysand. (Spiegelman 1991). I have suggested that these concepts of Jung properly belong to his conception of the "spectrum" of consciousness, beginning at the "infra-red" end, in which instinctive processes predominate (somatic unconscious), and rising through this spectrum to the "ultra-violet" end, in which spiritual processes (psychic unconscious) predominate, but both instinctual and spiritual comprise the dual-aspects of the archetype (Jung 1946 b).

I have also found it useful to further differentiate these concepts in the light of Kundalini Yoga and the Kabbalistic Sephiroth. In terms of the former, the somatic unconscious can be usefully symbolized by the first three *chakras* of the Kundalini, namely Muladhara, Svadhisthana and Manipura, whereas the psychic unconscious can be differentiated among the upper three chakras of Sahasrara, Ajna and Vishuddha. The central *chakra* of Anahata, located in the heart region, seems a good representation of their union. The symbolism regarding this system is of significant general psychological value (Spiegelman 1987, 1989) and of particular significance when one applies it to experiences in the transference (Spiegelman 1991). The Kabbalistic system of the Tree of Life, representing opposites from top to bottom, is an excellent paradigm for what goes on in this process and is one that the present writer uses as a basis for the daily work. This entails being in the work with "both hands"; the 'left hand' is open to the unconscious and what it brings forth, while the 'right hand' maintains the parenting, containing, and formative aspect. One attends to all that happens between and within each participant, follows the process with understanding and formulation, until wholeness is achieved, both within each of them and between them (Spiegelman 1988). How the chakra and sephira systems interact with our mutual process and field conceptions will become apparent later on.

To return to the differentiation of the mutual process conception, we can consider four aspects: (1) traditional analytic work in which there is asymmetry in the relationship, exclusive focus upon the psyche of the patient, with the analyst as mostly objective observer and the analytic situation is a container for the process. Interpretations of the transference are made, but there is little or no "self-disclosure" on the part of the analyst. This is sometimes called a "womb analysis" (see Spiegelman, 1992 Appendix); (2) "Womb-inter-action," in which there is occasional mutuality, but this is rarely the case and interpretations are generally of dreams and behavior. Transference interpretations are analysand-based and the analyst "uses" his reactions to tell him what is going on in the analysand, i.e., projective identification; (3) Mutual process proper, in which there is a realization of archetypal constellations as a "third," between and around the partners, so to speak. Complexes now take on an archetypal character, effecting both parties. Interpretations are at the archetypal level and "self-disclosure" may occur. What is disclosed is what the analyst is experiencing at the moment, particularly in relation to the analysand. This is a condition of symmetry; (4) Acausal field-conditions in which subtle-body experiences also obtain; there is energy exchange as well as work with images. The archetypal level of relationship predominates and mutual "self-disclosure" of what is being experienced is necessary for the continuity of the work.

One might think of these four types of transference as characterizing Freudian (#1), Kleinian and Object Relations (#2), Jungian (#3), with the fourth type as an evolutionary development based on all of these, with the addition of the body-therapies, particularly that of Wilhelm Reich, as influences. These are by no means to be considered as exclusive, since a Jungian, for example, might readily find herself going back and forth among these and any analyst, in his individuality, will be uncomfortable if "boxed-in" to one mode. Yet it is useful to use such categories when we examine the concept of the "field."

A field-condition might be manifested in any one of these four degrees of mutuality, but in (#1) and (#2) these are not particularly noticed nor worked with. For example, the archetype of the Great Mother and her Child may underlie aspects of the womb-analysis, as in some sand-tray therapy experiences, but these are neither interpreted nor commented upon. In (#3), however, this archetypal relationship constitutes the center of attention. Schwartz-Salant (1992), suggests that the analytic focus itself could usefully be centered upon the field, rather than upon the person of the analysand or analyst. In any case, (#3) is a mercurial one, in the present writer's experience, in which the archetypal constellation, and the opposites contained in it, shifts back and forth between the participants. This shifting process can be seen as a "third" between them, and ultimately is resolved as a union of these opposites both within each of the partners and between them.

The manifestation of the subtle-body, found in (#4), is often whole-making and always numinous. It is under this condition that synchronistic events occur, although sometimes synchronistic events appear without the subtle body experience as well. In the situation where the subtle-body is not experienced, the synchronicity is one pertaining to the psychic unconscious, although "matter" may also be effected, such as in the appearance of a squirrel on a neighboring roof when the dreamer is describing a squirrel in his dream. The union of psychic and somatic unconscious, as shown in the subtle body experiences, when combined with dream imagery or outside event, is the most compelling, although these are relatively rare.

We are confronted, then, with several kinds of variables here. First there is the degree of mutual process, as shown in the progression of (#1) to (#4). Then there is the presence of the field, with a similar progression, particularly when we add the factor of conscious recognition. It is notable that conscious recognition seems to be an important factor in contributing to both mutuality and the awareness of a joint field. Finally, there is the internal variable of psychic and somatic unconscious, differentiated into the Kundalini chakra system and the Kabbalistic play of opposites. Those therapies which become increasingly archetypal and field-oriented will be faced with such experiences and the task of consciousness is to work with such energies and images, as well as to be effected by them.

Jung's early reference to the chemical-like interplay which can take place between the analyst and analysand (Jung, 1929), can now be understood as a true energy-exchange going on in the process. Kurt Lewin, from academic psychology (Lewin, 1936), early on noted a field character to both social and psychological events, even employing the valuable mathematical conception of topology, but his concepts are not yet applicable, in the writer's opinion, to therapeutic concerns. Yet the hypothesis of energy exchange can also be addressed from other scientific perspectives, such as experimental psychology and biology, in which the somatic connection with the subtle body might be measured. The use of the galvanic skin response, such as Jung employed at the beginning of the twentieth century in the study of the word-association test, is possible (and is being examined by the present author and a physicist colleague). Secondly, the relation between field-phenomena in the transference and the concepts of quantum physics are also germane (see, e.g., Spiegelman and Mansfield, in press).

If we now recall Jung's classical four-fold model of the analyst-analysand interaction, including the unconscious of each person and the various possibilities of mutual effect (Jung 1946), we can glimpse the complexity, even including that of mutually unconscious exchange between the partners. This model proves to be a most accurate one in describing the work and even more so when the analyst consciously speaks about these processes with the analysand. Jung, it will be remembered, noted that much of this interchange could be and perhaps should be left "in the dark," yet present-day work permits more open discussion of such events.

These conceptions suggest both a broadening and a more differentiated understanding of the original idea of "libido" and hints at the possibility of bringing together a variety of views, including those of Reich on orgone energy, along with, as I have already mentioned, eastern conceptions of Kundalini and of Kabbalistic Sephiroth. The field is seen as activated when the collective unconscious is encountered. This activation also occurs when one is alone and takes up a relationship with dream figures, as in active imagination, of course (Von Franz, 1979). It may also take place after prolonged meditation practice or in body therapies. The subtle body is readily experienced in later phases of Reichian work, for example (Spiegelman 1992). But the joint experience of these things is quite impressive in the analytic situation. Questions and reflections arise as a consequence of these experiences, which we will now address.

What activates the field, either alone or in therapy? When alone, it is surely activated by the attention of the person, as in preparing for active imagination or meditation. Attention, which is direction of energy as well, provides a *vinculum,* a kind of bridge, perhaps, which invites the unconscious in. The first visitors, so to speak, may be the personal unconscious, followed by the collective, but not always, of course. The unconscious itself activates the field, quite autonomously. This happens naturally in effective dream interpretation and in spontaneous manifestations of all kinds (Meier 1939). When the ego addresses, invites in, or relates to such events or images, there is a conscious participation with the unconscious, as Jung has shown us. A relationship still takes place, of course, but in this case between the individual and the unconscious, with the crucial variable of awareness included.

How is the field activated in therapy? The patient comes in and the therapist focuses upon him/her, open to what happens. The splendid description of Bion as to how the analyst should address each session, "without memory, desire or knowledge," (Bion, W.R. 1970) is the ideal way to "invite in" the unconscious, since one does not immediately channel it into one's own theories, expectations or goals. After an indefinite period of work, the unconscious is activated, creating a field between the partners. It is "constellated," but how? Perhaps this is done by a complex of the patient touching something similar in the therapist. This is easy, since personal complexes have an archetypal nucleus which is set off. The therapist notices it, sensing that it is no longer just himself/herself who is responding, but that a "third" is present. Schwartz-Salant looks first to such things as projective identification (Schwartz-Salant 1992), but perhaps it is more parsimonious to think of this as an instance of mutual projection or of an incursion of a patient's complex, touching off the comparable one in the therapist, thus engendering a field. The field, comprising the unconscious within each of them, between them and surrounding them, has properties and these are being investigated by the present writer and his physicist colleague.

How does one know that the field exists, as a therapist? When a body reaction occurs or emotion is set off, since we know that emotion is a sign of the presence of a complex. The body reaction is not yet the subtle body. This occurs only after consciousness is registered and there is reflection as to what this might mean. For example, during a session I get a headache or stomach ache. I reflect on it, ask the patient if he/she has such a one or had it recently, and usually there is an answer that yes, he/she had it last night or has it now. Hence the field. At that point, the headache usually subsides (as a result of consciousness? Of sharing?) and one can move on to deeper understanding, energetically or in terms of imagery.

Another example is the experience of boredom, depression or chaos. In each case, I have found it valuable to register this condition and inform the patient. Often, as a consequence of education from books or other analytic sources, the patient will 'take the blame' for this as an induction. This may be true—and if this a strong reaction, I accept this—but I usually find it more fruitful to acknowledge that a field is engendered between us and I suggest that we both sink together, more deeply, into the registered boredom, depression, or chaos. After a few moments, imagery and energy emerge in either or both parties which is eminently suitable to be worked with. As proof of the pudding, one soon experiences an ending or profound lessening of the experienced boredom, depression or chaos. (See Spiegelman 1991 for other examples).

Another way to know about the field is the experience of the archetype as image. For example, the analysand is talking about father or mother and, after the usual questions and following of the story, I feel "the Father" in the room, not personal alone but collective as well. Interpretations or comments can then arise from the joint experience. I may be the father at one moment, then the son, changing about. This can be done either intentionally—a kind of psychodrama—or as one experiences it in its own mercurial flow.

Much of such exchange is largely connected to the personal unconscious. The collective unconscious manifests itself most clearly in synchronistic events during the session. For example, the patient and I are speaking about some matter and look to the dreams. There, sure enough, are images which speak to the condition and are often explanatory. This happens all the time. It cannot be forced, however. The most powerful events, such as a mutual experience of Jesus with a depressed former priest patient, are "miraculous" and connected to the synchronistic character of the field (Spiegelman 1992).

But why is there not more frequent synchronicity? Is it only then that the collective unconscious is truly activated? Maybe. But we must consider that the presence of images reveals the psychic unconscious whereas the presence of body reactions reveals the somatic unconscious. The synchronicity can be experienced in outer events—such as the burning out of a light-bulb as one speaks about the loss of consciousness. Or it can be inner events, such as mutual bodily symptoms, or mutual body images. Meier took the position that body and psyche were connected synchronistically (Meier, C.A. 1963), but Jung had his doubts about this. One can prove for one's self that this synchronicity happens at least sometimes in a session when one simply takes note of these "symptoms" arising within one's self while attending profoundly to the analysand and discovering that there are, indeed, meaningful psychosomatic connections—not causal—that are taking place in both parties.

Sometimes the subtle body can be worked with between us, especially if a meditative period has preceded our conscious work. I suggest the latter when I get sleepy or bored or enervated, knowing that the unconscious is pulling me down and that the same condition is plaguing the patient, as I mentioned earlier. We then meditate together for a few moments and I often feel the subtle body present. I can sometimes see the energy working between us, as well as feel it, as Schwartz-Salant also reports (1992), but I am not sensitive enough, alas, so that I can see auras, possibly because of undissolved Reichian armor. But I am reminded of a session I had with an ex-nun who was very connected with the unconscious. I felt myself as a "fallen angel," one who has descended to earth not as a sinner but as one who needs to "incarnate" in the human condition to do the work of God. She was feeling the same, and we both felt our "wings" were now absent but made present in the form of pain in the shoulder blades, typical Reichian armor. This revealed our joint, archetypal condition and resulted in weeping, in union and fellow-suffering, which also relieved the pain and resulted in more intense subtle-body and field experience.

This is a profound level at which to work, but it is not often that which is indicated or needed. There is always the necessary spade work of talking about life situations, complexes, feelings and thoughts, images, relationships, past and present. But it is when the complexes are engendered in the room that there is the best chance of their transformation, in my experience.

Jung emphasized the way of inner work, teaching active imagination and personal responsibility. My session with him, however, when I had completed my studies and went to him for a "blessing" for my analytic vocation, was filled with synchronicity and with powerful energy which stays with me yet, more than thirty-five years later! He continually 'spoke to my condition' without my having to even raise questions, an experience that many others have also reported. The subtle-body was present without being discussed.

Jung was partial to what I called the Rainmaker Model (Spiegelman 1980), in which the person, like the Chinese rainmaker, changes himself internally rather than trying to effect change in the outer situation; if he does so, the Tao changes and harmony is also restored in the outer surroundings. One also thinks of the Buddha, since the image arises of standing/sitting alone, facing the demons. But Jung also embraced the alchemical model for the therapeutic relationship, which implies two-persons and re-connects with a Christian image (Jesus said he would be present when two or three gathered in his name).

As for me, I fully accept Jung's recommendation of encounter with the Self via internal dialogue, which for me is deeply Jewish, as well as experiencing the Christ aspect of the Self in the therapeutic situation (when "two or three are gathered together in my name..."). Furthermore, I am profoundly conscious of the energies symbolized by the Hindu Kundalini serpent and chakras in both the personal and joint encounter, as well as seeking the Enlightenment promised by the Buddha. These are present as fundamental attitudes of approach, whereas the therapeutic material, as we know, is likely to be of an Animistic or alchemical nature, as well as of any other psychological content. A "psycho-ecumenical" myth is at the basis of what I do, hence my relatively easy connection, in the work, with people from different religions and cultures. Jung recognized that each of us needs to know our own myth, which much influences how we approach our therapeutic task. As Jungians, we share the myth, I presume, of service of the Self, in ourselves and the analysand.

There are certain historical implications of the foregoing reflections on the development of ideas about the therapeutic process. One might readily see the parallel between the field-idea in physics and that in transference. The original causal view of Freud seems parallel to that advanced in physics by Descartes, whereas the beginning of the field-idea by Newton (e.g., gravity as a field generated by a body) seems similar to the Kleinian analytic idea that the patient generates reactions in the analyst by projective identification. The field-proper, and its transcendence of space-time, discovered by Einstein, seems parallel with Jung's archetypal and synchronistic conceptions of the work. Finally, the idea of the field as engendering subtle-body and symmetry, with its acausal conditions, seems appropriately matched to the current quantum physics (Mansfield and Spiegelman, 1989). This connection between quantum events and transference brings us to a new possibility of integration of psychology and physics, parallel with the integration of spirit and matter, soul and body, long awaited in depth psychology.

Additionally, one can consider that the movement from asymmetry to symmetry, from the teacher/pupil and doctor/patient relationship to the alchemical model of the working pair (alchemist and his *soror mystica*) is consistent with the democratic development in society generally toward greater equality. This is also consonant with the shift away from hierarchical methods of relationship, associated with traditional patriarchy, to more mutual ones.

There are other implications of the mutual process experience and idea which are clinical, theoretical, social, and spiritual, but I shall limit myself here to the first two. The clinical issue of the analyst's self-disclosure has already been alluded to and constitutes a choice in stage three of the work, but becomes a requirement of stage four, when the subtle body is also at play. Schwartz-Salant has made the most advanced comments in this area (1989, e.g., Chapter 5 on the subtle-body), as I mentioned earlier, and has reported his own experiences of the "third area" very well, along with many clinical examples. He has linked up what I call the third and fourth stage of mutual process and interactive field with the theoretical principle of those working largely in the second stage, namely "projective identification" (Schwartz-Salant, 1988). He has also utilized the image of the alchemical couple in the "third area" to good advantage.

A more common experience for me, however, is for the "third area" to be manifested as the mercurial energy gripping the two participants, just as Jung has described, the opposites constellating between them and moving back and forth in a way which this divine spirit which has fallen into matter deserves his appellation as trickster. Opposites of parent-child, wise-man-woman and pupil-dullard, innocent and crafty devil, lusty animal and virgin, to name just a few, continue to manifest and incarnate in each of the pair—usually polarized—and, with consciousness and work, for both opposites to be found within as well. It is this latter condition which brings about both healing and consciousness and is experienced as a combined image and bodily/instinctual response. True wholeness, now constituting both union and separation of the couples, body and spirit, can result as a consequence of this shared alchemical work.

I have found that joint active-imagination, including moments of joint psychodrama, allow Mercurius to play out his/her forces and to eventually permit the conscious union of opposites within each member of the alchemical work. Each analyst must surely develop his/her own ways of dealing with this constellation of forces, but I think it behooves us all to realize that, at last, when in the "naked confrontation" with the analysand, we need to sacrifice not only interpretations but any and all preconceptions as to how the analysis should go, except for our holy commitment to "do no damage."

This kind of experience is also shown in the following quotation from Hester Solomon, of London, (Solomon 1994, p. 96):

> It is possible to think of the development from less to more differentiated imagery as being achieved in part through processes facilitating the formation of what has been called the subtle body. An unconscious couple is created and interact together in the consulting room, by virtue of the consistent containment of the therapeutic setting and through subtle communications that can occur within the interplay of projective identification, or in Jung's terms, through participation mystique.

Solomon also refers to a theoretical consequence of these relational factors, in the alchemical process of analysis, which leads us to some of the theoretical implications mentioned earlier. She speaks of the "pivotal issue in analytical and psychoanalytical theory building (which) concerns the question of whether there is something like a primary self, which can be thought of as existing prior to any influences coming from the eternal environment, or whether the relating function is so primary that, in Winnicott's phrase, 'there is no such thing as a baby.' (p.92)"

Solomon concludes that the opposing views of Fordham and Winnicott can be reconciled by using Hegel's dialectical model, and she uses Jung's image of the *coniunctio* as a creative image of the dialectical self. This is a valuable step forward, but I think it is also important to remember that Jung pointed out that individuation is both a subjective process of integration, as well as an "indispensable process of objective relationship" (Jung, 1946, par. 448). We can close these reflections with Jung's observation regarding a fundamental spiritual necessity for us all:

> Looked at in this light, the bond established by the transference—however hard to bear and however unintelligible it may seem—it is vitally

important not only for the individual but also for society, and indeed the moral and spiritual progress of mankind. (p. 234, par. 449)

REFERENCES

1. Bion, W.R. (1970) *Attention and Interpretation*. London. Maresfield Reprints 1984.

2. Freud. S. (1927) Standard Edition. Vol. 20.

3. von Franz, M.-L. *Alchemical Active Imagination*, Spring Publications, Texas, 1979.

4. Groesbeck, C.G. (1975) "The Archetypal Image of the Wounded Healer," *Journal of Analytical Psychology*, Vol. 20, No. 2, pp. 122-145

5. Jung, C.G. (1929) *Problems or Modern Psychotherapy*, Coll. Wks., Vol. 16, Chapter V.

6. Jung, C.G. (1934-39) *Psychological Analysis of Nietzsche's Zarathustra*, Seminar notes, edited by Mary Foote.

7. Jung, C.G. (1946) *Psychology of the Transference*, Coll. Wks., Vol. 16, pp. 163-323.

8. Jung, C.G. (1946b) "On the Nature of the Psyche." Coll. Wks. Vol. 8, pp. 159-234.

9. Lewin, Kurt (1936) *Principles of Topological Psychology*, McGraw-Hill, New York, 1936.

10. Mansfield, V. and Spiegelman, J.M., (1989), "Quantum Mechanics and Jungian Psychology: Building a Bridge," *Journal of Analytical Psychology*, 1989, Volume 34, No. 1, pp. 3-31.

11. Meier, C.A. (1939) "Spontanmanifestationen des Kollektiven Unbewussten, *Zentralblatt für Psychotherapie*, 11, p. 284, Leipzig 1939.

12. Meier, C.A. (1959) "Projection, Transference, and the Subject-Object Relation," *The Journal of Analytical Psychology*, 1959, Vol. IV, No. 1, pp. 21-34.

13. Meier, C.A. (1963) "Psychosomatic Medicine from the Jungian Point of View," *Journal of Analytical Psychology*, 1963, Vol. 8, No. 2 103-121.

14. Schwartz-Salant, Nathan (1988), "Archetypal Foundation of Projective Identification," *Journal of Analytical Psychology*, 1988, Vol. 33, No. 1, pp. 39-64.

15. Schwartz-Salant, Nathan (1989) *The Borderline Personality: Vision and Healing*, Chiron Publications, Illinois, 1989.

16. Schwartz-Salant, Nathan (1992),"On the Interactive Field as the Analytic Object," Chiron Conference, Einsiedeln, Switzerland.

17. Solomon, H. (1994), "The Transcendent Function and Hegel's Dialectical Vision," *Journal of Analytical Psychology*, 1994, Vol. 39, No. 1, pp. 77-100.

18. Spiegelman, J. Marvin (1965) "Some Implications of the Transference," in *Festschrift für C. A. Meier*, edited by C.T. Frey, Rascher Verlag, Zürich, 1965, pp. 163-175.

19. Spiegelman, J. Marvin (1980), "The Image of the Jungian Analyst and the Problem of Authority," Spring, *An Annual of Archetypal Psychology*, 1980, pp. 101-117.

20. Spiegelman, J. Marvin (1988) "The Impact of Suffering and Self-Disclosure on the Life of the Analyst," in *Jungian Analysts: Their Visions and Vulnerabilities*, edited by Spiegelman, Falcon Press, Phoenix, 1988.

21. Spiegelman, J. Marvin (1989) *Jungian Psychology and the Passions of the Soul*, Falcon Press, Las Vegas, 1989.

22. Spiegelman, J. Marvin (1991) "The Interactive Field in Analysis: Agreements and Disagreements," *Chiron Publications*, Illinois, 1991, pp. 133-150.

23. Spiegelman, J. Marvin (1992) *Reich, Jung, Regardie and Me: The Unhealed Healer*, New Falcon Publications, Arizona, 1992.

24. Spiegelman, J.M. and Vasavada, Arwind, (1987) *Hinduism and Jungian Psychology*, Falcon Press, Phoenix, 1987

25. Spiegelman, J.M. and Mansfield, V. "The Physics and Psychology of the Transference as an Interactive Field" (in press).

CHAPTER ELEVEN

ON SUPERVISION
(1995)

For me, the concept of supervision is subsumed under that of training and I draw on what Michael Fordham has said about that: namely that the task of the analyst of a trainee is to help him/her find out if he/she is meant to be an analyst and, if so, to advance them on that path. By extension, I see the supervisory task as helping the therapist or trainee to individualize his/her way of working. Central in this conception is that the training analyst or supervisor is in the service of the trainee or therapist and not bound to any institution or theory. Furthermore the supervisor is in no way a "boss" or even a watch-dog. The word "control," used for the supervised condition of those in the final stages of training, can be misunderstood in this fashion, but I think it refers to the German use of that term, which is merely that of a border passport and customs inspector. So there is no hierarchy indicated. Implied in all this, but not stated, is that both pupil and teacher, trainee and supervisor, share the fundamental commitment to serve the patient first of all and to try to do no harm. Secondly, as in passport inspection, one helps to establish the identity of the people "coming through."

In order to accomplish the foregoing, I use as a model my own way of working. That is to say, in order to help the trainee find the Self in his/her work, I follow the Self in my own efforts. In my experience, the Self manifests not only as an inner event (e.g., the Rainmaker model, as I have termed it in various papers), but also in the relationship itself (the Alchemical model). I am, therefore, open at the beginning of each session the way that Bion described in his analytic work, "without memory, desire, or knowledge," and generally let the trainee and the mutual process between us decide what and where to go.

Usually, this results in the trainee bringing in dreams or reactions of his/her patient and we, in turn, examine this material for understanding the dynamics and the person's process. In time, however, the focus turns to the transference relationship between the therapist and patient and how this effects the parties. Since about half of my own analytic practice is made up of therapists, I often work with them on their own counter-transference issues as well. A rough contrast between the work with patient-therapists and that of supervision is that in the latter situation I tend to defer the personal material to the trainees personal analysis and deal largely with the archetypal aspect. Ultimately, both therapy and supervision result in a kind of "mutual process," as I have called it, or "interactive field," in which the very archetypes evoked in the supervised relationship now manifest in the situation between my trainee or therapist-patient and myself.

I think this is a good thing, since it results in further understanding and real transformation between us, leading to changes in my supervisee's patient as well, sometimes as a result of further interpretation, and sometimes even synchronistically. We have all noted that on occasion the patient dreams about the psyche of the therapist with some accuracy. I have found that sometimes even the supervisor gets into the drama and that changes in either of the two relationships effects the other one.

I shall give some examples of this kind of effect in several different supervisory situations, which demonstrate the variety of ways in which this can happen. The first of these is with a Freudian analyst who is also a specialist in medical intestinal difficulties and sees patients in both modalities. The second is with a Japanese physician who specializes in psychosomatic problems. The third is a Catholic priest who is also a trained psychotherapist and sees patients in both spiritual counseling and in therapy. Finally, I will make mention of a person who was in Jungian training at the time.

I select mostly examples of those who are not connected with our training program or Institute since I am aware that even our discussion of these issues or cases can have an unknown effect on the analysand or supervisee. Even though I am not opposed to such presentation, I think it is wiser to forego such examples and avoid possible negative consequences. I shall leave for the end the question of whether this expansion of the field can be understood or dealt with us as a collective body.

I mentioned a core concept of my work, namely the "interactive field." I have written about the transference as a field for a number of years, initially referring to the condition as a "mutual process" and, in recent years, with the addition of somatic unconscious processes as well as those from the psychic unconscious, I use the "field" idea, originally used by von Franz to characterize the collective unconscious, similarly to the way that Nathan Schwartz-Salant understands it. We both find Jung's distinction between the psychic and the somatic unconscious useful in this regard. Schwartz-Salant also conceives of the transference as an alchemical field and finds the presence of an "alchemical couple" as a "third" factor in the room as the central place of work. I have experienced this on occasion, but usually find that the work centers on the "third", namely the archetype manifested, and that this mercurial process of incarnation of the alchemical couple, as parent-child teacher-pupil, etc., happens between the analytic partners themselves. Mercurius divides himself and his opposites between them (us) and is a "third" around and in them (us), bouncing about, often resulting in wholeness, and this is where the transformations are particularly effective. Such events also occur in supervision, as I now describe.

The first example, as I mentioned earlier, comes from a man for whom I have been a consultant during the last five years. He is a physician specializing in intestinal problems but is also a trained Freudian psychoanalyst and carries on a partial practice in the latter modality as well. We had been acquaintances and friends for some years and sometimes, naturally, talked about Freudian and Jungian approaches to therapy. Some years ago, he asked me to consult with him about some cases that he was seeing that were giving him difficulty and I gladly assented. One of these is a middle-aged woman attorney who has suffered from debilitating depression and physical and emotional hyper-sensitivity to such an extent that she has been periodically hospitalized and for a number of years has been essentially confined to her apartment. She comes out of her isolation only to see her analyst, twice a week. Fortunately, after early hospitalizations, she managed to purchase disability insurance which takes care of her and her therapy quite well. She has been in treatment for six years and has gradually improved over this time. My supervisee consulted me about her since all his work with reductive analysis, over years, accomplished very little. The woman is very intelligent, sensitive, and acutely aware of any behavior or attitude on the therapist's part which she experiences as a withdrawal of interest or connection. He is by temperament a warm and connecting man as well as a natural healer. He has found that he is endlessly challenged to be totally honest with her, since she is uncannily aware of any deviation in this regard. He consults with me about her on an irregular basis, about four times a year and our discussions always gradually lead to our experiencing her presence, imaginally, "in the room." As this happens, we both feel a heightened sense of life-and-death drama, the profound uncertainties and ambiguities of life and our joint desire to be as straight and honest about and with this person as possible, as if we are participating in a kind of trial in which divinity is present. That is not quite right; I experience the divinity in the room while my friend/supervisee experiences the profound dilemmas in an existential way.

Our most recent session found us discussing what had transpired since last time when we both suddenly had an image of this woman, truly borderline in every way, hanging on to her therapist by her fingernails. It was clear that all the reductive work on dependency, parent-child relations, etc. was long since accomplished and this was that issue raised—or lowered—to another level. I then was aware of a drop in my own psyche, as if I were just in the same condition, dealing with my anima or myself or a loved one, either the one hanging on or the one supporting. Actually, I experienced both conditions sequentially. My supervisee experienced the same thing. At that moment, this man and I were together in a psychosomatic field of vulnerability and sensitivity, knowing the precariousness of existence, for the patient and for ourselves. I was deeply moved by this moment, particularly since my supervisee is an unusually successful and highly thought of doctor, happily married and with teen-age children doing well, so I had never thought of him as being able to connect with such fragility from the inside, although his compassion surely made him understand it from without.

As I felt this condition and mentioned it to him, he nodded and we both broke into tears. We both understood, at that moment, the importance of what this woman was carrying and the centrality for existence itself, and for us as healers, to stay connected with her agony, not only as therapists, but as human beings and fellow-sufferers, each in our own way. After this session, as happens after almost all of our consultations, the patient showed significant improvement. It is my understanding that our supervisory work is a continuation of the field of the therapy and that as we carry that archetypal condition in its increasing profundity, the patient is relieved of being alone in that state and that the unconscious manifests itself in a replicated duality, resulting in a threesome composed of two dyads—patient and therapist, therapist and supervisor, three people. Finally, our own conscious connection with the archetype of human vulnerability and dependency upon the Self, constitutes a fourth and, thereby, the wholeness which heals.

The second example is that of a Japanese physician who is a specialist in psychosomatics. She and her husband, a psychiatrist, both worked with me for about a year more than ten years ago, some time after they had both completed an analysis in Japan. Her own work continued with me for another year or so, via correspondence, when they returned to their country. Then, some three or four years ago, she began to telephone me to consult about her cases and also her own dreams. This telephone work has continued on a weekly basis ever since. The focus on her patients' symptoms has often resulted in a comparable somatic experience of my supervisee and myself, in a field which, obviously, is not limited to the space in a therapy room. We sometimes experience together what I refer to as the "subtle body," a combination of somatic and psychic unconscious along with a conscious realization of this. I have written about this subtle body experience in three of my last papers and think that it is this area of experience that the quantum aspect of matter and the psyche coalesce in the analytic work, as "psychoid." Such experiences are healing for both parties and can generally be brought back to the patient in some constructive way. Dreams are often very helpful in this, presenting imagery upon which both my supervisee and I can focus. The joint subtle-body experience, however, is autonomous and happens of itself, can not be "manufactured."

Most recently, my supervisee found herself drained of energy and enthusiasm in her work. She, like many of her hard-laboring countrymen, is normally an indefatigable worker and this condition of depletion was particularly distressing. We tried hard to understand this condition, but it was only when I, myself, found that I was drained and depleted that she began to recover. This sort of thing happens frequently in both analysis and supervision, but usually I recover when I see that the field condition is effecting both parties. In this situation, however, I could not do so and it required her healing efforts, back with me, for me to regain equilibrium. This was useful for both of us and further reduced the dependency that my supervisee had been experiencing.

The third example is that of a Roman Catholic priest I worked with analytically, beginning twenty years ago. Our work came to a temporary end after about two years, and he then began and completed his own training as a therapist, functioning in both capacities. He then resumed analytic work for three or so years. Some time after termination, we became friends and colleagues in various ways. Over the years he has returned for consultation on his own cases or aspects of his development. More recently, our consultation work has been largely via the telephone and is also on a weekly basis. We proceed in the usual way, although, since we are friends, there is a lot more informality and play in our discussions and I am just as likely to bring in some of my own personal reactions and material, in a way which goes beyond my spontaneous responsiveness in other situations. Here, too, a powerful image which often comes in to help us is that we are in the presence of Jesus or God-the Father or, on occasion, the Madonna, in which we experience the psychic unconscious readily and, on occasion, the subtle body, as well. Such experiences occur only after we have worked hard on whatever it is about his patient or their or our interaction which is occupying us. It is then, usually, as a result of our joint active imagination with that figure, that resolution of dilemmas occurs.

Finally, I shall briefly mention tho work with a person who was in Jungian training at the time and I was the supervisor. This trainee, a woman, had worked for some years with a woman patient who suffered from a most sadistic kind of animus figure called "Doctor D." This inner figure, brilliant and cruel, could utterly undermine her, despite all efforts. Active imagination was impossible for the patient and very difficult, almost impossible, for my supervisee also. Over months, the trainee and I would become increasingly embedded in an alchemical *coniunctio* which was, in turn, resting on the female aspect of the Self and provided subtle body connections which were convincing in their psychic reality. This helped produce increasing solidity and confidence in my supervisee and she was able, thereby, to undertake joint active imagination, during the sessions, with her patient in relation to the latter's destructive animus. This had increasingly positive effect until the dark side of the feminine Self also appeared, and now the quaternio was present, both in my supervisee's work with her patient and the former's work with me. This process provided a formidable vehicle for the transformation of both the negative judge in the supervisee and the dark animus of the patient, both provided by and resulting in greater totality of the feminine Self in both parties, as well as in me.

Now, what does this experience of the transference field in the supervisory relationship suggest? I think that at the deeper levels of the analytic work that the transference takes on this character and what takes place is nothing less than the synchronistic, psychoid union both within the psyches of the participants and that of the supervisory pair. I have wondered, over the last years, whether this is also possible in more than the pair relationship. Or is it, as a minister-analysand of mine once said, Jesus can manifest when two or three are gathered in his name, but this is the maximum number?

Over the years, I have had some experience in groups where this can occur, particularly when there is focus on this possibility through an initial meditation, but usually such a field seems to dissolve too easily. The requirement for a field, as it is when working with transference, is for the parties to be focusing together on the unconscious and how it manifests at the moment, something not usually considered in any kind of group situation. Nonetheless, some small groups may be able to work in this fashion and this might make it possible to have archetypally-oriented group process, which is rather different from customary group therapy. It is in this area, perhaps, where advance in archetypal theory can occur.

CHAPTER TWELVE

On the Physics and Psychology of the Transference as an Interactive Field (1996) (with V. Mansfield)

To clarify these creative possibilities, we would have to have a group of physicists who are willing to take on a deep Jungian analysis—not because we want to rule them or influence them—simply that they learn. And then we would have to have a few Jungian analysts who would take the trouble to study physics. I think that's what first would have to be done, so that both knew really deeply the other subject.
— M.L. von Franz (von Franz 1992, p. 162)

INTRODUCTION

Unfortunately, we have not fully embodied the ideal suggested by von Franz in the opening quotation. Nevertheless, we have moved in the direction she proposes. Our discussion of the therapeutic interaction results from the shared attempt of a senior Jungian analyst (JMS) and a physicist (VM) to understand the reciprocal action between analyst and analysand engaged in what we describe below as "mutual process," and "interactive field." Both the observed psychological phenomenology and the physics of fields inspire our understanding. Although our suggestions for evolving the therapeutic interaction toward mutual process are natural outgrowths of classical Jungian theory and practice, the interaction we describe involves richer possibilities than are usually reported about the therapeutic encounter.

As we will show, the attention to awakened bodily reactions and subtle body energies in both the analysand and analyst, during sessions, and the use of joint active imagination, raise fundamental questions about the relation of psyche to soma and analyst to analysand. Ideas from the physics of fields are particularly well-suited for understanding the phenomena and moving toward answers to some fundamental questions posed.

We fully appreciate the difficulty of bringing ideas from physics to bear upon the complexities embodied in the therapeutic relationship. In healing the wounds of the soul we first build an hermetic vessel, the *vas hermeticum*, out of trust, honesty, compassion, and openness. Within this vessel is expressed the connectedness of Eros—between the analyst and the analysand and between them and the larger, encompassing source of healing. Perhaps ideas from physics can increase our understanding of the therapeutic relationship without violating this inter-subjective mystery. We first discuss the notions of mutual process and interactive field by placing them in the historical evolution of the therapeutic encounter.

Four Levels of Therapy

Early in his development of psychoanalysis, Freud became acutely aware of the impact of the patient's projections upon the analyst. He attempted to elicit these projections and use them to illuminate the infantile fantasies from the unconscious, and yet mitigate their impact upon the analyst. He called this process the working through of the transference. On the analyst's side, objectivity and detachment were the bywords, with asymmetry of connection the desideratum. In his "Postscript to the Question of Lay Analysis," Freud (Freud 1927, p. 257) says:

> For it is not greatly to the advantage of patients if their physician's therapeutic interest has too marked an emotional emphasis. They are best helped if he carries out his task coolly and keeping as closely as possible to the rules.

Over the century, however, psychoanalytic circles generally recognized that the mutual impact of analyst and analysand was not only unavoidable but was useful in the healing process. This recognition produced such concepts as projective identification and the active embracing of counter-transference reactions to understand what was going on in the patient. This has been especially true in Kleinian and Object-Relations work.

It was Jung who soon realized that not only is mutual transference a critical part of the work, but that the analyst's effect on the analysand is proportional to that of the latter upon him or herself. As Jung says (Jung 1954a, p 71)

> For, twist and turn the matter as we may, the relation between doctor and patient remains a personal one within the impersonal framework of the professional treatment. By no device can the treatment be anything but the product of mutual influence, in which the whole being of the doctor as well as that of his patient plays its part... For two personalities to meet is like mixing two different substances: if there is any combination at all both are transformed.

This realization of "mutual influence" and that "both are transformed" raised the question of whether the therapeutic relation should really be asymmetrical. C. A. Meier, in a seminal paper (Meier 1959), advanced the hypothesis that the analysis became symmetrical when the analyst learned ever more about the partner, thereby advancing the "cut" of consciousness into the "analytic object." With this increasing knowledge and intimacy, it was no longer possible to assess to whom a transference content "belonged." In truth, the analyst and analysand jointly constellated a "third," and this was the collective unconscious itself, its archetypal contents transcending those of the personal mother, father, etc.

Following upon Jung's and Meier's formulations, Spiegelman, in a series of papers beginning with a contribution to Meier's *Festschrift* in 1965, has been advancing an understanding of what he came to call mutual process (Spiegelman 1965, 1980, 1991, 1995). Parallel with this development, the concept of the interactive field has been adumbrated, particularly by Schwartz-Salant (Schwartz-Salant 1988, 1992), although the original use of the field in connection with the collective unconscious was suggested by von Franz (von Franz 1980, p. 80). The mutuality of the process refers to both analyst and analysand jointly and simultaneously engaging the unconscious activated through their interaction.

The two concepts of mutual process and interactive field are not synonymous, but tend to be interrelated. As we will show, the more mutual the process, the more the interactive field manifests. Spiegelman (Spiegelman 1993, pp. 205-208), classified the degree to which mutual process occurs in four categories of increasing consciousness of mutuality in the relation to the unconscious and thus increasing expressions of the interactive field. We briefly summarize that classification here.

The first category is that of traditional analyst, the type von Franz described (when she supervised JMS) as "womb analysis." In this situation, the analysis is like a cave or womb, a vessel in which the analysand can safely explore and relate to the unconscious, while the analyst provides a protective and supportive environment for it. Much classical psychoanalysis is of this nature. A Jungian case example (by JMS, supervised by von Franz), is a doctoral student at the University of Zürich, who actually painted such a picture at the outset of his analysis. He continued to paint and draw his own process under the caring and watchful eye of the budding analyst who hardly spoke the German language in which the work was done! Nevertheless, this maternal container contributed mightily to the therapeutic effect.

Another example, in the United States, was that of a creative writer with considerable previous analysis who used the analytic hour to work, almost by himself, to associations to dreams and active imagination. The analyst's task was largely to provide comments on dreams, only occasionally remarking about what was happening in their relationship. Although the relation was essentially asymmetrical and traditional, on occasional image sustained the transference—a giant lingam of light between the two partners. In this situation, little or no mutual process occurred, yet an interactive field condition did occasionally arise.

By interactive field condition we mean the two parties are embedded in an imaginally perceived whole situation. They experience the unconscious or archetypes both "around" and "between" them, as well as "within" them—an encompassing, infusing, and mutually interactive field. This occurs when the collective unconscious is activated or, as the word is sometimes used, "constellated," in the therapeutic interaction. We do not use the term interactive field for the relation of one person with the unconscious, but reserve it for describing the interaction two or more persons simultaneously have with the collective unconscious. Fields can certainly be constellated when one is alone, e.g., active imagination or in connection with nature and numinous objects, but this requires a separate discussion.

The second category, "womb-interaction," shows more conscious attention to the relationship. This is the mode frequently experienced by those who focus upon projective identification, projection, and the interpreting of dreams, behavior, psycho dynamics, and the transference seen in the traditional sense. In short, it is the general activity engaged in by analysts of most persuasions when emphasizing transference-counter transference reactions. Examples from case studies routinely occur in the journals of the respective schools. "Womb-interaction" is probably the mode experienced frequently by those focusing upon projective identification.

The third category, that of mutual process proper, has a variety of conditions and examples, characterized by frequent and sometimes intense reference to what is happening in the analytic relationship. This can be the typical parent-child situation or other archetypal relation, like those depicted in Jung's diagram, in his *Psychology of the Transference* (Jung 1954b), in which analyst and analysand are "accompanied," by anima and animus or other archetypal figures arising from the unconscious. As we discuss below, these figures have their own relationship to both parties. Generally, in this kind of mutual process there is an active consideration and verbalization of what is happening, sometimes from moment to moment. This form of interaction sometimes develops in joint active imagination. The distinguishing feature of this type of interaction is the mutuality between the partners. The "third," as the unconscious shared between them, is constellated and the mercurial play of the opposites is simultaneously experienced in the relationship and made conscious. The alchemical model developed in Jung's (Jung 1954b) interpretation of the transference is the prototype. More recent followers have gone further by verbalizing and articulating such process with the analysand while they occur.

The fourth category includes all of the regular process conditions, sketched above, and often includes bodily experiences in the head, chest, diaphragm, etc. including subtle body energies suggesting the various *chakras* or *sephiroth*. In addition, one often experiences acausal synchronistic events in such encounters and exchanges. For example, a former priest suffered for some years from serious depression and anxiety not alleviated in a previous analysis. After many months of work and little positive results, despite interesting dreams that referred back to his initial vocation and loss of connection with the divine, JMS revealed to him a fantasy that he had during the previous few sessions. This involved the image of analyst and analysand praying together before a Dürer print in the room, of Christ Crowned with Thorns (hung between a brilliant painting of Hassidim dancing, the other of a magician with doves). The patient immediately wanted to do this concretely and both partners knelt and prayed. As they knelt there, shoulder to shoulder, JMS felt a Christ-like presence, with an arm on each of their shoulders. When he reported this to the patient, the latter responded, amazed, that he had felt this, too. JMS then had the strong impression that the analysand was much larger than himself, although they were physically about the same size. He reported this too. The analysand, having the same impression, knelt lower, feeling he was inflated, whereupon JMS exclaimed, "No! Not at all!" The analysand, after all, he went on, was truly much larger than the analyst within a Christian manifestation of the divine and it was exactly right that he acknowledge this. The analysand then wept with joy and the depression lifted. Henceforth, the analysand gradually reconnected with his inner priestly vocation, via a series of remarkable dreams. In this joint prayer experience, both mutuality and an interactive field condition occurred along with some subtle-body experiences, but this concatenation did not continue for most of the later sessions, in which asymmetry returned.

All these varieties of mutual process can change back and forth, from one category to another. There is usually a period intense "womb" work, accompanied or followed by an important realization and transformation in an interactive field-condition, and then a reversion to slow, traditional work, with dreams, fantasies, etc. leading to another striking appearance of the collective unconscious. In other words, there is the work "within," which the analysand does either at home or in the office, with the analyst as participant observer, and then they constellate an archetypal connection—an interactive field—in which the collective unconscious is now "between" the two partners, or encompassing them.

These four categories of increasing mutuality correlate to the increasing perception of the interactive field condition in the analytic encounter, but interactive fields play different roles in each category. The first type, that of the womb analysis, may also include a powerful, but unspoken, experience of the interactive field of the Mother-child archetype, in which both are embedded, even with experience of subtle-body energies, but they usually neither remark upon this fact nor work on it. It may actually be occurring in the unconscious without the parties registering it at all, until much later or never.

Indeed, this less explicit use of the field idea occurs in Jung and in traditional work with the transference. The patient's projective contents affect the analyst but he works on them quietly, by himself. Through working on his unexpressed counter-transference, the analyst helps the patient toward healing. As Meier points out, since therapy is a totalistic system, the analyst's capacity to sustain and integrate the difficult content himself induces a change in the system and thereby helps the patient. The unspoken metaphor for this comes from the frequently referred to story by Richard Wilhelm, who experienced a Rainmaker in a Chinese village who "brought rain," not by any magic or incantations, but just by meditating within the disturbed and inharmonious conditions of the village. When he managed to recover his own harmony, was in Tao, then, as he said, "Naturally, it rained." (For discussion of the Rainmaker Model, see Spiegelman 1980).

The Rainmaker model, we think, is used by Meier and often embraced by Jung. It is also close to the traditional method favored in the original psychoanalytic circles, tempered in the Jungian domain by attention to the numinous or the religious attitude toward the contents of the collective unconscious. We connect this method with the introverted condition of focusing upon an inner relationship to the unconscious. Since it is not explicitly an interaction between two persons mediated by the collective unconscious, this is not the interactive field we are stressing here.

Later psychoanalysis and those therapies functioning in extraverted countries, such as the United States, required more overt attention to the transference, so they discussed the interactions in the light of the patient's dynamics. Such a shift in focus—from an exclusively inward relationship to the unconscious to a shared relationship—is also in accord with the attitude of finding the central value in relationship itself, a view traditionally connected with women, or at least the archetypal feminine. Is this a sign of the shift in consciousness from the masculine or patriarchal values in ascendance, to those in which we equally attend to the matriarchal or feminine values? Recall the admonition, in early Christianity, that the divine, or Jesus, is present when "two or three gather in My name." A Protestant minister once said that this number of two or three was the maximum, in his experience, where Jesus might have a chance of appearing!

We suggest it is useful to add to the Rainmaker Model (always necessary in any deep analytic work) a second one we call the mutual process or alchemical model, in which we consciously and frequently address the interactions between analyst and analysand. We reserve the term of full mutual process for type four. JMS describes mutual process of types three and four as one in which he is carefully attentive during an analytic session to what is happening both "within" and "among." The goal is to stay simultaneously attuned with his "left hand" to the unconscious and with his "right hand" to "minding the store," maintaining the parenting aspect and containing boundaries for the work (Spiegelman 1988), thus using Kabbalistic imagery for this attention to the play of the opposites (Spiegelman 1995).

With such dual attention, there generally emerges the phenomenology many analysts address in various ways and understand as projection or projective identification. Many analysts have noted how the analytic work effects their energy—from the loss of energy in boredom, to depression, excitement, etc. Others, going further, use this energy experience as an indication of the projections going on (projective identification), with its causal explanatory model ("He put his rage into me…" etc.). It might be more parsimonious, as we hope to show, to consider these interactions as ever-deeper manifestations of an interactive field. What such energy is and how it plays out in the work needs to be investigated.

Before considering the nature and function of the energy exchanges going on in the work, it is worth-while to take up the issues of the imaginal and bodily expressions of the unconscious. As Schwartz-Salant has usefully pointed out (Schwartz-Salant 1989, Ch. V), Jung made early use of the related concepts of Psychic Unconscious and Somatic Unconscious (Jung 1934-1939).

Jung (Jung 1978c) articulated his "psychological standpoint" that admits the primacy of the psyche. However, as he goes to great lengths to show in "On the Nature of the Psyche," the psyche is bounded at one end of the spectrum by inscrutable matter and at the other end by a transcendental mental principle, spirit, which is equally unknowable (Jung 1978a, pp. 207-216). In analytic work, we are continuously oscillating between the archetypal realm of meaning on the one hand and the bodily sensations and responses to our work on the other hand. Each class of experience expresses the Psychic Unconscious and the Somatic Unconscious respectively, fully realizing along with Jung that there is "nothing that is directly experienced except the mind itself" (Jung 1978c, p. 327).

The Psychic Unconscious expresses itself in those images and fantasies that originate in the unconscious. The Somatic Unconscious, however, expresses itself in sensations and experiences arising from the body. These bodily or somatic symptoms are other than those occurring from normal bodily activity, but have a link to emotional conditions. Common examples are headaches, palpitations, stomach aches, etc. As we know, the emotions, via the autonomic nervous system, are central in linking psyche and soma. We believe it is useful to consider these two types of unconscious as expressions of Jung's idea of the continuum and interaction between spirit and matter, soul and body, with the descent from the ultraviolet end of the spectrum to the infrared (Jung 1978a). The ultraviolet links psyche with the spiritual aspect of the instinct (archetypal images) while the infrared links psyche with bodily expressions of instinct and matter. Image and bodily experience are thus linked together and yet separate, as we find in analytic work.

It might also be useful to consider the analytic experience of bodily energies being activated, the symptoms that occur in sessions (Spiegelman 1991), as a manifestation of the Somatic Unconscious. Experience of working with the transference in the mutual process manner results in both kinds of effects, somatic and imaginal. Schwartz-Salant (Schwart-Salant 1989) has been especially articulate in describing this kind of work, invoking the alchemical formula of Maria Prophetissa, among others, and noting that the image of the couple is frequently manifested. Whether we remain with a generalized "third" appearing in the work (the unconscious "belonging" to both parties), or differentiate this into a couple, an interactive field clearly manifests. The participants simultaneously experience the interactive field within themselves, or as between them, or as surrounding them.

Reflection suggests that the interplay of psychic and somatic is just what the work toward union and totality entails. Mind and body, image and behavior, within and among, are all aspects of the opposites that the participants engage in, as a kind of alchemical sibling pair—Mercurius, as Jung spoke of it. They also frequently experience the subtle body here. The understanding of the subtle-body as a manifestation of the somatic unconscious (as is seen by Schwart-Salant), or as a union of unconscious with consciousness (as seen by JMS), is less important than the realization that the work involves such processes. Consequently, those apparently mysterious events—often felt as telepathic by some analysts—occur when the analyst, for example, registers the headache or anxiety felt by the patient before the latter has said anything about it. As we suggest below, rather than considering these as causal telepathic phenomena, it may be better to understand them as acausal instantiations of meaning—as synchronistic.

Spiegelman (Spiegelman 1995) also calls attention to the subtle-body energies awakened in deep analytic work. They clearly connect with the kinds of experiences reported in *Kundalini* meditation, in Kabbalistic work with energies, and in the experience of the energy called "orgone" by Wilhelm Reich in the deeper body therapies. These energies are not merely the expression of normal bodily functions, but occur after significant kinds of spiritual and bodily work and in the relaxation period following them. Perhaps, as Reich had hoped, a redefinition of the concept of libido may ultimately be possible. It is less certain whether this can be a fully biological concept, as he believed, or whether it is one indirectly connected with bios and partaking of the latter when infused with psychic components.

Along with these conscious/unconscious questions, come the role of causality and acausality in these processes. Ideas of projective identification use causal explanations, whereas synchronistic experiences are acausal. Obviously both processes are at work, but at which level and in which way are not yet clear. With these questions in mind we now turn to the findings of physics, which may further our understanding of these psychological problems.

Characterizing Levels One and Two with Classical Fields

Classical Fields in Physics

In the early fifteenth century, René Descartes and others developed the mechanical model of the physical universe that consisted of impartible atoms racing around in the void. In this view, all forces were contact forces caused by particle collisions. It seemed natural to believe that, as in our normal sensory experience, objects must touch to exert force on each other. In the late seventeenth century, Isaac Newton's formulation of the gravitation interaction caused serious conceptual problems for this mechanical view of nature. Although there was no disputing the power, elegance, and accuracy of his formulation, it was nearly impossible to understand gravity as a contact force. Gravity seemed to work through a pure vacuum, a real action-at-a-distance, an idea utterly repellent to such thinkers of that era as Bishop George Berkeley and many others.

Fortunately, by the nineteenth century the notion of a field became the preferred way of understanding such interactions as gravity and electromagnetism. In this view, rather than the sun and earth gravitationally interacting through empty space, we understand that the sun generates a field, an actual modification of the space surrounding the sun. This modification of space, this field, contains energy and exerts forces on bodies like the planets or asteroids placed in it. The conceptually vexing notion of action-at-a-distance is replaced by the field—an invisible entity mediating the force between the sun and earth. The earth "senses" the field only in its immediate vicinity and responds to that. Simultaneously, the earth generates its field to which the sun responds. There is no more action-at-a-distance, but there is mutual interaction through the field. Or take an electromagnetic example. A pair of protons generate electric fields around themselves that mediate their mutual repulsion. An individual proton only responds to the electric field in its immediate vicinity.

Modern physics now considers classical fields as critically important models for understanding nature. Although the fields are not visible, they can be easily represented in visual diagrams. They are substantial, since fields carry energy and momentum and have measurable effects. Despite their invisibility, fields have become as real and substantial, with the same ontic status, as the particles they effect. In other words, classical particles and fields are equally substantial and real entities existing in space-time.

Even at this uncomplicated level, classical fields are appropriate metaphors for the action of the unconscious on consciousness. Take, for example, the gravitational field. It is invisible, pervades all space, and is always effective, even if we are not actively aware of it. Our physical presence also has an influence on the earth. Similarly, the unconscious is invisible, pervasive, and continuously influencing consciousness, even without our knowledge of the process. In turn, our conscious position effects the unconscious. As we will see, well beyond this minor application, the field concept has descriptive power in delineating the interaction of the unconscious with consciousness.

All classical fields are causal, local, and based upon the idea of independent existence. By causal, we mean that the field always interacts in a completely predictable way when the same body is placed in it in the same way. Identical initial conditions always give rise to the same interaction and subsequent system evolution. For example, if you repeatedly place an object with a given velocity and position in the same gravitational field, the identical orbit always results. Local means that any changes in the field or the system it characterizes must propagate at less than or equal to the speed of light. For example, if a giant cosmic hand suddenly plucked the sun from the sky, the gravitational field at the earth's location would not reflect this change for approximately eight minutes—the time it takes for light to travel from the sun to the earth. All classical physics is based on the assumption that the interacting particles and fields are independently existent, that is they have an autonomy, separateness, or an inherent existence that is fundamentally free from interactions and conditions. For example, we may conceptually remove a particle from the interacting field and consider the particle or the field independently. In other words, the *relations* are much less real or fundamental than the independent existence or *autonomy* of classical objects.

Conditions for Classical Field-Like Phenomena in Levels 1 & 2

In Jungian analysis there is usually an initial period of reductive analysis, in which present problems or psycho dynamics are reduced to past psychological experience. Although all four levels of therapy discussed above may employ reductive analysis, our emphasis here is its use in levels one and two. For a too simple example: one's anger toward those in authority is caused by father's harsh treatment in childhood. The beginning way of dealing with this problem is often a reductive delineation, an articulation of the anger and its causes. Although this analysis makes reference to the unconscious, at this stage the analysis is largely causal—a particular complex is understood to invariably cause a certain emotional reaction.

To clarify this point refer to Figure 1, which is a slight generalization of the famous four-fold diagram Jung developed in his essay "The Psychology of the Transference." The major difference between our diagram and Jung's is that we have removed gender references. To continue our simplistic example: the analyst explores the analysand's relationship with his father. This two-way conscious interaction is represented by the double-headed arrow (a). The questioning activates the analysand's personal unconscious and he is over-

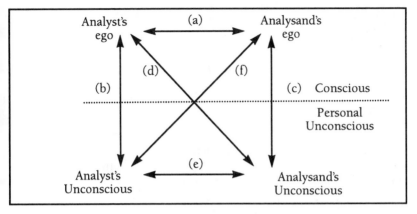

Figure 1

taken by feelings of anger and shame—represented by the double-headed arrow (c).The analysand unconsciously projects aspects of the father complex on the analyst—double-headed arrow (d). The analyst becomes aware of intuitions about the analysand by accessing his unconscious—arrow (b). The analyst may also project something like ungrateful son on the analysand—arrow (f). Finally, there may be some unconscious *participation mystique* between analyst and patient indicated by (e).

Of course, all these interactions are extremely difficult to disentangle in practice, since as Jung pointed out they are simultaneously present. Nevertheless, there are times when it is clear the interaction is dominated by one or a few of these modes. For our present purposes we have stressed the causal nature of the interaction. For example, the analyst questioning the analysand, arrow (a), causes the analysand to ponder his relationship with his father, which in turn causes the analysand to contact his father complex, arrow (c), which in turn causes the analysand's anger, projection on the analyst, and so on.

A more subtle underlying assumption here than causality is that the analyst, analysand, and the complexes are all relatively autonomous or independently existent. The analyst has a personality distinct and independent from that of the analysand. The analysand's ego can be considered independently from his complexes, from the analyst, and so forth. Of course, the assumption of separateness or independent existence in this reductive-causal method is thrown into question if there is a significant *participation mystique* interaction, arrow (e).

Although our example is necessarily too simple, it is well known that such reductive analysis can be extremely effective and is often taken up again at even advanced stages of the individuation process. Nevertheless, its primary locus of operation is the personal unconscious, although there is never an absolutely clear demarcation between purely personal material and more archetypal contents.

Classical Field-Like Phenomena in Levels 1 & 2

Let us continue the example of the father complex and first focus on the bodily phenomenology of the interactions. Soon after the analyst begins questioning the analysand about his relationship to his father the analyst notices the analysand's face flushing or twitching. The analyst may bring this fact to the analysand's attention. Although this "mirroring" is done on the conscious level along arrow (a), it serves in part to connect the analysand to his inner world along arrow (c). A more unconscious example of mirroring can occur along the following lines. The analyst senses tension between his own shoulder blades and is reasonably sure, because of is familiarity with his own unconscious and awareness of how this interaction is affecting him along arrow (b), that it is not merely his own complexes being activated. Let us assume that this awareness of tension came through some combination of unconscious channels (d) and (e). The analyst then tells the analysand about the tension he feels between his shoulder blades. In our idea example, the analysand realizes that he experiences this same tension when he gets into some power struggle with an authority. The analysand thereby increases his awareness of the functioning of channels (c) and (d). It may also turn out that the analyst then becomes aware of how he is projecting his disappointments and frustrations about his own son on the analysand—his reactions were not so pure after all. Then in the spirit of mutual process, the analyst may openly share this information with the analysand. Thus their mutual understanding of each other and themselves deepens.

Although the example is contrived, we hope it suggests how reductive analysis emphasizes consciousness, the personal unconscious, and how they causally affect both parties. Consistent with the needs of the analysand, the analyst may share his inner responses, limitations, and embarrassments, whether they are bodily symptoms or feelings. This is done even if such admissions are at the expense of the usual idea of the analyst as all-knowing healer—a projection of no lasting value. Naturally, such self-disclosure by the analyst is not a routine matter. What is usefully disclosed in analyst-analyst interactions are the experiences of the analyst in relation to the patient, which can then be of use to the latter, at least as indicating impact (See Spiegelman 1988, 1991, 1993).

Many persons working in depth psychology use the term, "field," in a variety of ways to characterize the powerful interactions between the analyst and analysand. However, there is little agreement on what, if anything, the term actually means. Nevertheless, there does seem to be a widely current intuition that some notion of field genuinely characterizes this type of interaction. We conjecture that when persons powerfully interact in the therapeutic mode as sketched above, that they then become aware of the unconscious acting like a classical field—invisible, pervasive, containing, causal and mutually effective. Naturally, since the unconscious transcends the categories of space and time, it is not sitting out in space like the gravitational field of the earth waiting for the perceptive analyst to sense it. It may be closer to say that we are constellating, instantiating, or concretizing the unconscious and it is experienced as a classical field. On the other hand, one could easily argue that the field is merely a convenient way of symbolizing powerful therapeutic interactions and that we should not literalize this experience by postulating a mediating physical field. At this stage, this is a viable argument. We return to this important point toward the end of the paper.

Next we move on to discuss even more dramatic and controversial suggestions about the therapeutic interaction. This type of interaction requires that we employ some ideas from quantum fields which we now briefly sketch.

Characterizing Mutual Process with Quantum Fields

Quantum Fields in Physics

The advent of quantum mechanics in the late 1920's not only revolutionized physics, but it greatly expanded our notion of fields. Now we understand quantum fields as not existing physically in space-time the way a classical gravitational or electromagnetic field does. Instead, quantum fields are potentials for manifestation in space-time, which are not directly measurable. Such non spatial and non temporal quantum fields provide us with probabilities for particles manifesting in space-time. Although quantum fields share many mathematical properties with classical fields, they are of a much more abstract order of being, especially because, unlike classical fields, they are neither in space-time nor directly measurable.

Probability occurs in quantum mechanics at a new and fundamental level, which many, such as Einstein, find deeply disturbing. There had long been probabilistic theories in physics before the advent of quantum mechanics. For example, in the classical analysis of an ideal gas, one of the early successes of thermodynamics, we concentrate upon the probability distribution for different particle velocities. It is not that the individual gas particles do not have definite positions and velocities, it is just that we do not have access to that level of detail. Rather, we only have statistical information about the distribution of velocities from which we deduce the properties of ideal gases. Here probability is an expression of our ignorance of the details.

In contrast, in quantum mechanics probability is introduced at a much more fundamental level. The quantum particles simply do not have definite positions and velocities and probability statements are all that we can make. It is not that we are ignorant of the details, but that there are no details. At this level, nature is inherently indeterminate and probability is an expression of its true indeterminate being. In other words, *quantum probability expresses the aontic indeterminacy of physical systems, not our ignorance of the fine details.*

Because of this fundamental indeterminacy, nature is acausal—there is no well-defined cause or causes for a particular event. For example, there is no particular cause for the decay of given radioactive nuclei. Although nature clearly reveals enormously varied and rich structures, there are no well-defined causes for individual occurrences at the quantum level.

Without a doubt, this introduction of acausality at such a fundamental level is an enormous shift in intellectual history. According to quantum theory, the most successful theory in history, we must now abandon our servitude to strict causality, the idea that all events have some well-defined set of causes and that the same initial conditions always generate the same effects. Now we must learn to appreciate that although nature is structured and lawful, it is acausal—the same initial conditions do not always generate the same effects. There are no well-defined causes for individual quantum events. This discovery inspired Jung when he learned about it through his long friendship with Wolfgang Pauli. It provided intellectual support for the introduction of his idea of synchronicity as acausal connection through meaning of inner psychic states with outer events. Jung repeatedly stressed that the inner psychic state (for example, the famous dream of the scarab beetle) does not cause the outer material event (the beetle flying through the window) nor vice versa. He wanted to supplement the notion of causality, so familiar from ordinary thought and classical physics, with the acausal principle of synchronicity, similar to the way acausality in quantum mechanics supplements causality in classical physics.

So quantum fields are invisible, non spatial, non temporal, probabilities for acausal manifestation. They therefore share many characteristics with archetypes. For example, in his synchronicity essay Jung advises us to resist the temptation to see the archetypes as causative agents in synchronicity. He says, "The archetype represents *psychic probability*..." (Italics are Jung's; Jung 1978b, p. 515). Although the archetype provides the fundamental meaning or intellectual structure for a synchronistic event, it is not causative of either the inner or outer correlated events.

More puzzling to the classical physicist—who lives in the heart of even the best quantum physicists like an inferior function or dark brother—than the acausal nature of quantum fields is its non local nature. This property has been dramatically and convincingly revealed in the Bell Inequality experiments of the last two decades. We have previously discussed the implications of non locality in quantum mechanics for understanding synchronicity

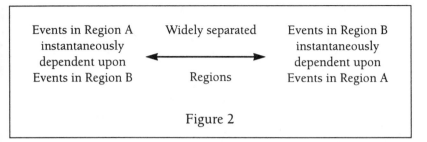

| Events in Region A instantaneously dependent upon Events in Region B | Widely separated ⟷ Regions | Events in Region B instantaneously dependent upon Events in Region A |

Figure 2

(Mansfield and Spiegelman 1989). Here it suffices to describe briefly the idea of non locality.

Non locality is the inability to localize a system in a given region of space and time. Stated positively, there are well-studied physical systems that show instantaneous interconnections or correlations among their parts—true instantaneous action-at-a-distance. For example, consider two widely separated regions, A and B, shown in Figure 2. In non local phenomena, what happens in region A instantaneously influences what occurs in region B and vice-versa. Surprisingly, *this instantaneous interaction or dependency occurs without any information or energy exchange between regions A and B.* The effect occurs without a definite cause—a truly acausal connection. For this reason alone, we cannot use non locality to develop a faster than light signaling scheme. Nevertheless, the effects are strong and do not weaken with the distance between regions A and B. This degree of interdependence between separate parts of a system has no counterpart in classical physics. Nevertheless, non locality has been clearly revealed in experiments that are independent of the present formulation of quantum mechanics. This means that *any future* theory of nature must embody this principle.

Our implicit belief in the independent existence of events in regions A and B greatly contributes to the sense of mystery in non locality. We unconsciously cling to the idea that the events in the two regions really are fundamentally separate and independent from each other. This false belief in their mutually independent existence then gives rise to the demand that we understand this interconnectedness in terms of effects propagating faster than the speed of light. Relativity physics, however, rules out such propagation. Instead, the view we have come to appreciate in the last two decades is that non local quantum fields are expressing a profound level of mutual interconnectedness and interdependence, a level impossible to understand if we cling to the old notion of independently existing objects causally interacting. In other words, classical, local fields cannot account for quantum interdependence. The assimilation of this revolutionary idea into collective consciousness will take time and without doubt have extraordinarily far-reaching consequences.

Most people who study the philosophic foundations of quantum mechanics agree that non locality is more mysterious than the dependency of system properties on the act of observation—illustrated in the famous wave-particle complementarity. They reason that in any measurement there must be some interaction with the system measured. In classical physics, because the systems are macroscopic, this interaction can be neglected. For example, when we precisely measure the Moon's distance from the Earth by timing how long a radar signal takes to be reflected from its surface, the reflected signal does not change the Moon's orbit. In contrast, quantum mechanical measurements involve energy exchanges comparable to the energy of the object measured. Because of these significant energy exchanges, measurement takes on a much more central role in quantum mechanics.

Depth psychology faces a similar "measurement" problem. In investigating unconscious contents, we inevitably transform them in the process. To expose a previously unconscious projection, for example, is to transform radically the thing known, a process central to individuation.

Let us summarize this subsection on quantum fields. They are invisible, non spatial, non temporal potentials or probabilities for manifestation. The processes governed by them are acausal in that they lack definite causes for particular events. Finally, the quantum fields are non local and thereby express the deep interconnectedness and mutual interdependence of quantum systems—a kind of interconnectedness that defies a classical characterization in terms of independently existent parts connected by faster than light signals or forces.

Conditions for Quantum Field-Like Phenomena in Levels 3 & 4

Quantum field-like phenomena in analysis evolve out of a deeper and more intense interaction than that described when we were discussing classical fields. The relationship between analyst and analysand and between the pair and the objective psyche are now more intimate, more mutual. We

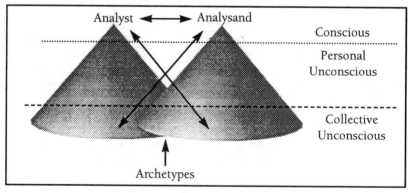

Figure 3

have moved to levels three and four discussed above. Eros is working his magic in drawing the analyst and the analysand together and toward the root of their own being. Here the growth and healing often born out of affliction and sustained by suffering becomes a voyage of discovery of the numinous archetypes of the collective unconscious. This relationship produces a diminishing of the sense of separateness and independence between the analyst and analysand. Through the therapeutic process they are now connected to the objective psyche. Now, rather than causal interactions there are, as we discuss below, acausal expressions of meaning. Simultaneously, there are expressions of the somatic unconscious and a variety of subtle-body experiences.

Figure 3 tries to embody these ideas by modifying our Figure 1. Here, two interpenetrating cones show that the conscious aspect of an individual, the ego-persona, rests on a much larger base of the personal and collective unconscious. The cone structure shows that consciousness is always influenced by and influencing the unconscious. The horizontal double-headed arrow depicts the conscious interaction. The diagonal double-headed arrows depict the transference, counter-transference, and projective identification discussed above. In Figure 3, the unconscious of the analyst is in direct contact with the unconscious of the analysand (*participation mystique*), because the two cones overlap both in the personal and collective unconscious. (Obviously, the clean demarcation between the layers of the psyche is a diagrammatic illusion, since there is no clear boundary between, for example, the personal and collective unconscious). What is perhaps most significant in the figure is the explicit reference to the infusion of archetypes into the relationship. In other words, when the therapeutic relationship becomes sufficiently deep, when we are profoundly and mutually immersed in the field, then we have prepared the conditions for direct mutual influence by the gods.

Quantum Field-Like Phenomena in Mutual Process

Here we attempt to describe some of the mutual process phenomenology in levels three and four by employing ideas from quantum field theory. Just as in physics, we are here faced with genuine complementarity, but in the psychological case between consciousness and the unconscious. If we wish to participate fully in the field, our sense of separate identity, along with its clearly focused ego consciousness, must greatly diminish. If we operate solely rationally, then the field experience fades. To be fully in the field requires an openness to fantasy, feelings, intuitions, sensations, and all the products of the psyche that are blinded by the effulgence of rational consciousness. When attending to the unconscious or affected by it, we frequently experience this complementarity, this tension, between rationally understanding the process and immersing ourselves in it.

When we feel we are truly "in the relational field," one that touches both the psychic unconscious and the somatic unconscious, with the latter definitely activated, we note that the interaction has dropped to a deeper level, that there is a qualitative shift to a more intimate connection. Often, the first manifestation of this arousal of the somatic unconscious is a definite and characteristic tingling in the palms of both hands. This is sometimes felt by the analyst and by the analysand at the same time. Often, this stage is preceded by the analyst experiencing physical symptoms such as stomach ache, headache, chest arousal, etc. When he or she notes this and asks the analysand what is happening in the latter's psyche, they frequently respond that something similar has happened or is happening. When the two are experiencing synchronization of phenomena, the mobilization of mutual process, in interaction with the collective unconscious, has taken place and the subtle body is aroused (see previous discussion). We surmise that the field has been present all along, but it is this attention or activation which has signaled its living presence.

Is the effect more than psychic? Are we hallucinating or inducing hypnotic suggestion, where the analysand is merely pleasing the analyst? We think not, since at least some of these field experiences are studied by other analysts (Schwartz-Salant 1989). Our considered opinion is that the effect has a physiological correlate and that the psyche is responding to something physical, an expression of the somatic unconscious in consciousness. We now believe that tingling hands are one reliable indicator of the presence of the field. Does this imply that the hands, richly supplied with nerve endings, are actually sensing in some mysterious way a field like those studied in physics? We cannot say for certain, however it is tempting to think this way.

Another possibility which we favor is that the subtle body, the psyche functioning through its material substrate of organized energy patterns, is the organ of perception of the field. Just as the psyche functioning through symbolic intuition is the organ of perception of the archetypes, it may be that the subtle body, the psyche conjoined with its physical-energic base, is the organ of perception of the field. This is another way of saying, as we did in the introduction, that the psychic and somatic unconscious are activated or constellated.

Beside the tingling in the palms of the hands, there is often a mutual reflecting or mirroring of somatic symptoms. In addition, a genuine archetypal presence is often experienced. The archetype seems to be present as a real third in the therapeutic relationship. The experience of the archetypal presence, the third, comes in two distinct but related ways: symbolically and through what we believe is the subtle body.

To expand on the symbolic mode, let us continue our simple example from the previous section. At this level of the therapeutic interaction it now feels like the archetypal father is present with the analyst and the analysand—actually attendant in the consulting room. God the father stands alongside or within the image of the personal father. Under the best of conditions, this becomes a numinous epiphany, a revelation of the archetype in the healing process. Now authentic healing takes place. We are again reminded of the saying in the New Testament, "When two or three of you are gathered in My name, I will be present." The self seems to be presiding over the process through the archetype. The field vibrates with power, emotion, and meaning.

Now there are more than intuitions that an archetype is present as the guiding third, as the presiding deity. Joint active imagination shows its presence more directly. When conditions seem appropriate, both analyst and analysand can elect the option of closing their eyes, turning inward, and engaging in active imagination. After a period of silence, which is broken by whichever person who cares to, they report their fantasies and inner dialogues. Then it become clear that the archetype so palpably present is simultaneously infusing both their fantasies and inner dialogues with meaning—a meaning that deeply connects them through the archetype. There can be genuine synchronicities between the eruptions of the psyche in both parties. The images are often different, yet the archetype simultaneously infusing the analyst's images with meaning provides an acausal bridge to the analysand's images. It appears that joint active imagination is separately going on in two individuals, but when the parties report the imagery they find, they are being simultaneously and acausally guided by an archetypal presence. Even mutual active imagination can take place simultaneously, with that third, archetypal factor.

The more physiological experience of the archetypal presence—the perception through the subtle body—may begin with tingling in the palms. It is often followed by energy perceptions in other parts of the body, especially in the various *chakra* regions discussed in *Kundalini Yoga*. Often the experience will be simultaneous for both parties. Sometimes it is reported by one and then later experienced by the other. No doubt, there is always the possibility of suggestion; however, we believe that the phenomena go beyond suggestion.

That both the somatic unconscious and the psychic unconscious are activated seems clear. How this becomes manifest in the therapeutic relationship depends upon the participating parties. Schwartz-Salant, for example (Schwartz-Salant 1989), uses the image of the couple as present in the relationship. This is drawn from the alchemical royal brother/sister pair and serves as the valued fourth which resolves the dilemma of the third versus the fourth in the famous Axiom of Maria Prophetissa. Schwartz-Salant also points out that this presence of the image of four helps to avoid the dangerous and potentially destructive effects of acting out the immensely powerful archetypal forces activated.

JMS's experiences, in harmony with those of Meier and others, confirms those reported by Schwartz-Salant. It seems that the "third," as the archetypes of the collective unconscious, is activated and, since most archetypes are relational (e.g., parent implies child, wise man implies pupil, king implies queen, aggression and sexuality imply a partner), these usually manifest initially as a polarity in the relationship. The analysand experiences the analyst as magician, for example, and themselves as apprentice or victim. The opposites are strongly constellated but, with the analyst's consciousness of this opposition, it is possible that both parties can arrive at a condition transcending this opposition. These opposites often bounce back and forth, so to speak, between the partners, until each of them experiences both sides within himself/herself. This is the desired equality and mutuality JMS has been trying to understand as far back as 1965 (Spiegelman 1965). Equality derives from being equal before God, he noted then, despite obvious inequality in every other way. We achieve this deep equality in the analytic work when both partners find the opposites within themselves and find the Self within and between them as the mediating condition. This gives an experience of both the "God within" and "God among" and is usually accompanied by interactive field phenomena.

We gave one example of this condition earlier, when JMS described his experience with the former priest. Another is one had by VM and JMS when they were planning this paper. They were seated under a tree in the latter's backyard discussing a father-son and brother-brother constellation that had happened between them, following a presentation of a dream by VM.

As they discussed fathering and being a son in each of their experiences with their own fathers and sons, the subtle-body experience of each of them grew in intensity. Besides this, VM began to experience the distinctive energy of the *Kundalini*, rising and descending within him. Then he heard a rustling in the tree above them and spotted what looked like a dove (it might have been another bird) and called JMS's attention to it. This was immediately thrilling to both and, naturally, recalled the picture in the *Rosarium Philosophorum*, where the king and queen join hands while a dove, a symbol of the holy spirit, is connecting with them from above. The energy released, along with the father and son images between and among them, provided a strong sense of bonding and brotherhood, as well as some healing of wounds that each of them had experienced elsewhere in the father/son connection. The spirit, as father and son to them both, was the uniting factor.

Incidentally, Jung notes that the Visio Arislei suggests that unification of male with male is not productive. It seems to us, and especially to JMS in many of his mutual process projects with others, that this is too pessimistic and such unions, in brotherhood, are very possible. This male/male connection has produced several "children" thus far, in the form of physics/depth psychology articles, as well as co-authored books on Jungian psychology and various religions.

Let us now employ ideas from quantum fields to try and characterize this interaction more fully. (In what follows, we use the modifiers "classical" and "quantum" when it is necessary to distinguish between the two types of fields, otherwise our remarks apply to both types). When using the idea of a field, we are acknowledging that the unconscious or the archetypal presence is not a visible entity localizable in a particular part of space. Rather, like a classical field, the invisible presence seems more pervasive of space. However, deeper reflection argues for the idea that the experience is actually of a principle that transcends our notion of space-time and that therefore it is more like a quantum mechanical field in this sense.

The meaningful correlations of the images produced in the joint active imagination and the simultaneity of subtle body sensations argues for understanding the experience as an acausal expression of meaning—more like synchronicity than a causal influence of the analyst upon the analysand or vice-versa. If we follow Jung and understand that "the archetype represents *psychic probability*," then we see that a quantum field description of the relational interaction mediated by an archetype is more appropriate. Because the manifestation of meaning in the field is acausal, many different images in the joint active imagination could incarnate the archetypal meaning. The critical thing is the archetype incarnating simultaneously in both the analyst and analysand, not what particular images carry it. Similarly, quantum fields describe probability distributions for a range of possible manifestations, all of which, despite their diversity, are expressions of the same field. In physics, the diverse expressions of the quantum field certainly have a pattern and order and they obey fundamental laws like conservation of mass-energy and momentum. Similarly, in joint active imagination, the manifestations of, say, the father archetype are diverse but easily distinguished in most cases from the archetypal expressions of the anima, although both may be present. They also obey certain structural laws of the psyche, such as what are the dominant psychological functions of the individuals involved. While active imagination is a significant exploratory tool in the mutual process exchange, it is far from the only one. *Joint active imagination gives us imaginal and symbolic access to the field while the subtle body gives us sensory access to the field.* Perhaps we can say that the two organs of perception for the interactive field are symbolic imagination and the subtle body.

One of the deep mysteries in this acausal field experience is the awareness that the presiding archetype is simultaneously and meaningfully structuring the individual psyches of both the analyst and the analysand. The temptation is to view this as some form of causal thought transference, to see the process as an expression of a causal field. However, the psychological experience is more like an acausal expression of meaning. The images are not the same or even necessarily of a similar type (for example, both of animals or mythological heroes), however the archetype organizing and infusing them in both parties is the same. In this way, we have much more an expression of acausal meaning, an instantiating of the archetype in both parties, without a causal interaction either between the analyst and analysand or between the archetype and the therapeutic partners. Because of our deep, and often unconscious, commitment to causality, accepting the reality of an acausal connection is difficult for us. This is true whether we are psychologists or physicists.

The quantum field seems like an appropriate explanatory vehicle because of its non local nature, because it implied a deep acausal interconnectedness, a profound and mutual interdependency between apparently distinct parts of a system. *Although the analysand and analysand surely have (at the level of the upper parts of the cones in the figure) a distinguishable and separable existence, at a deeper level (where the cones interpenetrate) they are both expressions of the same objective psyche.* Relationally there is a deep interdependency since there is no being an analyst without having an analysand and vice-versa. Substantially there is deep interconnection because ultimately we are all expressions of the same objective psyche. The non locality of quantum fields trenchantly expresses all this, reminding us repeatedly, both theoretically and experimentally, of the profound acausal interconnectedness of the universe, which depends neither upon distance nor upon the transmission of forces or information at speeds greater than that of light. From the psychological side, without the light of consciousness the interdependency in the *participation mystique* may be negative. Schwartz-Salant (Schwartz-Salant 1989) and others note this by "fusion states." However, if we can bring consciousness into it then we have the true root of our healing, the balm of Gilead.

Finally, we may consider that the four phases of mutual process can be seen as similar to the development, in history, of the physics and psychology of causality (Descartes and Freud), the initial realization of causal fields (Newton and Klein/Object Relations), the relativized field (Einstein and Jung), followed by the quantum field in both disciplines. We stress that this, of course, has nothing to do with better or worse, but is merely descriptive of different levels of reality, which often operate simultaneously.

CONCLUSIONS

We are fully aware that our efforts at discussing the relational field raise at least as many questions as they answer. Perhaps the first question that comes to mind is about the ontic status of the field. Is it a real, measurable field of the type studied in physics or is it merely a fitting and powerful symbolic characterization of a variety of phenomena experienced in deep mutual process? Schwartz-Salant prefers to characterize this as the imaginal, and although this is certainly true and we are as adamant about psychic reality as any other Jungian, the concept of matter and the somatic unconscious, as well as the experience of the subtle body, suggests something more encompassing. To help answer this question, we are investigating the possibility of making electrical skin resistance measurements (galvanic skin response) in the hands of both the analyst and the analysand when in this condition. Although we favor the possibility of finding physiological and material correlates for these experiences, von Franz (von Franz 1992, pp. 2-4) thinks that galvanic skin responses are insufficient as indicators for such complexes. We cannot at this stage definitely evaluate the ontic status of the field. We hope that by raising these issues some useful discussion and clarification can result. If, in the fact, the field turns out to be physical as well as mental, then we must address a whole host of problems surrounding the relation between psyche and matter. This is an exciting prospect for a deeper connection between physics and depth psychology, just as Jung and Pauli desired.

There are also practical problems. For example, for what type of analysts and analysands is mutual process appropriate and desirable? If it is desirable, at what stage in therapy do we employ it or, more likely, does it occur of itself? How do such individual differences such as the dominant psychological type affect the phenomena? If mutual process is as truly mutual as we believe it should and could be, then it challenges some of our most precious beliefs about the appropriate relation between analyst and analysand.

SUMMARY

An analyst and physicist combine their disciplines in studying the transference as an interactive field. Through a description of the history and evolution of the therapeutic relationship as one moving from asymmetry to symmetry, from reductive causal interaction to acausal, synchronistic expression of meaning, we describe four levels of interaction.

To unpack the notion of interactive field we describe the physics of local, causal, classical fields and directly connect them to the therapeutic encounter of the first two levels. The second two levels require discussion of non local, acausal, quantum fields. In this connection, the subtle body and joint active imagination provide a physiological and symbolic experience of the interactive field.

Fundamental questions and challenges arise from this study regarding the relationship between analyst and analysand and psyche and soma. This continues and deepens the hoped-for interplay between physics and depth psychology espoused by Jung, Pauli, Meier and von Franz.

REFERENCES

1. von Franz, Marie-Louise (1980). *On Divination and Synchronicity*. Toronto, Inner City Books.

2. von Franz, Marie-Louise (1992). *Psyche and Matter*. Boston and London, Shambhala.

3. Freud, S. (1927). "Postscript to the Question of Lay Analysis," Std. Edn. 20

4. Jung, C.G. (1934-1939). "Psychological Analysis of Nietzsche's Zarathustra," Seminar notes, edited by Mary Foote. Privately printed by C.G. Jung Institute, Zürich.

5. Jung, C.G. (1954a). "Problems of Modern Psychotherapy," *Coll. Wks*, 16.

6. Jung, C.G. (1954b). "Psychology of the Transference," *Coll. Wks*, 16.

7. Jung, C.G. (1978a). "On the Nature of the Psyche," *Coll. Wks*, 8

8. Jung, C.G. (1978b). "Synchronicity: An Acausal Connecting Principle," *Coll. Wks*, 8.

9. Jung, C.G. (1978c). "Spirit and Life," *Coll. Wks*, 8.

10. Mansfield, V. and Spiegelman, J. M. (1989). "Quantum Mechanics and Jungian Psychology," *Journal of Analytical Psychology*, 34, 1

11. Meier, C.A. (1959). "Projection, Transference and the Subject-Object Relation," *Journal of Analytical Psychology*. 4, 1.

12. Schwartz-Salant, Nathan (1988). "Archetypal Foundation of Projective Identification," *Journal of Analytical Psychology*, 33, 1.

13. Schwartz-Salant, Nathan (1989). *The Borderline Personality: Vision and Healing*. Wilmette, IL. Chiron Publications.

14. Schwartz-Salant, Nathan (1992). "On the Interactive Field as the Analytic Object," Chiron Conference, Einsiedeln, Switzerland. Printed for participants.

15. Spiegelman, J. Marvin (1965). "Some Implications of the Transference," in *Festschrift für C.A. Meier*, edited by C.T. Frey, Zürich, Rascher Verlag.

16. Spiegelman, J. Marvin (1980). "The Image of the Jungian Analyst and the Problem of Authority," *Spring, An Annual of Archetypal Psychology*.

17. Spiegelman, J. Marvin (1988). "The Impact of Suffering and Self-Disclosure on the Life of the Analyst," in Jungian Analysts: Their Visions and Vulnerabilities, edited by Spiegelman. Phoenix, AZ, Falcon Press.

18. Spiegelman, J. Marvin (1991). "The Interactive Field in Analysis: Agreements and Disagreements," *Chiron*.

19. Spiegelman, J. Marvin (1993). *Reich, Jung, Regardie and Me: The Unhealed Healer*, Phoenix, AZ, Falcon Press

20. Spiegelman, J. Marvin (1995). "On Transference as Mutual Process and Field," *Chiron* (in press for Fall, 1995).

Appendix

"Some Implications of the Transference," in Speculum Psychologiae: Festschrift für C.A. Meier, Rascher Verlag, Zürich, 1965, pp. 163-175. Italian translation: "Alcune Implicazione del Transfert," Rivista di Psychologia Analitica, Vol I, No. 1, 1970 Japanese translation: in Shinri Rinshoka No Jikikaiji To Kizutsuki (Self-Disclosure and the Suffering of Psychotherapists: Mutual Process in Psychotherapy). Sanno Pub. Co., Ltd., Tokyo, 1992.

"Notes from the Underground: A View of Sex and Religion from a Psychotherapist's Cave", Revision of a lecture delivered at the University of California, Los Angeles on Sep. 4, 1969 and published in *Spring: An Annual of Archetypal Psychology and Jungian Thought*, New York, 1970.

"Transference, Individuation, Mutual Process", Revision of a lecture delivered to Jung Group, San Diego, 1972, not published in English. Japanese translation in *Shinri Rinshoka No Jikikaiji To Kizutsuki*.

"The Image of the Jungian Analyst and the Problem of Authority", *Spring*, 1980, pp. 101-116 Italian translation in "Limmagine dell' analista junghiano e la questione dell' autorita," (translation by Paola Donfrecesco), *Anima*, Florence, Italy, 1995 Japanese translation in *Shinri Rinshoka No Jikikaiji To Kizutsuki*.

"The Impact of Suffering and Self-Disclosure on the Life of the Analyst", in Spiegelman, J. Marvin, editor, *Jungian Analysts: Their Visions and Vulnerabilities*, Falcon Press, Phoenix, 1988, 181 pp.) Japanese translation in *Shinri Rinshoka No Jikikaiji To Kizutsuki*.

"The Interactive Field in Analysis: Agreements and Disagreements", presented as a lecture to the Chicago Society of Jungian Analysts and to the Independent Group in London in spring and summer of 1989 and published in "The Chiron Clinical Series" as a chapter in the monograph, *Liminality and Transitional Phenomena*, edited by N. Schwartz-Salant and M. Stein, Wilmette, Illinois, 1991, pp. 133-150). Japanese translation in *Shinri Rinshoka No Jikikaiji to Kizutsuki*.

"The One and the Many: Jung and the Post Jungians", *Journal of Analytical Psychology*, 1989, Vol 34, 53-71.

"The Unhealed Healer and the Unpublished Writer: Thirty-Plus Year Report to Alma Mater", Lecture for the C.G. Jung Institute, Zürich, Spring, 1991, also published in *Reich, Jung, Regardie and Me: The Unhealed Healer*, New Falcon Publications, Arizona, 1992.

"The Self in Psychotherapy: Present and Future", A Lecture for Japanese psychotherapists visiting Los Angeles, Spring 1994. Unpublished.

"Transference as Mutual Process and Interactive Field", Chiron *Clinical Series*, Fall, 1995.

"On Supervision" Lecture for a professional meeting of the Society of Jungian Analysts of Souther California, Feb. 21, 1995. Unpublished.

"On the Physics and Psychology of the Transference as an Interactive Field" (together with V. Mansfield).*Journal of Analytical Psychology*, (in press) 1996 or 1997.